# WINNING THE CUSTOMER LOYALTY MARATHON

## How to Achieve Sales and Service Excellence in the Beverage Business

Darryl Rosen

authorHOUSE®

*AuthorHouse™*
*1663 Liberty Drive, Suite 200*
*Bloomington, IN 47403*
*www.authorhouse.com*
*Phone: 1-800-839-8640*

*First published by AuthorHouse  2/9/2009*

*ISBN: 978-1-4389-5424-0 (sc)*

*Printed in the United States of America*
*Bloomington, Indiana*

*This book is printed on acid-free paper.*

Welcome to the start of what I am sure will be a successful journey towards *winning the customer loyalty marathon!*

Is this book for you? I think so.

Do you interact with customers on a daily basis? Do you rely on your customers to pay your bills – to put food on the table? Then this book is for you!

I am delighted to share my lessons from a lifetime of wine, beer and spirit retailing and my recent interactions with so many intelligent, thought-provoking, hard working beverage professionals. In the following pages, you will find literally hundreds of ways to build, cultivate and maintain better relationships with your customers.

If you have the courage to start the race – then you will be well on your way towards achieving sales and service excellence in this business or any other. You *will* be more successful. Why?

*That's just the way it works!*

I dedicated my first book to my wife, Jill Rosen

So, staying true to form, and in full acknowledgment of the place in my heart that my *much better half* occupies,

I am pleased to dedicate this book to Jill, *yet again.*

Also, to my boys – Josh, Danny and Ben. I can't forget those guys!

I love you all!

# CONTENTS

# The Start

December 5, 2008, marked 75 years since Prohibition was officially repealed in the United States with the ratification of the 21st Amendment to the United States Constitution. The 21st Amendment not only officially ended national Prohibition, which began with the 18th Amendment in 1919, but also established an effective, state-based system of alcohol regulation that today works efficiently to provide American consumers with unparalleled *choice* and variety of wine, beer and spirits.

But what about retailers? Do they have a *choice*?

**Well, not exactly.**

Consumers have choices. They can choose where to buy that esoteric 6pk of beer or that *gotta have* bottle of wine, but the bar, restaurant, or store that sells the consumer, in most cases, has no choice as to what distributor or wholesaler to use.

One could argue over beers (or in court) as to the need for the 3-tier system, but *I'm not going there.* It is what it is, and it is likely never going to change. The real question is, how does this lack of *choice* affect the distributor/retailer relationship?

I believe it has led to complacency. I believe it has led to some distributor and supplier sales people taking their customers for granted. Some act like it is a mandate that business has to be done a certain way. Many do not try as hard or provide as much value. The worst part is

1

that they act like they have some pre-ordained right to have the business.

Not all sales people – but enough to make a difference.

I want to put an end to that behavior and help improve customer relationships – which is why I use my persepective (from a lifetime of retail) to write, and say - what I write, and say. I believe the following:

***The best distributors and suppliers create an environment where their customers do business with them, not because they <u>have</u> to, but because they <u>want</u> to!***

This one simple phrase will work wonders for your beverage career. If you take one thing from this book, I certainly hope you remember that phrase.

I think you will get a lot more than just one phrase; however, that is a biggie. Here are a few other things I want you to know about this book:

## All customers are created equal

When I say retailer (or customer), I am referring to any company that sells products purchased from distributors. It could be a bar, restaurant, country club, store or tavern. It could be an independent store or restaurant, a chain store, a warehouse club, or the corner tavern. To be sure, your customers come in different sizes and shapes, but inside, they are staffed, owned and operated by people just like you and me.

People that want to be treated well.

### *That's just the way it works!*

I used this phrase in a presentation some time ago, and it really resonated with the audience. Now I use it all the time – including at the end of every chapter of this book. Here is what that phrase implies in my view: There are certain principles that have force in customer/human interaction no matter the situation. For example, if you insult your customer's intelligence, he or she will rightly take offense. Your business will suffer and ***that's just the way it works.***

Someone in an audience once asked me, *"So, what do you do - just give up? Accept the fact that it's just the way it works and stop trying?"* Not in the least bit. My point is that the best sales people, when sales decrease due to a situation or circumstances, spend more time fixing the situation than trying to figure out why the situation occurred or lamenting its existence. At some point, all great sales people accept the situations they are in, fix the problems, get creative, and then, and only then do they sell more products. ***That's just the way it works!***

## Say *"Hello" to* Vending Machine Man

Throughout the book, you will find a modestly handsome character named *Vending Machine Man,* a bizarre creation of my mind. I created this dude to show sales people what <u>not</u> to do. Vending machine Man exemplifies the worst of all sales people. That person is an order taker, and not much else. He or she takes an order and runs out of the account like the police are giving chase. That kind of person is unprofessional, cares only about self, and is more interested in the next cup of coffee than the success of a customer's business. That person has many other habits and personality traits, *as you will see,* that are all detrimental to the end goal of creating motivated customers. I created Vending Machine Man to add some life to the very worst kind of sales person.

## Partner versus Pretender

Another distinction I draw repeatedly in this book is the difference between partners and pretenders. Simply put, a partner is a sales person that cares about your business and your success. Conversely, a pretender is self-serving. A sales person that *pretends* to care about you and your business but in actuality cares only about his or her paycheck.

## Questions From the Field

As I travel the country, sales professionals ask me how I would handle certain situations. Several of the questions and answers are captured at the end of the applicable chapters. I hope you will find these additions useful!

## The Marathon Analogies

Maybe you are thinking – *why all the marathon references?* Well, I started running marathons when I was 13 years old and did not stop until my mid-thirty's. I love the sport of marathon running, despite the fact that I hardly see myself running 26.2 miles anytime soon. Today, 26.2 feet would be more appropriate (because of the 26.2 extra pounds!), but I digress.

Have you ever heard the phrase *it's a marathon, not a sprint?* The applications to business are endless. Building, cultivating, and maintaining long standing, win-win customer relationships takes a long time and tons of effort, just like a marathon. It is not a sprint, and it certainly will not happen overnight.

To keep with the theme of my first book, *Surviving the Middle Miles,* this book also has 26.2 chapters - 26.2 ways to win the customer loyalty marathon. If you want to know what the New York Times said about my first book, look it up on the web. Oh, whom am I kidding? *That book* is critically acclaimed…only by my family (barely).

Anyway, in this book you will notice a section at the end of several chapters called the final straightaway. Why do we need the final straightaway, anyway? Well, 26 miles does not make a marathon. 26.2 miles is the full distance. The last 385 yards are the most important. Without those last yards, a runner never has the thrill of hoisting his or her arms in the air while smiling for the finish line photo.

In my writing, I use it to denote the most important point in a chapter or article - the part you cannot do without.

What do you get at the end? You know - the finisher's tent? What do you get when you *win your customer's loyalty?* If you do as I suggest in this book – what is the payoff?

You get customers who are motivated to do business with you, and customers who embrace more of your products. Customers who are determined to support your company (like you support their company!). Customers who are more accepting when things go wrong. Be real and face it, if you are great, you will be forgiven for your mistakes but if you are bad, you will eat your mistakes. The biggest payoff is having customers who resist the overtures of your competitors. That is truly the end game.

Are you going to sell every bottle in your territory? Of course not, but you will certainly sell more with the right approach than the wrong demeanor. You also get the pride and satisfaction of a job well done – which is pretty nice!

*You will get customers that do business with you – not because they* <u>have</u> *to but because they* <u>want</u> *to.*

Congratulations, by reading this book, you seemingly have the courage to start the race – and courage is perhaps the most important factor. *That's just the way it works!*

# A Word about Changing Habits

There is nothing in the next few pages that will seem earth shattering. Much of it is simple, straightforward, and common sense. Yes, loads of common sense, but you know what they say about common sense? There is nothing common about it.

I am just asking you to change some habits. Simple tips and strategies that will help you attack your work and your customer interaction (*don't actually attack your customers*) with zeal and purpose. Changes that will help you be more professional with your work and more compassionate with your customers. Changes that will help you distinguish yourself from a lot of the bitter, nasty sales people who do not understand why their customers do not want to do business with them.

I realize that it is *simple, but not easy*. Very simple to want to bring change into your life, but not easy to have the courage and commitment to make it a reality.

In writing this book and working with sales people, I wanted to understand how the brain handles change. Just how does the brain allow you to create new habits? Before I go any further, please understand that I am far from perfect on the subject. I struggle just like everybody else. (Wait, let me grab *another* Diet Coke)

In my research, I came upon the work of Dr. Jeff Schwartz, a noted professor at UCLA and the author of *The Mind and the Brain*. It seems that there is an area of the brain called the caudate nucleus (say that 10 times fast). This is the area of the brain that helps you successfully implement both good and bad habits. His suggestion, based upon his research, is this:

### *Do something consistently for two weeks!*

Yep, that is what his research shows. Do something consistently for two weeks and you will be able to establish whatever habits you wish to establish. See how it cuts both ways. Be careful, because, according to Dr. Schwartz, your brain will kick into a higher gear. The habit will be ingrained into your brain and two things will happen. First, you will begin doing the task without thinking. Second, if you try to skip it, you will miss it. Be careful what habits you wish for!

As author John C. Maxwell puts it, "*The choice is yours!*"

Do you have the courage to change when it is easier to remain comfortable? There is great distance between *I will* and *I am* and an even bigger distance between *I am* and *I have become*. Bridging that gap is the key. Moving forward each day is essential.

Take notes as you read this book. Jot a few ideas down on a piece of paper or in the margins. If you like, buy a note card and write the phrase *Change Card* on the top. Keep the card in your pocket and refer to it as often as possible. Always remember, you win your customer's loyalty one order, one idea, one suggestion, one act, one gesture and one case at a time.

*That's just the way it works!*

There is a great distance between I will and I have become! Similar to the distance the Bears usually need for a first down - that they fail to get because they run the same play 3 times in a row!

# Distilling the Ingredients of Success

Now that the curtain has closed on 2008, the beverage industry can look back on one of the craziest years in memory. For starters, the economy slumped tremendously, causing pundits to bypass the R word (recession) and head straight for the D word (depression). Consumer confidence fell to bargain basement levels, the financial system almost crashed, and oil prices (and prices at the pump) moved up and down like a yoyo.

I am sure many people were happy to see the ball drop in Times Square!

While all this was going on, major changes were taking place in the beverage business at both the distributor and supplier level. In June 2008, Miller and Coors officially became one company, and later in the year, InBev completed its purchase of Anheuser-Busch. Is that enough change? On the wine and spirits side, major brands like Absolut changed hands, and big distributors continued to merge and gobble up smaller houses.

Yet the more the landscape changes, the more it remains the same.

To be sure, brands move around and big changes take place, and that will probably continue in the years to come. I firmly believe, however, that there are certain ingredients necessary to distill success in the beverage business. Remember, the best distributors and suppliers create an environment where their customers do business with them not because they <u>have</u> to, but because they <u>want</u> to. Is that your goal? If it is, keep the following factors in mind.

- **This is a SERVICE business** – despite all the company sales, consolidations, supplier quotas, industry trends, internal company changes, and Nielson data, people still buy wine, beer and spirits from other people.

There has been innovation and change in all corners of the beverage business. At the end of the day, though, the industry has kept the human touch that now seems so foreign in other industries. Every day in bars, stores and restaurants, human beings are knocking on doors and selling to other human beings. The best are sales professionals, but more importantly, customer service professionals. They resist the urge to be completely absorbed by new product introductions and internal company changes, and understand the end game: happy customers! The most successful sales professionals understand that service is the name of the game. Those professionals will be the ones who win their customer's loyalty.

- **Customers aren't like buses** – there isn't a new one coming along every 20 minutes.

Sales professionals typically have a finite list of customers. In other words, the list does not get any bigger! Sure, some businesses will expand, some new businesses will open, but at the same time others will fail. The total number of customers will probably be somewhat constant, so the math is pretty simple. The more customers a sales professional has a good relationship with, the better. Despite the fact that customers in the alcohol beverage business have to buy from specified distributors (by law), if you start alienating accounts, then you will surely see your sales receipts begin to fall. New customers will not magically appear like the bus does on a cold morning (after a while, anyway).

- **If you don't take care of your customers** – someone else will.

Another sales professional will always be lurking around to become your customer's preferred provider, and his or her partner. Many industry veterans try to convey the importance of consistently being the customer's *vendor of choice*. The goal is to be known as a confidánt, a partner, and an advisor. That goal requires that you are there to take care of problems, not create them.

If you have seen my workshop, you may know that I liken this phenomenon to the 2001 romantic comedy, **Serendipity**, starring John Cusack and Kate Beckinsale. Yes, I like chick flicks. Anyway, in the movie the two star-crossed lovers find each other through luck, fortune, and coincidence, but mostly through chance. Destiny, if you will.

The same thing happens in the beverage business. Try to picture the following scenario: a beverage professional drops the ball on something (does something wrong or fails to complete an important task) and leaves an account with his or her head slumping, mood dragging. They have made a mistake, but do not yet know the repercussions. What they do not see as they head for the nearest coffee house (possibly shedding a few tears in the process) is that their competitor was sitting in the parking lot. Unfortunately, the competitor saw the face, the demeanor, and they smelled blood. They spring out of their car like a jack-in-the-box and head for the door. The opportunity is now theirs!

The next time the professional visits that account, hoping to make amends, he or she may notice some things have changed. Maybe the manager is not as friendly. Maybe a floor stacking has been moved, perhaps the back bar looks a bit different. Small things. The point is that *the law of serendipity* unofficially states that someone will always be there to pick up the pieces. You need not worry if you fail to take care of your customers - someone else will!

- **True customer loyalty** – is won one relationship, one act, one gesture, one case, one placement and one customer at a time.

We are not talking rocket science here, friends. The truth is that it takes a long time to build a strong relationship, but just a few short minutes to destroy everything. Since we are talking about *winning the customer loyalty marathon*, I have a example from, you guessed it, the world of marathon running.

Many runners who fail at the marathon distance (26.2 miles of pain) do so because they dwell on the enormity of the task and fail to break the adventure into pieces. Success at the marathon distance and in the beverage business is measured step-by-step, mile-by-mile. Many professionals try to be everything to their customers instead of focusing on small aspects of the relationship.

While it takes great time and effort to win customer loyalty, it takes just a bit of greed and stupidity to lose trust in a *New York minute*. It can be lost in just one simple act. Trust is a huge factor, as we will discuss throughout this book. Break a bond of trust and your dealings (if you are still on the account) will be mainly transactional.

Successful beverage professionals realize that *Rome was not built in a day!* Those individuals pick small things to work on each week while steering clear of actions that could destroy everything. In time, they arrive at the finish line - sometimes not quite sure how they got there!

- **Your customers may not say it** – but they want your help to make their businesses more successful. It is your job and your responsibility.

Correction: your customers may not have asked for your help in the past, but they probably are asking (requiring) it now. Tom Cole, President of Republic National Distributing Company was quoted in Impact Magazine in its December 15, 2007 issue as saying, *"As the retailers and restaurateurs have become bigger and more sophisticated, they've become far more demanding of us."* Have you noticed?

In the good old days, top sales professionals advanced by going above and beyond – which is why they are still selling today. These days, though, the tide has turned. It is much harder for younger (and newer) sales professionals to be successful. One of the requirements is to be constantly on the lookout for ways to increase your customer's profits, but not to achieve that goal by lowering your prices! It is not a simple task, and there will be much more on that later. Keep reading!

- **People buy and sell the brands of the people they like** – that's just how it works. You know it and I know it.

In my former life as a retailer, I saw this firsthand. Whether it was a small batch bourbon, a lesser known craft beer, or an esoteric burgundy from Beaune, we had the size and power to make brands. In many cases, we did so only because we liked the people who brought us these products. Maybe we trusted them more than others. Maybe those sales professionals instilled more confidence in us; maybe they just made us feel good. Whatever the case, we were able to make things happen for them.

Some have said, "*Sure, it's easy in a big retail environment to build brands. What about those of us who deal with smaller businesses?*" Good point! One thing I have learned over time is that all over this country, from California to Florida and all points in between, there are bars, stores, and restaurants (big and small) that are building brands, customer-by-customer and product-by-product. It takes time, but all good things come to those who wait.

- **You represent your company; you are your company** – in the eyes of your customers and consumers, you represent your company and your brands.

You are first and foremost your customer's most critical link to your organization. When sales go up, you (well, actually, your managers) get the credit. Unfortunately, when sales go down, you take the blame. So the onus is on you to build, cultivate, and maintain healthy, profitable, mutually enjoyable, win-win customer relationships.

Is building, cultivating and maintaining long term, healthy, profitable, mutually enjoyable relationships a <u>big part</u> of your job?

Is building, cultivating and maintaining long term, healthy, profitable, mutually enjoyable relationships the <u>most important</u> part of your job?

I imagine the answer is YES on both counts, and I know it is pretty daunting at times. So it bears repeating: The onus is on you (beverage professionals) to build, cultivate, and maintain long term, healthy, profitable, mutually enjoyable relationships with your customers. Nobody is going to do it for you!

*That's just the way it works!*

The good news is that this book will help you through the process. Keep reading!

The customer (the gentleman on the right) is happy to see
the sales person.  That's what you want! The question all sales
people have to ask is would my customer do business with me
if he or she didn't have to?

# Questions from the Field

Q: Should sales people be doing anything different in difficult times?

**A: Absolutely! During tough times, your customers need a friend (and a positive light), more than a sales person.**

Reminds me of an interesting chat I had with the President of a Midwest beer distributor last year. We talked about the state of the economy and what his sales people do to help customers through difficult times. No doubt about it, (as I type this chapter) *consumer confidence* is low right now. Really, really low. Lowest it has been in years. He shared that many of his customers (especially on-premise) were hurting both financially and emotionally.

What is the distributor's role as it pertains to their customers' confidence, especially in difficult times?

Well, a distributor cannot really affect *consumer confidence*; but an individual sales person can help his or her *customer's confidence*. Yes, their psyche; their outlook.

But, *I'm not a psychologist*, you say.

No, not by training anyway, but you can help create a positive atmosphere. Anyone can help create a positive atmosphere. Just ask Dr. Phil. You just have to do a few simple things:

- **Leave your accounts better off than you found them**

Do something that leaves your account in better shape as a result of your visit. Make sure you are cleaning, maintaining, re-arranging, dusting, wiping, affixing (signs), correcting (errors), educating (anybody that wants to be educated), smiling, and bringing (as in bringing breakfast, lunch, coffee, doughnuts, bananas), and most importantly, sharing (creative ideas for increasing customer counts, bar rings, average tickets, etc.).

- **Enter accounts with a smile on your face. Be enthusiastic!**

Move with a sense of purpose, a sense of urgency. Act like you have not seen your customer in ages. You might know that smiling is good for your health. Lowers the bad stuff (chemicals in your body) and raises the good stuff (Please note: no medical journals were consulted for this paragraph, but you get the idea). Smile! Be enthusiastic! Not only do happy people live longer, but they also spread more joy. Never miss an opportunity to create joy for others.

- **Be a therapist**

Resist the urge to ruminate about the stock market, home industry, tax code and other situations that are out of your control. Talk about the positives, not the negatives. Point out the *light at the end of the tunnel.*

- **Lead with a compliment**

Be observant. Take just a few extra moments to find something good in your customer's business and mention it. Give a sincere compliment. Give your customer reasons to believe in his or her business.

- **Say "thank you!"**

Thank your customers *big and small* for orders *big and small.* Make sure they know you appreciate their business. It can mean a lot.

- **Tell the truth and keep your ethical standards**

Especially in tough times, nobody should have to be suspicious of his or her sales person. Be straightforward and candid. Do not run away with the truth! Always remember: integrity is not an expendable line item on the budget; something you cut at the first sign of trouble. No matter how tough times get, never compromise your integrity, even if your competition is fighting with dirty tricks.

- **Share new ideas**

The truth is that a boon makes average performers look brilliant. When the bottom falls out, however, the real cracks are revealed. Now is the time to create better ways to serve your customers. Rethink your offer. Brainstorm for more creative selling ideas. Find out what your customers want and do it better than anybody else.

I firmly believe that when a recovery starts after an economic slowdown, customers truly remember who helped their businesses when they needed it the most.

- **Leave your baggage in the overhead bins**

Help create a productive environment by leaving your personal troubles behind before making account calls.

Watch less TV, especially the news. What does the news tell us? It tells us about everyone's problems. Does it help us? No. Keep informed, but use extra time to either visit/help customers or educate yourself.

*Don't be a vending machine.* Reflect on your customer visits. Ask yourself: Was what I did in there any different than what a vending machine could/would have done? Did I add value? Did I create a positive environment?" Or did I just add to the negative feeling gripping our country?

Handle problems quickly. Call people back immediately and keep in touch with customers that may not be ordering as regularly.

Realize that there are certain times, and now is one of those times, when your customers need a friend (and a positive light) more than just a sales person.

*That's just how it works!*

Every person entering an account can make a difference. Keep that famous expression in mind, "A smile a day, keeps the Doctor away!"

Vending Machine Man thinks his problems should be his customers' problems. He is a pretender. He doesn't realize that baggage is best left for the overhead bins. Your job, as a partner, is to bring your customers up, not down! Especially in tough times!

# Knowing What your Customers Think of You

Do you ever wonder what your customers are thinking about you? Is this news you can use? Absolutely! It should be of great interest to you. Some of you may be thinking, *"I don't want to know!"* Uh, probably not a good idea. This chapter is all about taking a good hard look at how your customers see you, and I will begin that process by suggesting different questions you should ask, or at the very least *want* to know the answers to. The goal will be to find ways to ask these questions on a semi-regular, or regular basis. Some questions drive at how a sales person is performing within an account, while others are about how your company is performing. Both areas are vital.

Think about it this way: have you ever started a new fitness regimen? Typically, if you are a new exerciser, over a certain age (35 or so) and you have been sedimentary in your lifestyle, it is recommended that you consult a doctor. The goal is to start with the right plan, one that takes your health into consideration. Younger people have it a bit easier. Their major decision is what color shorts to wear and what to listen to on their Ipods. The point is that everybody has to start somewhere.

Sales people have to start the relationship-building process somewhere also. You <u>must</u> know where you stand with your customers.

Why is this so important?

These days, customers have less time, attention, patience, and energy, and every day they are bombarded with new products, new initiatives, and lots of other stuff coming at them in ramshackle fashion. Sales people (and companies) that **win the customer loyalty marathon** remember that every time they call or visit a customer, their attitude, their feelings (their future), are front and center and on display for all to see. Simply put, the best professionals always know where they stand and are not afraid of the answers.

Are you ready to get started?

Imagine you are face-to-face with your customer right now. Imagine asking (and contemplating) the answers to these two questions:

### *What are we doing well?*
### *What could we do better?*

In workshops, I ask sales professionals why we should ask the first question. Common responses are *"so we can continue to do what we're doing well"* or *"so we know our strengths."* Others say we *"can show our customers that we care."* The correct answer is all of the above, but there is something else. In my view, the most important reason for asking *what are we doing well* is to make sure we are concentrating on those tasks that are meaningful to our customers. The truth is that just because *we* think something is important does not mean our customers agree. As noted author Brian Tracy says in his legendary book *Eat that Frog, "the biggest crime is to do something well that need not be done at all!"*

Every day I hear of unfortunate situations where well-intentioned professionals excelled at tasks that just were not important (or wanted) by their customers. The result was time wasted, and in this environment, that is a recipe for disaster. Ask, and you shall receive the truth on what is really important to your customers.

The second question is a bit more straightforward. This is information we need to be successful. Look for trends. Are many customers saying the same things? If so, you know your opportunities and where you can improve. A few words of caution, though about how your customers may respond:

- Many customers may automatically (as if conditioned by Pavlov) speak about price, discounts, or other monetary variables. Push a little on this. Beyond the world of price, there are always other variables that help your customers make decisions. (Read more on *price* in Chapter 3.)

- Do not ask the questions if you will automatically dismiss the answers. In other words, the more serious you are, the more beneficial the process will be. Automatically dismissing what your customers say will do more harm than good. *"Denial" isn't just a river in Egypt,* as they say. Besides, if many customers point out the same issues – take the lesson and run with it. The truth is that if it walks like a duck and talks like duck….(well, you know how that one ends)

- Accept feedback with a good nature. Sure, it is not easy to hear criticism, but remember the following: a) you asked the question, and b) feedback (especially negative) is how sales people grow into better sales professionals.

Accept your customer's comments with a smile on your face. As long as their feedback is well intended and not vindictive, you can always learn from it.

Once you ascertain some basic information about how you are faring, it is time to dig a little deeper. For the questions below, imagine a professional research firm is going *in depth* (with your customers) to truly determine how they feel. The first questions would be about trust.

- Do you trust your sales person? (Much more on trust in Chapter 14)

- Do you believe that your sales person has your best interests at heart?

- Do you believe that his or her company has your best interests at heart?

- Do you enjoy working with your sales person?

- Do you enjoy working with his or her company?

- Does your sales person *proactively* help you sell inventory that you already own?

- Does your sales person *proactively* suggest a plan for sell-thru before asking you to buy something?

- Do you believe that your sales person is a strategic resource?

- Do you rely on your sales person?

- Does your sales person educate your staff on product attributes, but more importantly, teach your associates how to sell the products?

- Does your sales person offer solutions?

- Does your sales person follow through and keep commitments?

- Does your sales person arrive on time and prepared for meetings?

- Does your sales person answer all your questions in a patient manner?

- Can your sales person verbalize how his or her product is different from the competition?

- Does your sales person know how his or her company is different from the competition?

- Does your sales person know how your company is different from your competitors?

- How is your relationship with your sales person? Is it smooth? Do you have to work at it? Is it tense? Does it come naturally? Are you happy to see your sales person?

- Does your sales person lift you up or bring you down? Is he or she a joy to be around?

- What do you like least about your sales person?

- What do you like most about your sales person?

- What do you value most in a sales person?

- Can you name 3 acts of outstanding service over the last 3 months?

- Have there been *more* acts of outstanding service than acts of terrible service over the last 3 months?

- **In the last 3 months, has your sales person gone out of his or her way *in any way* to help you or your company be more successful?**

- If your sales person transferred to a different market, would you care?

One last note: your goal and the real question that you must always consider is – do your customers think and perceive (remember, perception is reality) that you (and your company) help to make their businesses more successful? Do they think you add value? Are you their strategic partner?

*"Yes, of course"* is what most sales people say to me! *"I am a strategic partner."* I hope so! The real question is, *are you held in a higher regard than competing sales people?* If you are a wine sales person, is there a beer or food sales person that occupies a higher rung on the ladder?

Are you a trusted advisor? Are you helping to build your customer's business? Are you liked and beloved? Do you add value before asking for value? Do you provide valuable information? Do you understand the situation that your customer is in? And most importantly, can you drop by (and see a decision maker) without an appointment?

A great exercise is to make a list of your accounts and try to accurately determine if you are a trusted advisor to the decision makers in each account. Be honest or do not do it. What is the percentage of your total accounts? Always try to improve upon that number.

### You must be known for something:

*At the end of the day (and the beginning of the day for that matter), If you're not known for something special, and your customer cannot remember (or identify) ways that you stand out (or noteworthy things that you have done) – you are probably not differentiating yourself from your competition. You are just like all the rest, and that is not the best place to be!*

Take a moment to consider. Maybe you have always been the go-to person. Perhaps you are known as someone who is very creative. Are you great at follow-through and following up? Are you a sales person of impeccable integrity, honesty and values? What do they say about your honesty and integrity when you are not around? Do you always enter an account with a big smile on your face and tons of enthusiasm? Does your customer trust <u>you</u> for support and wisdom?

It can be any of the above, but remember, it must be something (preferably positive).

One FINAL thought on this subject. It does not matter what you think, it matters what your customer thinks. Be strong, ask the questions, and the answers will help you win your customer's loyalty.

*That's just the way it works!*

# QUESTIONS FROM THE FIELD

**Q:** In a recent workshop I shared with my audience the need for sales people to stand out and to be memorable in at least one positive way. After the session a young sales person asked what she could do to stand out?

**A: This is really a 2-part question. The first question is how to stand out and the second question is how to convey the manner in which you stand out to your customers.**

**Part 1**: How to stand out. There are many ways to stand out as a sales person but the most important variable is that you stand out in a way that is *uniquely* you. Yep, sounds exactly like what your parents used to tell you. *Be yourself!* Nothing is more irritating to a customer than fake, contrived and manufactured personalities.

So how can you stand out?

- You can convey the most information

- You can be the most prepared

- You can be the most knowledgeable about what is going on in the marketplace

- You can be the most cheerful (not over the top exuberance, but being known as someone who has a positive frame of mind).

- You can help out the most at your customer's place of business

- You can be known as a person of incredible integrity

Unsure? Ask your customers what they like about you. The point is that run-of-the-mill will not get it done these days in your customer's hectic lives. You must find ways to stand out.

**Part 2**: How to convey the way in which you stand out? This calls for a little bragging. Yes, bragging. You cannot wait around for people to notice; you have to be gently, but consistently, reminding them. For this I call upon a book called Brag! *The Art of Tooting Your own Horn Without Blowing it.*

Author Peggy Klaus expertly suggests that to brag is to talk about your best self with pride and passion in a conversational manner. Your customers these days have much less time, attention, patience and energy. They are simply not going to take the time to figure out what you stand for or what you bring to the table. First, show them and second, show them consistently. After a while, you have to tell them.

*That's just the way it works!*

# Understanding What your Customers Really Want

*Your customers don't buy everything at Costco....*

It's no secret that price is important. But is it the only consideration that people have when they shop? No! If it were, then your customers would buy everything at Costco! They do not, and the reason is that many other variables loom equally as important when your customers spend amounts big and small.

One year we raised a few prices at our family's chain of wine stores. After many years of matching competitors' prices, we came to the realization that we needed fair, healthy margins to be viable.

*It didn't go so smoothly at first. Not in the least bit.*

One day, a woman called and mentioned that we were priced higher than Costco on a case of water. My Dad immediately sought me out. "How can we be higher than Costco?" Veins were popping in his forehead. Kind of scary! I calmly (sort of) explained that, to save a few dollars, the customer would have to drive to Costco, park two football fields away, grab her own cart, pull the cases off the shelf, pay for them, and then haul everything to her car, *all by herself.*

Does this sound familiar? Is this what you go through when you shop at price clubs and discounters?

Silently, I reminisced about my one trip to Costco. I remembered how we parked so far from the entrance that I thought I was at Disney

World! I imagined that once the price shopper completed the task of buying the water, she would still have to get the cases to her 14th floor apartment!

Or, in return for a few dollars more, we could deliver the cases right to her refrigerator!

*Money isn't everything!* She bought the water from us after we explained that the benefit of doing business with us was a fair price and, much more importantly, convenience.

Maybe you are thinking *nice try, pal,* but *my* customers only care about price. Yes, it is important. Please understand, however, it is not the only criteria your customers use when spending their money – both personally and professionally. Your customers may steadfastly hold to the '*price is everything*' argument; however, the more you get to know them, the more you understand their needs, and the more you are able to ascertain their problems - for which you have solutions - the more likely it is that your customers will pay your prices.

Still not convinced? Okay let me try another way. I imagine some of your accounts care about price and price alone. I get it! Not every customer demands the lowest price *every time.* Your job is to maximize your company's profits, and the more you are able to accentuate the other positives of your company, the better off you will be. It is not easy, but it is worth a try.

Review the list below. Educate your customers about the overall quality of your offering, and always keep these other attributes in mind. There really is much more to the experience of dealing with you and your company than just the price of your products. (This is why I feel so strongly about Chapter 2 and sales people being known for something!)

Your customers probably care about the following, in addition to price.

- **They want on-time delivery** – your customers want the products you promised, at the time and day that you promised them.

- **They want respect** – everybody wants to feel important. Never fall into the trap of thinking your customer is stupid. Assume that they understand what they are paying for.

- **They want help and guidance** – conversations (for the purpose of educating your customer) represent a tremendous opportunity to sell. Become an educator and teacher to your rushed, stressed-out customer.

- **They want to feel like they are learning something** – everybody wants to feel like they are growing and learning. Sharing what you know contributes to their sense of well-being, and a sense of well-being leads to sales. Customer confidence goes a long way.

- **They want to stay free of embarrassment** – they want everything to run smoothly and successfully. The more *certainty* you can provide them, the better. Nobody like surprises except, of course, people that throw surprise parties.

- **They want to have a hassle-free day/week/month/year** – the more you do to help your customers in as many ways as possible, the more you will be a trusted and valued resource. – and partner. From the water story at the beginning of this chapter: the act of bringing three cases of water to our customer's doorstep was helping her avoid a real hassle. She just needed help thinking of it that way.

- **They want to look good in the eyes of their superior or boss** – always help your account contact get ahead. Do you deal with the corporate buyer? Be of assistance as he or she moves ahead in his or her career. Help your customers achieve their dreams. Give them more reasons with which they can persuade their superiors to pay your price.

- **They want a performance-capable vendor** – your customers want to make sure you can actually do what you say you can do. If you say the cases will be there, your customer simply wants to see them there.

- **They want courtesy, speed, and timeliness when they ask questions**. Call people back right away! Remember, the person calling is probably reporting back to the decision-maker. The sooner you handle the problem/crisis/opportunity, the better it will be for your sales. I know a top insurance professional who makes the following promise to his clients: He promises that he will always call back the same day. Lip service? Not a chance. I have spoken with a few of the thousands of clients he has helped who say that he has lived up to that promise every time.

- **They want speed and accuracy in invoicing** – some prospects want specific information on an invoice. Some want information itemized a certain way. Do everything you can to accommodate their special requests. Handle discrepancies in a timely manner.

- **They want help minimizing their costs** – help your customers realize economies in their operations so they can enhance their organization's bottom line. Give genuine help. Provide advice and assistance to make your products and services more useful for your customers.

- **They want consistent follow-up** – periodically check with customers to make sure their plans are being executed as they had hoped. Stay on course with your customers. The more face time, the better. Stay relevant to your customers. Always review open items before launching into a sales pitch. Pay careful attention to slow moving items.

- **They want your willingness to "go to bat" for them when problems arise** – you can win your customers for life if you help them when they truly need the help. Your customers want the earliest possible notification when unavoidable problems occur. Look, nobody is perfect; however, the sooner you *candidly* notify people of problems, the more choices everybody has to amicably resolve those problems.

- **They want you to have knowledge of their products and services** – your customers expect you to know everything about your products and services, but also, they expect you to know everything about their products and business. You cannot help them if you do not know what they are trying to do.

Help your customer gain a competitive advantage. Ask the tough questions. Help them peel back the layers of the unknown until they have the information they need to make the best possible decisions. Does your customer understand what differentiates your excellent product from another that might not be the best? Yes? How so? If not, why should your customer stock it in the first place?

Show your customer how to use, position, and market your products. Give them good reasons to get behind your products. Share reasons that help your customer, not you. Demonstrate how your items will help the customer gain a competitive advantage!

Does the competition have similar offerings? How are they similar? How are they different? How does the competition display the product? What is their merchandising strategy? Are they seeing better results? Why?

I remember (back in the day) that the best salespeople took an active interest in our success. They educated us. They helped us understand *how-to* profit from the sale of their wines, beers and spirits.

Be your customer's advocate in all areas of business, not just when it concerns the products you are selling. A salesperson once mentioned a new advertising approach, something that was new to me. It was a new avenue that worked out very nicely. He showed that he wanted our business to do well and his reach extended beyond traditional boundaries. I appreciated his initiative.

Your customers also want the following:

- **They want you to know a lot about what you are selling** – so you can help them to make the best choice about what to buy from you.

- **They want you to be prepared for sales calls** – too many people simply "wing it." If you cannot back up your request for a fair price with genuine "know how," you are not going to be successful. Woody Allen said, "90% of success is just showing up!" *Yes, Woody, but you can't show up unprepared.* (See Chapter 10 for more on sales calls.)

- **They want predictability** – your customers do not want to work with an unpredictable vendor, no matter what the price!

- **They want simple interpretation of price lists** – confusion erodes trust. Lack of trust costs money, and if your customer doubts you, the price *actually* goes up because the customer has to spend time looking over your shoulder and checking up on you. You must be able to clearly point out what the price is, in simple, understandable terms. Have you ever done business with someone simply because you trusted him or her? Of course! We naturally gravitate towards clear, transparent and trustworthy people. *That's what your customer wants.*

- **They want superbly written materials** – when you leave informative materials, your customers can study those materials at a time that is convenient for them. That is showing respect for their time and appreciating that they may learn and process information in their own way. Very powerful!

- **They want to work with people they like** – assuming you have proven the value equation, being likeable, genuine and caring may tip the scale in your favor.

- **They want to know why other customers buy from you at your prices** – do a little name-dropping. Build credibility. Let prospects know why others buy from you. Always convey your competitive advantages in a clear, yet understated manner. Don't brag. Inform!

- **They want to work with companies that do the little things** – always have the mindset that the *devil is in the details*. For example, if you make signs for your customers, make them in an accurate and timely manner.

- **They want you to have confidence in your products, your price and your people** – everybody wants to make the right decision. The more you back up your words with solid data, the more you educate your customer. The result: they will be more confident in their decision to do business with you.

- **They want creative solutions to their problems** – prospects want and need help solving their problems. A partner that can develop cutting-edge strategies will have a better chance of winning business. Think outside the box. Come up with new and exciting ideas. Different ways of moving products. Different ways of advertising products. Different ways of merchandising products.

- **They want to be part of a valued relationship** – your prospects want to be around likeable people. They want to feel part of a process, part of a team. Oftentimes, your primary contact with a customer is with an individual who assists the ultimate decision maker. It is conceivable that you are more knowledgeable, and more educated about your products (or the beverage business) than they are at the present time. Educate them. Ask them what they think. Listen to them, not just to appease them, but so you can hear what they have to say. Take their feedback seriously. Create a comfortable environment for your customer, and price will be less and less of an issue.

- **They want partners not pretenders** – your customers want their distributor and supplier partners to take a vested interest in their business and their success. They want a trustworthy business partner - not a self-serving pretender.

### The Final Straightaway

If they know you, like you and trust you, then they will want to do business with you. Do not concentrate on price. Keep selling. Keep pointing out your advantages. Never stop educating and informing your customers. Keep asking questions. Keep trying to uncover what they really want. Be strong, point out why customers should buy from you, and over time, they will buy an awful lot from you!

*That's just the way it works!*

# UNDERSTANDING THE STAKES
# OF THE GAME

*"I don't care what you think; you have to buy from us!"*

An actual quote! Seems like it was just yesterday. We were talking about a program for a popular domestic beer when the conversation turned sour and he blurted out these unfortunate words. I was stunned! Clearly, I understood *that I had to buy the beer from his company (if I wanted to carry it)* but his attitude shocked me to the core.

First, it is true. In nearly every state, retailers (stores, restaurants and bars, etc.) in your territory can only buy products that you distribute *from you*. Sure, some states like New Jersey have slightly different rules, but your state's right to regulate the sale of alcohol is not going away any time soon, despite the best efforts of some major retailers. It is a situation not likely to change.

Second, does anybody care about this lack of choice? Are you kidding?

Your retailer cares! And he or she cares a great deal! In every other consumer goods industry, customers who buy products have a choice as to where to buy those products. Regular consumers certainly have choices. Want a steak for dinner tonight? There are tons of places to choose from. Have you bought a new TV lately? Again, you have many choices. Big stores like Best Buy and a variety of smaller chains and independents dot the marketplace.

The same choice does not exist for the third tier of the beverage industry.

Absent this element of choice, the trick in this industry, for distributor and supplier sales people, is to *create an environment where your customers do business with you,* **not because they have to, but because they want to.** Heard that phrase somewhere before? Just this simple shift in your thinking will pay dividends. A beverage professional should always have in his or her head that he or she is right on the verge of losing this customer to a rival. Similarly, sales people should **pretend** that their customers could go elsewhere. **Make believe** that the corner bistro can buy the same exact product just down the street.

Treating customers right is just good business. A positive relationship forms the basis for successful selling. Besides, customer animosity is not a good thing. Life is hard enough. I have seen the fear in a sales person's eyes as he or she walked in our stores. How uncomfortable! Also, in this day and age with all the mergers, brands moving around, people moving around - you just never know. Your actions **(and your service philosophy)** will determine your customer's willingness to develop a relationship with you and your company. And that willingness, ultimately, will be the true measure of your success.

With all this in mind, here are **26.2 ways your customers can make your life more difficult.** The reason that I have included this chapter in the book is because I think it's important for sales professionals to always keep in mind that, although their customers cannot choose where to buy most products, they can choose whether or not to create an environment where your products will thrive. You may chuckle (or shed a tear) as you remember some of these things happening to you.

- Your customers can refuse to take Monday deliveries, making it hard for beer distributors to balance their weekly delivery schedule. (We wanted Monday deliveries! The driver would come in and straighten up, throw away the empty cartons, and make sure we were adequately stocked. We loved the help.)

- Your customers can ignore your phone calls and delete your emails without reading them.

- Your customers can grant you limited access to associates and make it impossible for you to see the decision makers.

- Your customers can give your competitors, but not you, opportunities to conduct training programs with your associates. To be sure, some states would legislatively frown upon this practice, but clever sales people will always find ways to give to one, while withholding from another.

- Your customers can give your competitors, but not you, opportunities for tastings and other events and refuse the same to you. (see legal disclaimer above!)

- Your customers can put your products on a *really, really* high shelf in a low traffic area!

- Your customers can put your products on a *really, really* low shelf in a low traffic area!

- Your customers can put your products on **no shelf!**

This is important stuff. According to studies published in *Progressive Grocer Magazine*, a display located in a low traffic position can achieve sales increases of 50%, while the same display located in a high traffic position can achieve increases of as much as 600%! Wow!

What else can your customers do?

- Your customers can take you at **1:30 p.m.** for a **1:00 p.m.** meeting.

- Your customers can take you at **2:00 p.m.** for a **1:00 p.m.** meeting.

- Your customers can let you show up in your Sunday's finest, with your sales manager, regional sales manager and national sales manager in tow, listen to your presentation, and then simply and arbitrarily say something to the effect of "Nah" or worse, "Thank you for thinking of us, but no thank you."

Yes, even though your product may be a great value, be well advertised, and in a growing category, your customers may arbitrarily decide to keep it hidden just to make a point. Your on-premise customers could do the following if they were so inclined: remove your by-the-glass program, remove your products from the back bar and/or remove tap handles from behind the bar. Or they could remove your products from the wine list or eliminate tabletops. *You know what I'm talking about!*

Can your customers do anything else? Absolutely!

- Your customers can ignore your products so they get messy, dusty, and disheveled looking. They can choose to place your products *off the beaten path*. They could choose to not maintain the products *off the beaten path*. The truth of the matter is that if your products are in the main aisle (instead of the aisle *leading to nowhere*), they will be better maintained.

- Your customers can do things to get under your skin like moving your products to the stock room when they know you (or worse, your boss) will be stopping by.

- Your customers can take forever to make simple decisions. They can make you wait until the last minute for a decision they made weeks ago just to make you sweat!

- Your customers can let your products run out of stock so consumers buy a different product.

- Your customers can arrange a meeting with you, your sales manager, regional sales manager and national sales manager and cancel the meeting at the last minute. *(As you are pulling into the parking lot!)*

- Your customers can go over your head and make you look bad.

- Your customers can complain incessantly about every little thing, like the way you affix shelf-talkers.

- Your customers can destroy your confidence over time by questioning everything you do.

- Your customers can advertise and promote other's products.

- Your customers can resist your attempts to use cutting edge shelf management techniques and other creative ideas to increase opportunities.

For example, according to Paco Underhill's (1999) legendary book *Why People Buy,* there are definitely specific places that *you* want your products that you would prefer not to see anybody else's products.

For example, most people read left to right and consequently, most consumers reach with their right hand. How do they know this, you may be thinking? Paco Underhill's research consists of thousands of hours of watching video of consumers shopping (fascinating, huh?). Anyway, they suggest placing your product to the right of the category leader. That placement will increase sales while a placement to the left of the category leader will not help. This is important for the following reason:

When consumers come in a store it is almost like a jump ball in basketball. Half the time the ball will go one way, and half the time the ball will go the other way (unless of course the Bull's are playing. Then the other team always gets the ball!). Consumers act in a similar fashion. Many studies (and my own personal observation as a long-time retailer) indicate that consumers know what they want half the time, and need help picking products out the other half of the time. Sometimes consumers ask the retailer for help, but in many other cases, they make their decision while staring at the shelf.

Have an eye on impulse purchase opportunities. Here are a few examples: (a) try to increase facings (b) look for high-traffic display opportunities within the alcohol beverage department, (c) look for high-traffic display opportunities outside the alcohol beverage department - industry studies show that displays located in other departments increase sales substantially, (d) look for cross-merchandising opportunities, (e) look for space near the door handle and away from the hinges in the cold box, (f) try to group your products together for maximum influence.

Now back to our show!

- Your customers can advertise and promote your products at really low prices, ruining your margin structure and causing you to receive messages from every retailer in the land demanding to know why other customers are getting better prices.

This is an important one. Many sales professionals believe that retailers run low prices not only to anger other retailers, but also to get their distributors and suppliers in trouble. Come close - I have secret for you. It is true, but the good news is that it is an inverse relationship. That is, the better a job you do for your customers, the less likely they will wreak havoc (and cause you trouble) in this manner.

- Your customers can sell your products for brief periods of time at really high prices to kill the brand, a particularly good irritant for beer guys!

- Your customers can arbitrarily discontinue your products (we used to be really good at this one) or reduce the amount of your facings.

Facings are a very visible and powerful statement of your brand's image, and they lead to increased sales. In fact, studies conducted by Progressive Grocer magazine suggest that the simple act of reducing three facings to two may cause a 66% sales decrease. Not good!

- Your customers can act in many vindictive ways (like placing your product behind a **post** or some other obstruction) with the sole purpose of taking money right out of your pocket and hurting your company.

- Your customers can refuse to suggest your products to customers!

## The Final Straightaway

We recommended the products of the people we liked, and ignored the others, much of the time. **We simply did a better job merchandising, selling, placing, promoting, maintaining, recommending,**

**cleaning, stacking, displaying and caring about products** that were sold by companies that created an environment where we did business with them – not because we <u>had</u> to but because we <u>wanted</u> to!

I guarantee your customers do the same thing.

Oh yeah, I forgot the final straightaway (in my view, the most important point).

They can decide against carrying your many <u>line extensions</u>. Most brands these days have a few little brothers and sisters that are very important to their companies and not nearly as important to their customers. And for every Bud Light Lime, a tremendous success story in 2008, there are numerous situations where, although the products may be good, your customers will have very little interest. The pressure on these brands is just incredible.

Further, it seems that 18 new vodka brands are introduced into the market every hour. Have you noticed? Yes, and the pages of Beverage Dynamics, Market Watch Magazine, and other publications are always brimming with new releases, not to mention the star brands, growth brands, improving brands, fast track brands, and the infamous category, comeback brands, all vying for attention in a crowded marketplace.

A new flavor, new size, or new package could be the most important item on the suppliers or distributor's agenda that year. To the companies that supply and produce these items, new items are exciting and raise great hopes in the boardroom and on Wall Street; however, to your customers, they are often *just another item.*

Remember the guy from the beginning of this chapter? The one who said, *"I don't care what you think?"* Well, thankfully, his superiors cared *about our thoughts,* and you should care the same about what your customers are thinking. Treat them like they can go elsewhere to buy the same products. *Care what your customers think* and you will win their loyalty.

*That's just the way it works!*

# MANAGING TASKS AND TIME

It does not matter if I am out East or down South or shoveling snow in the Midwest; I always hear a similar refrain from sales people and their managers: *"How do I manage a steadily increasing portfolio with my already voluminous amount of items?"*

No small problem to be sure. While some distributors report having 30-40% more products than just a year ago, customers have less T.A.P.E. (time, attention, patience and energy). They are facing their own issues (slumping sales, less people to do the work, etc.) and opportunities (how to grow their businesses). Taking in a new product every week and helping sales professionals make their goals may not be on the top of their to-do list.

Come to think of it, distributor sales people have less time, attention, patience, and energy as well. As a supplier executive put it one morning in Harry Schumacher's newsletter (Beer Business Daily), *"I have noticed wholesaler personnel being really, really stretched. Poor response time and/or voice mail boxes full, sloppy on details, an ambivalence toward brands. It seems the new wholesaler era is a race to lock-up cases to achieve case drop yields and step away from service and brand building."*

When you take a few moments to consider the changes in the industry, do you agree? The truth is, wasting time on unproductive tasks is a killer, and accomplishing more with less time may be one of the biggest contributors to your success both with suppliers and customers.

I believe your ability to steadily introduce new products and manage a larger by-the-minute portfolio relies on the following:

- Your time-management and organizational skills.

- Your ability to creatively get customers interested in new products. Often, new products are introduced as placements based upon perceived entitlement instead of tangible business reasons.

- Your ability to build, cultivate, and maintain healthy and enjoyable relationships. In other words, your ability to create a situation where your customers do business with you and your company, *not because they have to, but because they want to.* There is that phrase again. I use it a lot because I know it is vital to your success!

For the purposes of this chapter, we will concentrate on time management and organization. We already know that your customers have less time, attention, patience, and energy, while at the same time, you need more of their time, attention, patience and energy! Not to mention, all the new items you have to sell and the fact that you are probably doing a whole lot more than you were hired to do.

So what do you do?

Now more than ever, sales professionals must strive to make every second count. Now more than ever, sales professionals must be able to easily prioritize and focus on the most critical tasks. Now more than ever, sales professionals must be able to turn work around quickly and have an efficient way to track to-dos. Now more than ever, sales professionals must resist the urge to get caught up in minutiae and unproductive tasks. Now more than ever, sales professionals must stick to the activities that positively affect their company's revenues.

You know it and I know it!

There are so many great sources for effective time management and organization. To help readers gain clarity on this subject, I have reviewed the works of many personal productivity experts and combined their insights with my ideas from watching sales people operate and talking with many successful sales professionals to gather their best practices. I also bring in my experiences and tools from a lifetime of managing people in our family's retail business.

I am firmly of the opinion that many sales people in this industry are waiting for someone to come along and motivate them. ***It is not going to happen.*** Nobody is coming to the rescue. Getting organized and managing your time wisely is (you guessed it) your choice. Is it easy? Absolutely not! Does it take a time commitment up front? Yes, and thankfully, it is extra work that will make you more efficient.

**<u>Getting started</u>:**

- **Know where you stand** – so you know where to get started.

Yes, some sales professionals (say they are organized) but many are hiding unanswered calls and emails and un-delegated tasks. Many have projects that have been on the to-do list forever. Others feel a particular anxiety caused by lack of control, lack of organization, lack of preparation and lack of action. Perhaps you are one of the many who have half a dozen things you are trying to accomplish right now – but not having the ability to get anywhere.

So I have to ask. Are you completing the tasks you set out for the week? Are you organized or disorganized? Is your desk a mess? Do you look at a project and think *how in the world am I going to get this done?*

If you are – please recognize that better time management and organization are skills, which can be learned. That is the first step.

- **Focus on the long term picture** – and have more short-term successes.

Have a sense of where you are going with a customer or project. For example, say you want to achieve 80% penetration with your top 25 customers. In other words, if your goal is to have 4 out of every 5 of your items in your top accounts, it only makes sense that you know the level of your current penetration. Many sales people would immediately think (in a knee-jerk manner), *I have to get more items in XYZ restaurants.* But then what?

Begin by comparing your current penetration at XYZ restaurant with your desired penetration and set reasonable targets for improving this metric.

For the purposes of knowing where you stand, I suggest you build a spreadsheet that captures (at a minimum) the following data:

- The number of SKU's your company has
- The percentage of penetration you have in each of your top 25 accounts
- The top 10 most profitable brands at your company
- The top 3 brands not currently placed at your top accounts
- The top brands (in terms of profit) that are not placed in your top (or fastest growing) accounts
- The names of your top accounts that are less price resistant than the others (i.e. the ones where you can make fair margins)
- The names of brands that your fastest growing accounts do not carry

Here is another example. If you determine (and can see visually) that your 8th biggest account has only 6 of the 10 most profitable brands (for your company), then you have good information for what to work on. With the amount of SKU's in your portfolio, it is very easy to understand why some important items get lost in the shuffle.

As I stated earlier, this takes time but once you have made that initial investment, you will reap the rewards of your effort (and organization)

- **Get it all in a system**

A great source for personal productivity is a book by David Allen (2001) called *Getting Things Done.* The premise of this book is this: If you fail to *download* everything you have to do into some sort of system – your mind will never be clear. If your mind is not clear – you are not going to operate at peak productivity. Does that make sense?

Allen argues that until you generate a *next step* for each project or task, each project or task will be an *open-loop* continually pulling at you. When these items pull at you, the result is stress, distraction and a lack of clarity. If, on the other hand, you capture *open-loop* items in a system, your mind will be clear and you will spend your time more constructively. In my view, this is one of the strongest concepts in all the information out there on time management and personal productivity.

Do as Horace, the Roman philosopher says: *"Rule your mind or it will rule you!"*

- **Be willing to change**

If you have made great strides in your career, you are probably used to being able to rise just above everyone else. Somehow, you always come out looking pretty good. At the higher levels, though, you may notice that everyone is very skilled. Suddenly, your competitors (both in your company and out) are aggressive and ambitious – just like you. There comes a time when you have to *kick it up a notch*. To succeed (and continue to prosper), you must take a good hard look at how you handle time and tasks and make some changes to be more productive.

<u>**Task management:**</u>

- **Prioritize, prioritize, prioritize** – remember the old adage in real estate - location, location, and location?

Same concept applies here. Maybe you are familiar with Pareto's principle. This widely held logic holds that 20% of your activities will likely account for 80% of your success. Make sure that you spend the most time doing tasks that make the most sense, specifically, those tasks that move you closer to the finish line with your customers – a place where they are inclined and motivated to *embrace* more of your products.

*You are never going to have enough time to do everything and the time is going to pass regardless of how you spend it. So the question*

*(should you ask) is how can I be the most effective and what are my highest value activities?*

The key to effective procrastination is ignoring the small tasks and handling the big tasks that help you win your customer's loyalty. I believe that the difference between high performers and low performers is what tasks they choose to place on the backburner.

- **Study your tasks** – to determine which tasks are most important

Which tasks contribute the most to your success? Which tasks are most important to your company's success? Which tasks help you make money? Which tasks constitute real or implied promises made to your customers? These are the ones you should get started with right away. As author Dan Kennedy puts it, *"Tasks don't get better with age like a fine wine!"*

The secret to getting ahead (and getting things done) is getting started. Think about it this way. When you wake up in the morning, you have to accomplish nearly 100 different tasks to get out the door – but you probably do not think of it that way. The first task is to get out of bed. It makes very little sense to put your shoes on right away, even if the floor is cold. We do this all naturally. Professionals need to have the same thought process for their day-to-day tasks.

Do the following activity: think of a challenging task that you recently completed successfully. Write out all the steps you went through to complete the task. Step-by-step. Now apply the thinking that made you feel good about the completed project to another project that you have not started yet because it is overwhelming the living daylights out of you. Learn from one of your project management successes.

- **Do tasks that are close to your company's revenue line**

Author Julie Morgenstern (2008) suggests, in her book, *Never Check Email in the Morning,* that the largest portion of your time should be spent on tasks that are *"close to your revenue line."* She goes on to say, *"the tighter the economy, the more important it becomes to evaluate all the tasks on your to-do list in terms of their relationship to directly making or saving your company money."*

Sounds like a good plan for this environment.

- **Break tasks into pieces** – so your un-completed tasks seem more manageable.

You can overcome fear and procrastination by taking your mind off a huge task. Focus on a single action to move forward. Many people become so overwhelmed by the sheer enormity of a task, that the only response is to put off starting. Break the task into pieces. There is an old saying, *by the yard it's hard, inch by inch it's a cinch."*

Start with the biggest task. Take action. What are the tasks that, upon their completion, would give you the greatest feeling of success? What are the tasks that, upon their completion, will have the greatest effect on your company's bottom line? Do those tasks first. Brian Tracy, author of *Eat That Frog* talks about eating the ugliest frog first. His point: if you have to eat a frog (or handle a distasteful task), you might as well get it over with. If there are two frogs and one is uglier than the other – eat the uglier one first.

Use this logic to handle your important tasks.

- **Make lists** – so that you remember important tasks, stay focused and have direction. It is a good feeling to check off accomplishments.

Writing things down is liberating. The more you get on paper, the less you have to worry about forgetting important priorities. It is all about organizing and managing ideas. Your goal is to not let ideas slip by. Write everything down. Keep a pen and pad of paper with you at all times. Write ideas down on note cards, project files or customer files and/or notebooks. Anywhere, just get the idea out of your head!

French philosopher Emile Chartier said, *"Nothing is more dangerous than an idea when it is the only one you have."* Get tasks and ideas out of your brain and into a notepad of some sort.

For example, I give many different types of workshops and presentations but there is one I am giving in the next several months that I do not do that often. To me – that is intimidating. I think to myself, *I'm going to be traveling a lot and doing other presentations. When, oh when am I going to have time to prepare for that one?*

I imagine you have similar challenges. The most normal reaction or emotion is to silently ruminate over these challenges. Or, you could take charge. In my example, I could take out a piece of paper and jot down all my thoughts for that particular presentation along with some next steps and suggested completion dates for components of the project. Now, it will seem more manageable. The point is I will feel better by doing a quick brainstorming session (with myself) and clearing my *mental calculator.*

Once your thoughts are down on paper – then what? Do you use a priority system like labeling tasks A-B-C-D-E? Do you use a calendar to classify your to-do items by day? This is actually an age-old question for productivity experts. Some say *yes;* label your tasks from low priority to high priority and do only the A-B items. Maybe the C items if you have some time. The problem is that you never have enough time so how would you ever get to the C-D-E items? What ends up happening is the continual movement of uncompleted tasks from Monday to Tuesday to Wednesday, etc. Do you get the picture?

This is demoralizing as the end result is that tasks are not being completed.

I like the following instead. Have a list of *next actions* for calls, errands, customer-related activities, etc. Try to keep only one list and carefully consider what the next step is for each task or project. For example, if you need to call the winery to get a lesser-known piece of information for a restaurant customer, but you have to ask your sales manager who to call at the winery, *that is your next step.* **Getting a hold of your sales manager.** Write *that* on your list. Move the project from the *how in the world am I going to get that information* stage and think to yourself, *if I am to accomplish that task, what is the next step?* Now you have some clarity.

If important tasks need to be completed by a certain date, put those on your calendar, but other than that, lists are more effective for helping you manage your tasks and their completion.

- **Plan your week and work your plan** (not sure where I heard that one, but it really applies here).

Decide what you want to achieve every day, every week, every sales call, and stick to it. *Always know what the* <u>next step</u> *is.* Again, according to author David Allen, too many discussions end with only a vague sense of what the next step is. To reduce stress and uncertainty, always determine the next step.

It used to be (way back when) that the organization in our lives was more static. We would go to work, take a break, work some more, eat lunch, work some more and then go home. Not the case in today's world. Now, our organization is more dynamic in nature. Our work-day requires constant adjustments. Shifting priorities, shifting tasks and shifting workloads affect us every day and make our days unpre-dictable.

## Time management:

• **Use a time log** – to see where the time goes

Record how you use your time for a few weeks. You would be amazed at how much time is wasted on unnecessary tasks. Your most precious asset should not be squandered.

Plan more time into your schedule. Allow for more time going from meeting to meeting. Allow for the fact that your customers may take you late for a meeting. (Customers do that from time to time - remember the last chapter?) Avoid squeezing every task into one day. The key is how you handle your time when you are running ahead of schedule or when you have a few extra seconds. Have your *next action calls list* with you. Make important calls and return emails. Better yet, stop by unannounced at a customer's place of business to help out.

Write a schedule as it relates to time. How does your actual time compare to your estimated time? After reviewing your time log ask yourself – is this how I want to be spending my time? Analyze what you are getting done during your various blocks of time? We all know that it is not about the number of hours you put in, but more about what you actually accomplish. With a time log, you will be in a better posi-tion to pull the plug on unproductive initiatives that waste time.

If time always seems to fly (where did the time go?) or you have trouble managing your time, use an analog clock (as many executive functioning experts suggest) so you may visually see the passage of time.

- **Plan time for planning** - spend some time before the week planning and you will be sure to allocate more time to important tasks and less time to unimportant tasks.

Plan your daily schedule the night before. Experts say that spending just 10-12 minutes planning the night before can save you up to 2 hours the following day. What do *you* want to accomplish tomorrow? If you decide the night before exactly what you intend to conquer the next morning, you will hit the ground running. Alternatively, you could spend 30 or 60 minutes figuring out what to do that day, but that is probably a strategy that will not work out so well.

- **Don't waste valuable time** – by doing invaluable things

Avoid the water cooler chatter at all costs. It is your responsibility to sell products, and when times are tough, as they have been recently, resisting the all-to-common urge to concentrate on the negative is imperative.

Keep your time drains in check. As you review your time log, make special note of your biggest time wasters. Ask yourself the following questions: Why am I doing this? And what will I (or my company) gain from doing this? The more you recognize these saboteurs the better.

Spend less time on the Internet. Call to check in on a customer instead of playing with your mobile device. Use every opportunity to take your customer's temperature. Use every opportunity to stop and visit with your customers.

- **Devote the first hour of every day to your most critical tasks**

Not only will you get a great jump on the day, but also you will feel great about your accomplishment. You will feel more in control and you will not have your most critical tasks hanging over you all day – weighing you down with guilt. Focus on the joy of completion. Numerous Gallup surveys sight a direct correlation between job satisfaction and achievement. Enjoy the thrill of task completion.

- **Review your schedule, calendar, to-do list, etc. every day** – so you have a clear picture of what needs to be accomplished.

Most personal productivity experts say that no entrepreneur will achieve success without reviewing what or she wants/needs to accomplish. *Wait, I'm not an entrepreneur. I work for XYZ Company.* Is that what you are thinking? I hope not! The truth is that successful sales people are just that – entrepreneurs. They handle their accounts, their routes like they are running their own businesses.

Review your lists at least once a week. File items that one day might serve as reference in the appropriate place – a file in your drawer clearly labeled. Empty your head.

Make a list of what you are putting off. Next to each item - list the fear that is preventing you from acting. Is the desire to be perfect playing into any of these items? If you look at the *fears* and think it over, you will probably realize that the fears are unrealized.

### Overcome Unproductive use of time:

- **Understand why you procrastinate** – and get more done with your free time!

Develop strategies for identifying and eliminating the causes of procrastination to be more productive. Why are you unable to get started on a particular task when you know that getting started is half the battle? Consider the words of President Abraham Lincoln who said, *"You cannot escape the responsibility of tomorrow by evading it today."*

- **Identify your common excuses** – and the reasons you tell yourself why it is okay to not complete important tasks.

Get the upper hand on the excuses. When you catch yourself putting off a task – identify the reasons why you are allowing that to be acceptable. Get a hold of the self-talk and turn it into a motivator. Stop accepting old excuses.

Do not delay starting an important task or project because you want everything to be just right. Realize your tendency to obsess and ask yourself – *if this is not absolutely perfect, is it really going to make a difference?*

- **Focus on the payoff** – keep in mind why you are doing whatever it is you are doing!

- **Have rewards to motivate the completion of disliked tasks.**

Just like when children complete an undesired task. Do the same for yourself. Go out for ice cream, watch a ball game, or chill out for a while. Give yourself a reward to look forward to. Appreciate the sense of energy and enthusiasm and self-esteem from completing important tasks. Completing an agreement with another or yourself is a little victory. A win! That is why people write tasks down on to-do lists only to immediately check them off because they are already complete. Everybody wants to win!

The motivation to complete tasks needs, first and foremost, to come from within. No, it should not come from the person signing your paycheck although *your boss does have some influence.* The most productive people find the resources (within themselves) to break down tasks and find the time to work through them.

- **Organize your bag or briefcase**

Organizing your bag or briefcase has as much to do with effective sales calls as time and task management. If your bag is disorganized, there will be two results. One, you will not be able to find what you need, *when you need it* and two, you will end up rummaging through your bag in a meeting and, again, you will probably not find what you need in a timely manner. The result: you will be embarrassed and your customer will find you unprepared.

Establish different sections for different aspects of your life and business. Keep customer files in one place – where they can be accessed in a hurry. Limit what you carry. Be realistic and do not haul around what you know in your heart you will not get to. Clean your briefcase daily and bring that organization into other parts of your life.

### Other strategies for becoming more productive:

- **Resist having long phone calls that mean nothing to you** – unless, of course, you're checking in on your mother!

- **Be decisive** – as being wishy-washy wastes a ton of time. If a task will take you less than 2 minutes to accomplish – do it!

- **Beware of the pitfalls of multitasking** – and use your brain-power to do one thing very well.

You may think that multitasking increases productivity. I used to think that, but I now know that is not the case. The editors of NeuroImage, a science journal, set out to study this behavior. They determined that managing two mental tasks at the same time significantly reduces the brain-power available to concentrate on either one, ultimately damaging the quality of your final product.

- **Be a self-advocate** – ask for help.

For example, pretend you are a new sales person in the beverage industry and you are overwhelmed by all the magazines and web sites with industry relevant information. For a while you try to keep up with each and every source – but that does not work very long. Be your own advocate. Ask your sales manager or a friend with more experience to help you wade through the information jungle. You can count on one thing. You have to ask for the help. Nobody is going to offer it up unless you ask.

- **When in doubt** – throw it out.

If it seems like junk, it probably is. Stay one step ahead of unruly piles by tossing as much as possible right off the bat. Unless, of course, it is a piece of marketing titled *Winning the Customer Loyalty Marathon*. Keep that stuff and examine it thoroughly.

Seriously, though, according to Rita Emmett (2000) and The Procrastinator's Handbook, *"You can't do it all. You can't learn it all and you can't read it all. The wastebasket can actually be your friend!"*

Ask yourself – does this piece of potential junk relate to a viable opportunity? Will it help me make money? Will my job be affected if I throw it away? If the answer is no, aim for the basket and try for a three-pointer!

- **Fight the fear of imperfection** – learn to accept flaws but understand the potential consequences of incomplete tasks.

Nobody is perfect. The sooner you accept that, the better you will be with your customers. We all lose our keys from time to time. It has nothing to do with our intelligence. So, if you are late for a meeting – it happens. Just do not make a habit of it! Your customers do not expect perfection; they expect *effort* and *fairness* and many other traits you will read about in this book. Get over the little mistakes and keep going. Your goal is improvement, not perfection.

- **Fight the fear of judgment** – do not postpone worthy goals and ideas because you are afraid of what your bosses and co-workers may think.

- **Keep a tickler file** – to keep miscellaneous papers straight.

Go to the office supply store and buy tabs numbered 1-31 and tabs with the months of the year. When you have to review a proposal next Tuesday (or the following Tuesday), place it behind the appropriate folder tab. This will help reduce the mountains of piles that may inhabit your desk and office. If anything, keeping papers in a tickler file will help you save time when you are looking for a particular document.

- **Create a workable schedule**

Consider the following suggestions from the Harvard Business School Press. Don't book every minute of your day. Leave some time for surprises or just for getting easy tasks out of the way. Schedule creative activities for times of the day where you have peak energy. For example, if you need some quiet time to tackle a new initiative, allocate some time while you are still fresh – and not after downing a double cheeseburger. Also, keep your schedule and (next steps) list handy and check your progress throughout the day.

- **Put a date** - on everything you touch.

You may have heard experts say *touch every paper only once.* I do not agree with that premise. I believe if you subscribe to that philosophy, you may be rushed into acting impulsively just to clear your docket. On the other hand, I do know that it is important to know when you last touched something. If you handle a piece of correspondence every day for 2 weeks without taking some action, you probably need to review you organization strategy.

- **Handle people** - that want to abuse your time.

You know the type. They wait until you are back in the office for a day and then interrupt you every 5 minutes with *pressing matters* that are *not really so pressing.* Make appointments with these individuals, much like you would with other people. Guard your time as the precious resource that it is. Also, be wary of other peoples' emergencies. As it has been suggested in many places, *lack of planning on your colleague's part does not constitute an emergency on your part.*

- **Make the decision** – do not get busy with a thousand little things when it comes time to make a decision.

Determine the time of day that you think most effectively and make headway on significant projects during those hours. *Just do it,* as the Nike slogan goes. Consider the words of Ralph Waldo Emerson, *"What you are afraid to do is a clear indication of what you need to do next."*

- **Understand the cost** - of *not making a decision.*

Yes, there are costs inherent in stalling and procrastinating. Understand the financial risks of dragging your feet. Some costs may be financial but the main cost in not making a decision is emotional. Not sure about the rest of you, but when I am avoiding a decision, it eats away at my insides. Being agitated and frustrated is no way to go through the day and fear is paralyzing and counterproductive. Anyway, the person who never makes a mistake is probably not doing anything.

- **Say no once in a while** – so you do not get unnecessarily over-loaded.

The trick is how you say it. Do not over-schedule. Leave some time for unexpected events. Okay, okay, I know: easier said than done. At the very least, keep it in mind! The price you pay for breaking agreements in the world is disintegration of trust in the relationship. Often, you say *yes* to win people's approval and then when you break an agreement, you feel anxious because you have not only potentially harmed a work or customer relationship, but also a little agreement with yourself.

### In summary (because time is a wasting)!

I said this earlier in the chapter and it bears repeating. You will never have enough time to do everything you want to do. The most productive sales professionals do the tasks that help them win their customer's loyalty and move them closer to their goals. The most productive sales professionals have an entrepreneurial mindset. These motivated individuals realize that (although they may not own a company), their *business* is their career. These individuals make the decision to change some habits. Now, do not procrastinate and move on to the next chapter. But first, as you contemplate the role of time management in your life, consider the words of the ultra-famous, quote machine anonymous. *"If you always do what you've always done, you will always get what you've always got!"*

*That's just the way it works!*

Vending Machine Man is oblivious to the fact that good organization will help him with his customers. He is a pretender. Partners understand that great organizational skills create more efficient use of time, which, in turn will help them win their customer's loyalty!

# QUESTIONS FROM THE FIELD

Q: Why can't I be more productive?

**A: There are many reasons why sales people fail to reach maximum productivity.**

This is a great question and while just a few professionals are brave enough to ask me this, I believe it is a concern for many others.

Here are a few suggestions for improvement:

- **Never take your *eye off the ball***

Said another way, some sales professionals *run in place*. To pursue success, one needs to be aware of the impulses that lead to running in place and taking ones' eyes of the ball. Much of the time it stems from a lack of concentration. Sales people meet with customers with their minds drifting. When you meet with customers, take special care to listen to them and stay focused. Another reason often given for lack of focus is uncertainty and fear. Always remember that courage and action lead to success.

- **Multi-tasking is counter productive**

Yes, doing too many things at once! I am referring to being marginally productive at many tasks instead of supremely productive at any one task. Have you ever been on the phone discussing an important topic and you hear the other person typing away furiously in the background? I know we all have been in that situation. Give your undivided attention to anyone you are talking to, especially when conversing with customers. The funny thing is that those who make the worst use of their time are the first to complain of its shortness. Give important tasks (and phone calls) 100% of your attention.

- **Looking past a golden opportunity**

Stop by any tasting or industry event and you will see people greeting each other. As you observe them, pay careful attention to where these individuals are looking. Many are looking <u>past</u> the person they are talking to. Who are they looking for? Are they searching for the proverbial *better person* with whom to speak? Instead of talking to someone, and looking at the nametags of others in the group, or at a group elsewhere who might be more important – or the refreshment table - give your partner or customer your undivided attention.

- **Thinking of unfinished business instead of the business at hand**

In Chapter 10, I suggest taking care of unfinished business early on in the sales call. The reason is so that once you have completed that part of the call; you can concentrate on solving problems and creating buying opportunities.

- **Waking up in the morning with no idea what to do that day**

I am not talking about running a sales route. Over time, anybody can learn a sales route. I am speaking more about *what to do* (above and beyond the ordinary) to be successful. One thing you can do (before you go to bed each night) is to review your *next actons* list so you know what to handle the next day. You will sleep better, feel a sense of peace and *have a clue* when you wake up in the morning about what to do first!

To improve your productivity, sales experts suggest you chart your progress. Try measuring the following:

- **How many sales calls you make per week?**
- **How many requests you make per week?**
- **How many people are saying *yes*?**
- **How often are your customers saying *yes*?**
- **What your customers are saying *yes* to?**
- **What is the time of your first call? Your last call?**
- **When you do things differently, what happens?**

The only way to be more productive is to study how you use your time <u>now</u>. That is why measuring your time is so important. Your analysis will help you see where improvements can be made. Some companies have tools in place for measuring productivity, and if yours does not, then the onus is on you to take the initiative to understand the productivity process. The choice is yours and you should listen to the words of heavyweight boxing champion, George Forman, who says, *"Success begins with a decision!"*

*That's just the way it works* (and I wouldn't argue with George Foreman!)

Creating a next actions list will have a profound
impact on your career

# GUARD YOUR COMPANY'S IMAGE, AND YOURS, WITH YOUR LIFE

Last summer my wife and I picked up our son at overnight camp in Southern Wisconsin. On the way home we stopped at a gas station. As we pulled into the parking lot I immediately noticed a big brewer's beer truck. On the way to the bathroom I encountered the driver and a salesman having one of the most *profanity-laced* stories I have ever heard - and I grew up in a liquor store! It was a bit much for me, and my son Josh, still only 13-years old at the time, did not need to hear such an interesting interpretation of the English language!

Here is the point we outlined in Chapter 1: sales professionals (and drivers) are the most critical link between distributors and their customers. They are always on the clock, always in the spotlight, and always expected to represent the company in a professional manner. These professionals spend the most time in an account, and often make or break the overall service experience. When salespeople wear clothing that identifies their company and brands, their behavior is even more critical.

Good manners and proper etiquette are more important than you think. Consumers do not always know the difference between a store or bar's employee and someone who is only there to conduct business. National distributors and suppliers of alcohol spend millions upon millions of dollars promoting their brands, and I guarantee upper management of the big brewer whose salesperson and driver I overheard would be quite disheartened by the display. That is why good behavior is so important. The fact is that distributor professionals in customer accounts can either really help, or really hurt the sales process.

Here are a few things to keep in mind to make positive impressions.

- **Watch the language and keep it clean**

Some people do not mind locker room talk, but others do. Keep it clean and professional at all times. Many groups of people find certain topics of discussion *offensive,* so stay away from areas like religion, politics, and sex. Avoid stereotyping at all costs. Years ago in our retail wine business we revamped our buying structure. I met with many distributors with the hopes that some smaller houses could help us with our needs. I remember meeting with a gentleman one afternoon. The conversation was going really well. I remember thinking to myself, *I could do business with this company!*

Then the guy dropped a religious stereotype on me – and did not even realize he did it. That was it! Suffice to say, he never got the opportunity to help us meet our needs. Be careful with borderline topics.

Avoid complaining and ripping on your competitors. It is potentially hurtful, usually destructive, and can really harm your career. Instead of pointing out your competitor's weaknesses, which makes you look like an amateur, spend your time laying out reasons why the customer should do business with you. Besides, mentioning your competitors and giving them a sincere compliment here or there shows that you can be objective. Just do not go *so* overboard (with your compliments) that your customer is more interested in their products than yours!

- **Dress neatly and professionally**

Usually, the women do not need any help in this area, but the men – well that is a different story. Men: keep the shirts tucked in. Hats should not look like they were run over by the truck that delivers your products. Also, hats should be worn straight, not crooked and not backwards. Numerous studies have proven time and time again that proper dress instills more confidence in your customers, and that is the goal. Be as professionally dressed as your customer. On the other hand, just because your customer wears a golf shirt, does not mean that you should do the same. Ere on the side of caution!

Do your customers judge your grooming? Absolutely. Is it fair? Probably not! They do judge, however, and your best bet is to appear professional as that simple act will help build your customer's confidence in you.

One caveat: Do not rely on personal appearance alone. A great appearance might help sell magazine covers but will only take you so far in the beverage business. In the long run – preparation and professionalism are far more important.

- **Smile**

Smile – and portray the illusion that you are happy to be there – even if you are not. Ask yourself – am I a joy to be around? Do I lift others up with my presence and attitude, or am I like the Saturday Night Live character "Debbie Downer" – always bringing people down? Usually we look for ways to lift *ourselves* up. Do the opposite for a change. Look for ways to lift others. Remember: smiling is actually medically good for you – as I mentioned at the end of Chapter 1. It raises the level of good chemicals in your body and lowers the bad chemicals.

That is the end of the medical lesson and please note: no medical textbooks were consulted in the writing of this paragraph, but you get the idea! So with great liberty I say, *a smile a day keeps the Doctor away*; make sure to smile as often as possible.

Enter accounts enthusiastically. Move with a sense of purpose. No, you need not move around your accounts with sweat dripping from your brow. Move in a manner that suggests you have a job to do and you take that responsibility very seriously. One day last year, I flew from Dallas to San Antonio. Just before the flight was scheduled to depart, the captain announced that there was a liquid dripping from the landing gear. They were going to check it out. "Good idea!" I thought to myself.

I was sitting on the left side of the aircraft. I saw the mechanic park about 40 feet from the airplane. Now, I have seen plenty of people going pretty slow at the end of marathons (*and who wouldn't be after trudging along for 25 miles*), but this guy was ridiculously slow. He shuffled ever so slowly towards the landing gear as most of the passengers on the left side of the aircraft watched in disbelief. Airlines constantly beat into their customers' heads the terms *on time departure and on time arrival,* but here was a mechanic strolling along as if he was taking a walk along a beach.

I have said it before and it bears repeating. The moment you enter an account, you are on display. Your every move is watched. Make sure to smile, share your passion, and move with a sense of purpose.

- **Be helpful**

Help the consumers you come across in your accounts. Hold the door for someone. Show the way if a customer seems lost. Because you go there frequently, you know the *lay of the land* as well as anyone, so help those in need of help or directions. Remember, the consumer will not distinguish between who works there and who is servicing the account – they just know that they had a positive and pleasant shopping experience - or the opposite.

Also, guys, please stay away from the tasting girls. One of my most interesting (and frustrating) memories from all the vendor tastings we had over the years was how the sales professional would always hang around the tasting girl, like she needed help or something. The most professional of salesmen kept their eyes properly placed in their heads and helped customers instead of stalking and staring. Remember, it is all about the experience for consumers. As a retailer, I shared the following expression with our associates: *"Make the buying of wine, beer and spirits as wonderful as drinking them!"* Do your part to make that a reality for your customers and *their customers.* Make sure to help consumers!

- **Treat people with dignity**

When brands move around in the beverage industry, people can instantly become stars with their new portfolio. In some cases, unfortunately, the inevitable occurs - an inflated ego. This is where the trouble starts, and in a multitude of ways, sales people begin to thumb their noses at the little people.

Try this instead: treat everybody with whom you come in contact with great dignity. Remember that many of the people in your customer's businesses have dreams, goals, and aspirations, just like you. Never make people feel small. Resist the practice of gossiping behind people's backs. Do not join the party that makes fun of people. If you have to give feedback, then do so in a professional manner. Have fun with others, but not at their expense. Always remember that what goes around, comes around.

- **Maintain your areas**

Replenish the stock that has sold since your last visit. Do you need to maintain an on-premise account's by-the-glass program? Make sure to do so. Take care of the little details. Pay special attention to priority items. Continuously monitor the back bar to make sure products are visible to the consumer. Rotate the stock in your displays, in the cold box, and on the shelf to name a few areas. Help to assure that older products get sold first!

Make sure your stock is maintained in the back room in a clean and professional manner. On the shelf, make sure labels are correct. If you notice a mistake on a store-generated label – say something. There is an old saying in retail: *"If it doesn't have a price on it, it's not for sale."* In my past life, I saw this play out hundreds of times. A consumer would be drawn to a display, pick up a bottle and look for a price. If the price was not clear, he or she would quickly put bottle down and move on. What a shame! All the marketing and promotion in the world will not rise above such carelessness. Always make sure your items are correctly merchandised!

In summary, the challenge with beverage professionals using foul language (in this example) or acting in other unprofessional ways is that he or she represents the weakest link for management. As the expression goes, *you are only as strong as your weakest link.* I used to employ over 200 people in my business. I dealt with all kinds of moods, problems, and attitudes. People brought a whole host of personal garbage to work. Sales professionals must save their baggage for the overhead bins, so to speak.

Managers may ask - so how do you achieve some measure of uniformity, some sense of customer service standards?  By *articulating a customer-focused vision.*  By constantly sharing why it is so important for sales people and drivers to maintain a professional demeanor in public.  By emphasizing the *results* of good manners and etiquette, and why it is so important to achieve those *results.*

So keep the following in mind.  Your job is more than delivering beer, selling a new wine label, or taking an order.  It is making your customers more successful by taking an active, heartfelt interest in their businesses and by instilling confidence with your words and actions. Just keep repeating the following phrase: **The more professional I appear, the better I will fare!** You win the customer loyalty marathon one step at a time (pun intended), and the image you portray in your accounts should be a big part of your strategy.

*That's just the way it works!*

Vending Machine Man is terribly unprofessional.  He's a pretender. Your job, as a partner, is to realize that the more professional you appear, the better you will fare! Professionalism builds confidence in the eyes of your teammates and your customers.

# DEVELOPING STRATEGIES
# FOR BETTER COMMUNICATION

Last summer our oldest son was away at summer camp. He was 13 – and it was our first experience having a child away. Our son (in all his teenage wisdom) opted for the "very limited" communication package. Suffice to say, I can count the letters we received using just a few fingers.

Apparently, he enjoyed the lack of communication, but it begs the question – do retailers, bar owners, and restaurateurs like it when a distributor or supplier fails to communicate? My guess is 'no,' and when I consider that dynamic, I am always reminded of the great movie *Cool Hand Luke* when the late Paul Newman says, "*What we have here is a failure to communicate.*"

There are a whole host of factors that lead to successful relationships, and communication is certainly near the top of the list. Please understand that I am not naive about some of the larger changes and challenges buffeting the supplier/distributor/retailer relationship, particularly consolidation and the intense pressure to produce quick fixes and profits. But now more than ever, it is important to open and improve channels of communication - it is not a cure-all, but it is a start.

Creating an environment where retailers (be they bars, restaurants, or stores) are motivated to sell your products (whether you are a distributor or supplier) is always the goal. Better communication leads to reliable and consistent service to retailers, and that is the key.

Here are 26.2 questions distributors and suppliers should ask to be sure their communication skills are not leading to the rifts, rancor, and recriminations so prevalent in today's industry.

- Do I communicate my company's objectives to my customers?

*You don't roll a keg down the driveway and hope it gets to the cooler.* Nor do you try the same tactic to achieve mutually beneficial relationships. Sometimes you need a roadmap to show what you are hoping to achieve. You should be asking - do I communicate the supplier's objectives? Do I communicate cohesiveness in the supplier/distributor dynamic? Do I communicate that we are on the same page?

- Do I communicate problems or issues when they occur, or do I wait until the last minute (i.e. showing up on the last day of the month *in need of cases)?*

- Do I communicate relevant pricing information in a timely fashion, or do I spring price increases on my customers at the last minute?

- Do I communicate with my customers *even* when I do not want anything?

In other words, do I ever stop by an account just to see how my customer is doing, not necessarily with the intent to take cash out of his or her pocket? (See Chapter 17 for much more on the topic of *giving value.)*

- Do I communicate a sense of partnership?

- Do I communicate *why* the category is hot instead of simply pointing it out?

- Do I communicate relevant market information, or do I share information from far-away lands (in an effort) to make a sale?

- Do I communicate ways to sell products through the retail channel, or do I just dump my products and move on to the next customer?

- Do I communicate with multiple levels of my customer's organization? (In other words, do I say hello to the bartender or walk right past in search of the owner/manager?)

- Do I communicate ways that retailers can sell my products in a profitable way?

- Do I communicate my appreciation when my customers do things for me?

Do I share my appreciation when my customer expands his or her business, or when he or she spends his or her hard earned money to fill a new store, bar or restaurant with my products?

- Do I communicate my appreciation *even* when my customers say no? (If your customer says "no," hopefully you are learning something about your sales approach.)

- Do I communicate creative ideas to help sell products? (Not the same tired promotions, but creative *out of the box* ideas.)

Often sales people find it difficult to create and communicate new ideas. Sales people erroneously feel that they have tried everything. Usually, there are other tactics that they can try and they will come to that realization with a bit more communication. Talk to senior level performers for suggestions. List ideas that have worked in the past. Have senior level people act as mentors with the goal of communicating new and exciting ideas to the company's customers. Especially in tough times!

- Do I communicate what is interesting and exciting about my products?

- Do I communicate how my products stand out from the competition? (If not, why should my customer buy my products?)

- Do I communicate with a positive attitude? (In other words, am I an upper or a downer to be around?)

- Do I communicate why my customer should do business with me?

In other words, do I communicate my company's unique selling proposition?

- Do I communicate fully what I am trying to accomplish with my brands – including price, image, demographic appeal, etc?

- Do I communicate changes in my company before my customers find out *on the street?*

- Do I communicate and share results in a timely and constructive fashion?

- Do I communicate the truth in an open, honest and straightforward fashion?

Will I communicate the hard truth if I feel my customer's business is tanking? (See Chapter 14 for much, much more on trust!)

- Do I communicate in a direct and succinct way? (Do I understand that my customers have less time, attention, patience and energy?) Do I communicate in a way that will save my customer time?

- Do I communicate ways to help make my customers more successful? (In other words, if you do *this*, I feel that it will help your profits in *this* manner.)

- Do I communicate with my customers when I say I am going to? (In other words, do I keep my appointments and return phone calls and emails?)

- Do I communicate with body language in addition to verbal language? (Remember that only a small portion of your communication comes from what you say, and a much larger percentage comes from how you say it.)

- Do I communicate with my suppliers to create a unified front and to provide the best situation for my customers?

## The Final Straightaway

Do I communicate in a way that creates an environment where my customers will do business with me, **not because they have to, but because they want to**? (In other words, do I foster an inviting environment?) Is my conversation friendly and nurturing? Do I communicate in a way that makes my customers enjoy my company? Do I act like I want to be there? Do I communicate that I care about my customers, and do my actions back it up?)

I'm hoping that the answers in the final straightaway are mostly *yes* because these are the skills that will lead to your success.

*That's just the way...*wait! I have more. I have some tips for communicating better in 2009 and beyond – beginning at the top of the next page!

## Additional tips for handling of emails and calls more productively:

- **Use the subject line** – Prepare the reader for what is coming. I learned this the hard way (thank you, Jennifer). Apparently, I had a nasty habit of ignoring the subject line. She correctly reminded me that I was not showing a healthy respect for her time. It is true! Include the subject line in your emails. That simple note will help your readers to manage their emails more effectively.

- **Open an email only one time** – This is a great idea that I will actually try again this year. Sadly, we often read emails several times before we *finally* act on them. What a waste of time! Delete them, respond, or take some action. Do something! Anything, just do not let it take up permanent residency in your inbox. Looking at emails over and over only increases pressure and anxiety. Try this test, and ask yourself the following question: will answering this email move me closer to the finish line with my customers? If so, take care of it right away. If not, hit the delete key.

- **Train a trusted assistant to help with your email** – Let us face it. Most emails do not really require our attention do they? The typical inbox these days - is filled with junk. I do not know about you, but I get one good email for every four or five junk emails. Sorting through them all is something your trusted assistant can handle! Spend a few hours showing him or her how to disperse your emails. Odds are he or she will be doing a great job by lunchtime, and you will have more time for other tasks.

- **Be brief** – Nobody wants to read anything the length of the Magna Carta, except for history buffs – I suppose. Spell your thoughts out in a few words and move on. *This isn't the NBA. It's ok to be short.* A big key to winning the customer loyalty marathon is respecting your customers' time. Often, we are verbose because it is more difficult to whittle our thoughts down. Mark Twain once famously said, *"I would've wrote a shorter note but I ran out of time!"* Take a few extra moments, and deliver your thoughts in a clear, concise fashion. Your readers will appreciate that!

- **Put the Blackberry in your pocket** – Yes, this one again! The person you are with at that moment should feel like the most important person in your universe, at least for the time that you are together. To be fair, I admit I have been a work in progress on this one. Not anymore! I am over the hump; I have made it up the hill. Here is the point: give your undivided attention to make your conversation partner feel important. That is the goal, right? Make others feel that they are special in your world. I have a buddy that sets his Blackberry right on the table like it is part of the dinnerware. That is rude and insensitive. Hopefully, he is reading this article (on his Blackberry, no doubt).

- **Respond quickly via email** – Ok, I realize that I just advised you to check your email less, but it is important to realize that we live in vast electronic times. Your customers expect immediate replies. Checking your email once at 10:00am may not cut the mustard in some circles. Get back to people as quickly as possible. Admittedly, most emails do not require immediate attention; however, somewhere, someone in cyberspace (probably me) is waiting for a response. Follow through and respond quickly and accurately, just not at lunch or dinner with your significant other.

- **Never forget the power of the written word** – Send a handwritten letter once in a while. On second thought, do it more often than once in a while. Do it as often as possible. Do you want to rise above the clutter? Your business associates are inundated with several emails and calls every day. Imagine their delight at getting something in the mail. Last week, I received a greeting card from a company for which I gave a speech. It was short, succinct, and very nice to receive. It made me feel great. Here is your challenge. Each day, send one handwritten note. Just one. You will enjoy doing it, and your recipient will relish the walk back from the mailbox!

- **Make good use of the signature block** – Most email software packages give you the ability to include some information at the bottom of your outgoing emails. With Outlook, you even have the ability to choose different signatures for different types of emails. For example, when I email members of the wine, beer, and spirit industry, I use a specific signature. It includes testimonials from some of my clients in that industry. Accordingly, I have a different signature for other emails. This level of customization allows me to share more applicable information with respective email recipients. Make good use of this tool.

• **Say "thank you" for calling** – The only acceptable way to answer the phone is by saying, "Thank you for calling XYZ Company." In second place, try "Thank you for choosing XYZ Company." I have said it before, and I will say it again. Your customers will most vividly remember what happens first and what happens last. Start the encounter off on the right foot.

• **Be patient on the phone** – The human brain can process information much faster in person than over the phone. Why is this? Because when we are face to face with someone, we use *non-verbal* clues to derive meaning almost as much as what we hear. On the phone, we cannot see what the other person is doing. Sometimes a good thing? All kidding aside, we do not get the added benefit of seeing how our customers react to our words, gestures, and movements. We do not see their facial expressions. Take a deep breath, and be patient. The result will be more rapport and increased understanding.

• **Make sure to hang up last** – Do not let your customers feel as if they are speaking to someone in a rush. Let them hang up first. To be sure, it is an acquired skill. Just take a deep breath and wait. They will hang up, soon. Trust me on this one! Never, ever let your customers feel like an interruption.

• **Do not enter a vocabulary contest** - According to Leil Lowndes (1999), in *Talking the Winners Way*, winning communicators use "rich, full words, but they never sound inappropriate." This makes perfect sense. Do not try to impress others with your vocabulary. Chances are you may use the word incorrectly or miss-pronounce it. The results may be egg all over your face. Play it safe, and your conversations will go according to plan.

• **Talk to hear yourself talk** - Listen to your written words spoken to hear how they sound. Always read your emails and memos out loud. Try it! Your words will actually have a different ring to them.

The benefit of this is that by doing it, you will more closely simulate what your readers will hear or see. Typically, when I take this step, I find things I want to change. Like this chapter, which I keep changing!

- **Speak in layman's terms** – Keep informal communication short and simple. Do not overwhelm readers or listeners when giving a brief sales pitch. Your readers and listeners only have so much in their attention spans. Just ask my wife! Pick a few key points, and try to hammer those home.

- **Pre-determine the length of the call** – If you need 5 minutes, specify up front that you need 5 minutes, and keep the call to 5 minutes. Do not go over by 5 minutes. If you need more time say, "Can I have a few more minutes to cover the last few points?" Be upfront. Most all of us have the innate need to feel that what we do on a daily basis is important, just like the next guy. Our time is important to us.

- **Make sure it is a good time to talk** – I love when the phone rings, and the caller dives right in, seemingly oblivious to the fact it may not be a good time for me to talk. Some sales courses teach you to dive right in, to not ask if the time is good because that may give your prospect an out. NO! Make sure it is a comfortable time for the other party to talk. A big component of making customers feel comfortable is rapport. Our customers must feel *at ease* with us. Do not dive right in until you have established that this is a comfortable time for everybody, not just you.

- **Make sure to communicate for the right reasons** – Always try to determine why you are doing something. Is it for you, your career, or for *someone else?* Follow the advice of success coach Jim Rohrbach: "Ask yourself: do I really want to do this, or am I afraid to refuse because of what this person will say or think?" Do not get fired, but stop being an approval-seeking junkie. Make more productive decisions in 2009!

- **Get a headset** – Want to sound more energized and more passionate on the phone? Get a headset, and walk around while talking on the phone. The good news: movement stimulates your thought processes and increases blood flow to the brain. When you stand, your diaphragm is open. You will sound friendlier, more open, and confident. Renee Walkup (2006), in *Selling to Anyone over the Phone*, cautions one to always "Be aware of the tone of your voice and your body language." If you are having a bad day, you could be sending negative messages. Better to save an important call for a time when you are in the right frame of mind.

• **Avoid vague wording** – Do not say "yeah;" say "yes." Do not say "no problem;" say "I'll be happy to take care of that." Use can-do wording. Differentiate yourself by being more respectful in a world where graciousness is not the norm. Eliminate the need for follow up emails to clarify simple points by being more direct with your words.

• **Plan for your call** – Ever try for a long time to get someone on the phone, only to blow it because you did not prepare? It is a terrible feeling (I have been there) to know that you squandered an opportunity. *Try getting that individual on that phone again!* When you are fortunate enough to make a connection in the rush-rush times of 2009, it may be your only opportunity!

**Communicate more effectively than your competitors.** Do a better job with written, verbal, and electronic communication than your competitors. Can communication be a point of differentiation? Can it be a critical component of your product or service offering? Absolutely! Competition is everywhere (like I had to tell you that). As markets get tighter, companies get more aggressive. So how do companies set themselves apart? How do sales people set themselves apart?

Among many other things, make it a point to follow up quickly and efficiently. Do what you said you would do. Follow through! Pretend that you are right on the verge of losing the customer. Keep the lines of communication open. Check in with the customer every once in a while. Are you out of sight? If so, you may soon be out of mind, and you will be looking for a new customer - to fill the void created by the one that got away.

*That's just the way it works!*

# REMEMBERING PEOPLE'S NAMES

Ever watch a marathon in person? It is pretty thrilling for runners and non-runners to see so many people laying it all on the line in pursuit of a special goal or achievement. I have always found it very inspiring to watch. Many marathon runners even write their names on their T-shirts. Why, you ask, would they deface an article of clothing with a magic marker? Hmmm! I should ask my children that exact question!

The reason runners personalize their race day clothing is so strangers in the crowd will cheer for them and call out their names. Many running publications suggest this as a way to heighten and enjoy the race-day experience. I once was a runner myself and ran alongside many people who decorated their clothing like this. They seemed to feed off the energy coming from the crowds. The simple sound of hearing names called would motivate tired runners as they battled towards the finish line.

If your goal is to create an environment where your customers do business with you not because they *have* to but because they *want* to, knowing people's names is a big part of the equation. This is true not only with your customers (the people that work in bars, restaurants, and stores) but with the people at your company with whom you interact on a daily basis. Drivers, warehouse staff, office workers – people react with a little "pep in their step" when they hear their names.

There are many benefits associated with learning and remembering people's names. The best is that addressing someone with his or her name is a relationship booster that is completely free! It is motivating, inspiring, and works wonders on morale. Learning and knowing the names of your customer's employees, recognizing their faces, and knowing little things about them is easy (if you try) and very rewarding.

Here are some easy ways to help you remember people's names:

- **Make a concerted effort** – to remember people's names.

I used to have trouble with this because I simply did not try hard enough. Making a concerted effort is half the battle. *You get back what you put in*, just as our parents taught us. Does that sound familiar? Be interested! Take the time. Often, we do not get the name of another person when meeting him or her because we are focused on ourselves and not on the person we are meeting. Our minds wander because we assume we are going to forget the name anyway.

Have you ever been in the following situation? In rapid-fire succession, you are introduced to five people, maybe a group of servers at a new restaurant in town. You hurriedly repeat, "Nice to meet you," again and again, knowing all too well you are not going to remember any of the names! According to an article on CareerBuilder.com (July 22, 2005), "The first and most important step is to pay attention when you're being introduced." Try to get some names and features down on paper as soon as possible after the meeting, anything to help you remember.

- **Observe details** – notice something about the new person.

Look the new person straight in the eye. Really see his or her face. Pick out something unique. Make it a practice to learn something different about the facial structure or voice or anything else unique about this person. If you look closely at people, you can easily detect special characteristics that will help you remember them. According to Tony Buzan (1991), author of *Use your Perfect Memory*, "If you can sharpen your observational powers, you will have made a giant step toward the improvement of your memory. Blank looking, instead of real seeing, is one of the major causes for poor memory."

- **Repeat the name** – force the new name into your memory.

After you hear a new name, call that person by his or her name several times so it will be stored into your long-term memory. Each time you repeat the name, you will have a better chance of remembering it later. If you need to, politely ask to have the name repeated if you do not think you heard it right the first time. Ask to have it spelled out. Verify the pronunciation. You could even ask for the origin of the name. If the name sounds foreign, ask where he or she is from. These days, many distributors have a much more diverse customer base than ever before. Many names are challenging to pronounce. Take extra time to learn the most complex of pronunciations. Trust me, asking a foreign customer to repeat his or her name will show great respect and courtesy and will help bridge the gap between cultures. Being flip about a foreign name will convey just the opposite. So if you are not going to *really* try, do not try at all.

The added by-product of asking these questions is that it reminds you to express interest, which helps develop bonds with people. Remember the following thought that I echo over and over: all things considered, people would rather do business with a friend. Make friends by remembering names!

- **Associate the name** – connect it with someone or something noteworthy.

Many memory experts suggest that if you associate someone's name with a famous person, then you will have a better chance of remembering his or her name. A friend of mine recently attended a presentation and recounted an extraordinary story to me. The speaker stood at the door to the room and welcomed each of the 50+ attendees into the room. A few minutes later, he went around the room and addressed everybody by name! Wow! His trick was to immediately think of somebody famous as he was shaking his or her hand. For me, maybe he would have envisioned Darryl Dawkins, the former NBA superstar noted for shattering backboards with thunderous dunks. (An odd thought, to say the least, as I am all of 5 foot 8 inches tall, actually 5 foot 7 ½ inches without the hair. The only thing I dunk is a donut!)

Sometimes, however, the results are not so rewarding! While recently discussing this subject with a beverage professional, my friend also recounted the following story. His friend used the "association" tactic to remember names. While cultivating a new customer, he associated the potential customer's name with the iconic Chicago hotel, *The Conrad Hilton*. For several weeks, he addressed the person as *Hilton*, only to be eventually corrected by the gentleman – whose name was *Conrad*! Be careful with this trick, and use it at your own risk.

- **Show your cards** – admit it if you cannot remember someone's name.

Do not wing it! A few months ago, I was dining in a local restaurant. Someone stopped by my table and mentioned that I had spoken at his company. "Oh yeah, I remember you, Tom!" Wrong!! *That wasn't his name.* I was embarrassed, and he was probably more embarrassed. The young guy had taken a moment to say "Hello," and I had guessed at his name. I thought I remembered, but I guessed wrong. He was with his wife. I felt terrible and apologized profusely, but the damage was done.

If you do not know someone's name, fess up and move on. Be honest. Be real. Your contacts and associates will be a lot more forgiving if you genuinely say something like, "Your name escapes me at the moment," or "I'm great with faces, but lousy with names!" than if you try to bluff your way through an uncomfortable encounter.

- **Use the name** – repeat it instead of just nodding and smiling.

Use names in passing and on the phone. When passing your associate in the hallway, instead of simply saying, "Hello," say "Hello, Tom!" The result: the person whose name you use will feel good, and his or her name will be reinforced in your mind. Be careful not too do this too often, though. Using someone's name too frequently in face-to-face conversations can come across as a bit calculating. But when speaking on the phone, sprinkle your conversation with the other person's name. Remember that the phone affords us much less intimacy than a face-to-face conversation. We do not see facial expressions or other gestures that help us converse, which are actions that help us understand each other's meanings.

The ability to remember names is essential in both business and social situations. It builds instant rapport and friendship, and it does not cost a penny. With your customers, very few acts convey more respect or are as flattering. Do you have a special memory of someone unexpectedly addressing you with your name? Maybe it was your boss at your first job? How did it feel? Did you have a little more *kick in your step* for the rest of the day? Did it make you smile? Treat your customers and colleagues to that same feeling.

In an era where personal communication has become more and more important, the ability to remember and use people's names is a valuable skill in both business and personal interactions. Think about it this way. If we expect our customers to remember our names and want them to do business with us, then we should take the time and effort to remember their names.

One last thing about the people that work in your customer's businesses. Let us take cashiers as an example. As a retailer, I noticed two distinct ways that sales professionals interacted with our cashiers. The first distinct group walked past the cashiers as if they were not even there. The second group addressed them as valued members of the team. They learned their names and other little details about them. They asked simple questions like "What's selling these days?" or "Are you going to watch the big game this weekend?" It was great to see, and I often observed that the simple act of acknowledging someone and using his or her name could make someone so happy. To be sure, life is a complex equation; however, there is one thing that makes us each unique – our names.

So learn names. Learn little details. Ask questions even if the answer is not vitally important. Keep up-to-date not only with the people you sell to but also with the people who work at their companies. The cashiers, bar backs, stock people, servers, hosts and hostesses, etc. These are the individuals who make things happen. Your job is to sell not only to the president of the company but also to those at every other level of it.

*That's just the way it works!*

# Things to Think About
# While Driving Around

Do you log a lot of miles in the car driving between your accounts? Most sales people do. What do you do during those times? Do you listen to sports radio or contemporary rock? Do you make and return phone calls? Check in with the office? Call your spouse?

To be sure, all the above tasks are important, even listening to the radio. Sometimes you just need to get away from everything for a while. I understand that!

But when I am driving for long stretches or waiting for someone or exercising, I see ample opportunities to reflect on how I am approaching my vocation. You should consider doing the same. It is imperative to make time for honest self-reflection.

To that end, I have several questions you should ask yourself and contemplate during your free time, down time, or time just staring at the dashboard. You will notice that one question in particular is repeated several times. That is by design and not the product of shoddy editing. And yes, there are 26.2 questions (and then some)!

### Have a look at the following questions:

- Do I see the world from my customers' points of view? Do I ever "walk in their shoes?" Do my customers genuinely know that I care about them, their businesses, and their associates, or do my actions indicate that I only care about myself? Am I able to expand my universe to include those around me?

- If I worked 5 extra hours a week, would I make more money? Would my company be more successful? Would I get a promotion? Better accounts? More distribution? A bigger bonus? Better placement in package stores? More bottles behind the bar? More selections on the wine list? Would I be my customers' preferred provider?

- How did I handle my last disagreement with a customer? Could I have handled it better? Was I empathetic? Did I apologize or offer to make it right, even if it was not my fault? Was it my fault? Why? What could I have done differently?

- What am I afraid of professionally? Is it asking for the sale? Not reaching my goals? Do I realize that I am only as strong as my weakest skill? Am I willing to overcome that fear and improve that weak skill?

- How well do I know my products? Is there something I know about my products that might intrigue my customers? What is it? Do I constantly have to get back to customers with the correct answers? Do I ask for more time when I do not know the answer? Do I become defensive? Do I always have to be right?

- If I made calls for an extra half hour today, what would happen? Would my company be more successful? Would I get a promotion? Better accounts? More distribution? A bigger bonus? Better placement in package stores? More bottles behind the bar? More selections on the wine list? Would I be my customers' preferred provider?

- If I planned my day out the night before, what would happen? Would I be more organized? Would I be less forgetful? Would I execute better on sales calls? Would I have more time to pay attention to the "little details?"

- Am I exercising enough? Is my brain getting enough oxygen? (Be honest!) Do I feel good about my body image? Am I self-conscious to the point that I do not want to meet new people? Am I eating right? Am I healthy? Am I getting enough sleep?

- Do I act like a professional? Do I make inappropriate jokes? Am I a sexist? Do I share too much information? Do I make excuses or assign blame to others? Do I enter my accounts while talking on my cell phone? Do I talk just to hear myself talk?

- Do I know enough of the names of my customers' associates? Do I know the names of 50% of the people I see each day? 75%? Am I trying to learn names? Do I smile and acknowledge everybody or just buyers? Do I say hello to receptionists?

- Do I review my emails before I send them out? Do I answer my emails in a timely fashion? Do I know how to use the spell check feature on my documents?

- If I saw my first account one hour earlier each day, what would happen to my sales? Would my company be more successful? Would I get a promotion? Better accounts? More distribution? A bigger bonus? Better placement in package stores? More bottles behind the bar? More selections on the wine list? Would I be my customers' preferred provider?

- When is the last time I sent a hand-written note to a customer? When is the last time I thanked a customer for seeing me? When is the last time I thanked my customer for placing his or her weekly order or recommending my products to his or her customers?

- How recently have I asked my customers what is truly important to them? When was the last time I asked my customers how I could serve them better? Do I honestly want to hear that answer?

- How is my attitude? My outlook? Have I been complaining about my job or my company or my industry to my customers? Do I truly realize the damage that emanates from complaining *about my company* to my customers?

- Am I dressed professionally? Does my hat look like a beer truck ran it over? Do I try to make a fashion statement, or do I dress in a manner appropriate for business situations? Are my clothes freshly pressed, or are they wrinkled?

- Do I start smiling the moment I walk into an account? Can my customers see if something is upsetting me? Am I genuine? Does my response to a happy situation genuinely sound happy? Does my response to a sad situation genuinely sound sad? Am I real?

- Do I return phone calls and emails on the same day I receive them?

- If I have time to kill, do I go to Starbucks, or do I stop in to see a customer? Would my company be more successful if I skipped the coffee? Would I get a promotion? Better accounts? More distribution? A bigger bonus? Better placement in package stores? More bottles behind the bar? More selections on the wine list? Would I be my customers' preferred provider?

- Do I think hard enough about how I can provide better service to my customers? What was the last tangible suggestion I made to help my customers improve their businesses? Do I understand that helping to make my customers more successful is my responsibility? Do I willingly accept that responsibility? Do I understand that, if I am to make my customers more successful, I must help them to be more profitable?

- If I see a bar or restaurant and I do not know if my company has distribution there, do I stop in or keep driving? At 4:30 p.m., do I make another call or go home?

- Do I set goals? Do I know what I want to do and what I want to be? How far do I want to go? How will I get there? What are my strengths, and what are my weaknesses? How much money do I want to make? What do I have to do to get there? If I asked these questions and took my job more seriously, what would happen? Would my company be more successful? Would I get a promotion? Better accounts? More distribution? A bigger bonus? Better placement in package stores? More bottles behind the bar? More selections on the wine list? Would I be my customers' preferred provider?

- When is the last time I Googled my restaurant accounts, saw a positive review, and sent that restaurateur a congratulatory note? When something good happens to one of my accounts, do I acknowledge or congratulate them in any way?

- Do I cheer for others? When was the last time I paid my customer a sincere compliment about anything? Have I ever sincerely complimented my customers for something having to do with another vendor?

- Have I ever really listened to my customers? I mean, really listened so I could hear them and understand them? What would happen if I let them finish their sentences? Am I constantly jumping to conclusions? Do I really try to build a rapport with my customers? Do I pay attention to them?

- Am I topping off my mental tank? Do I embrace the idea that sellers should also be learners, or did I stop learning after I donned my cap and gown years ago? Do I realize that my base of knowledge *next year* will only be my base of knowledge *this year* plus whatever I learn over the next year? Do I ever read the type of books my customers would read? In other words, do I read books on retail, bars, restaurants, and other topics that might shed more light on how my customers' businesses operate?

## The Final Straightaway

Do I realize what a great industry this is? Do I realize that the products I sell are typically consumed in happy, joyous, and memorable occasions? That I get to work with a lot of really neat people? If I told myself this every day, what would happen? Would my company be more successful? Would I get a promotion? Better accounts? More distribution? A bigger bonus? Better placement in package stores? More bottles behind the bar? More selections on the wine list? Would I be my customers' preferred provider?

*But wait there's more!* **Here are a few more questions you can ask if you have time:**

- Can I name the last three significant events to happen in my industry?

- Can I identify the last three significant moves my competitors made?

- When was the last time I showed up unexpectedly at one of my accounts?

- When was the last time I showed up unexpectedly at one of my accounts and actually did something constructive?

- When was the last time any of my customers received something from me in the mail?

- When was the last time I spent my own money on a book, CD, training course, etc., to improve my skills?

- What are my strongest skills? Do I use those skills to help my customers?

- What are my weakest skills? Am I trying to improve in these areas?

- Am I hanging around with people who will improve my skills and outlook on life or the opposite?

- When was the last time I bought the top salesperson in my company lunch and asked him or her how I can be a better sales person?

## **Bonus Question**

Do I know more than I knew last week about any of the following?

- my business (or my company) and my industry
- my competitors
- my top customers
- my fast-growing customers
- my declining customers
- trends that might affect me or my company
- trends that might affect my customers
- ways that my customers could be more profitable

If you answer these questions once a week or once every two weeks (and if you use your *driving around* time productively), you will be light years ahead of your rivals.

*That's just the way it works!*

*Vending Machine Man* sleeps the day away dreaming about the "big sale". He is a pretender. What he doesn't realize is that his sales success will be *in his dreams*. Your job (as a partner) is to always ask: If I got out of bed 30 minutes earlier…Would my company be more successful? Would I get a promotion? Better accounts? More distribution? A bigger bonus? Better placement in package stores? More bottles behind the bar? More selections on the wine list? Would I be my customer's preferred provider?

# DESIGNING EFFECTIVE PRESENTATIONS AND PRESENTING EFFECTIVELY

Do you ever feel that you should give your customers a pillow so they will be more comfortable during your presentations? Do you have trouble capturing their attention? Does it take you forever to prepare for a meeting because you have no clue as to how to do it properly?

Often, sales professionals ask me how to design and execute effective sales presentations, and I usually break the question into two parts.

**Part 1:** How can I design effective presentations?

**Part 2:** How can I present effectively?

Let us examine each part individually, and along the way, I will offer some tips for designing presentations that will give your customers the information they need to make confident, sensible decisions. To round out the chapter, I will cover two additional topics.

**Part 3:** Other strategies for executing better sales calls…

**Part 4:** What to do if the call could have gone better…

## Part 1: How can I design effective presentations?

- **Ask first, present second**

The first question I always get is how much data should I show my customers? This is a common question because many professionals struggle to choose among the plethora of data at their disposals. Nielson reports, scan data, ad "run" schedules, and PowerPoints galore! The primary question here is "What should I do with all of it? Should I show it all to my customers?" My gut reaction was originally to say no. Do not show everything. *Stop* with the fancy PowerPoints and stacks of data. Your customers *do not care!* My opinion is just give your customer the basics.

After much thought, and some research, I realized that this was more my opinion from how I ran a large *independent* wine and spirit operation but not necessarily how all retailers (on and off premise) operate. In some cases, for example, at large chains, a buyer's pay and bonus may be contingent on metrics like inventory turn, gross margins, and other variables. The buyer may want to know more about national advertising campaigns because those ads will drive consumer traffic. He or she may need to see that information.

As a result, I have modified my answer a bit. I still believe that when you provide too much information, key data gets lost in the translation. It is all about how you prepare your presentation. Much more on this in a bit!

I believe in the following: *ask first and present second.*

What do I mean by this?

I always suggest that salespeople arrive prepared with a good knowledge of their presentations. However, they should leave the presentations in their briefcases until they ask the customer how **he** or **she** wants the presentation to proceed. Alternatively, you could find this information out ahead of time. The key is you knowing what your customer wants to see! Do you know what type of data (or benefits) will help **him** or **her** make a comfortable decision?

Not what *you* want him or her to see; what **he** or **she** wants to see.

I suggest you ask first and present second.

The majority of business presentations seek to convey, not persuade. When the message is not clear and the benefits to your customer are not vividly evident, the presentation will fail! You know it, and I know it!

- **Remember "who" *you* are doing this for** – and you will always keep the customer front and center.

Review the following questions and answers as you prepare your presentations. This is your litmus test. If you cannot come up with legitimate answers for sharing some tidbit of data, then keep it in your back pocket.

(Q) Why is this important to my customer?

(A) This is important to my customer because…

(Q) Who cares?

(A) My customer should care because…

(Q) Why am I telling you this?

(A) I am telling you this because…

- **Have an objective** – so you know what *point B* is.

Make sure everything you say and present ties back to your main objective (point B). Notice I did not say *objectives*. Do not overwhelm your customers with multiple objectives. Yes, you can have more than one request; however, any additional requests should be minor in nature when compared to the main objective. Determine the main discussion points, and discuss those points before anything else.

An objective is not to sell more beer because that is way too vague. What do you hope to accomplish at this sales call? What are you after? Be specific. "My goals with this call are to suggest some specific profit generating ideas, to obtain a placement, to share some market knowledge, and to relate the details of a plan that I created *on my own time* for kick-starting the sell-through of some slow moving inventory. Yes, the cases that are covered by cobwebs." *Now that is a plan!* Although planning sales calls will certainly be more detailed, at least you have organized yourself more effectively for a call.

While you are at it, share your *point B* with your customer at the beginning of your call so he or she is clear on your objectives.

- **Use data effectively** – share information that actually makes a difference in your customer's world, not some far, far away land.

This reminds me of a supplier that I dealt with several years ago. He wanted us to take his price up 10% and expected his unit sales to rise 15%. Not his dollar sales but his unit sales! When I asked how we were supposed to achieve that goal, he said, "We have scan data from Ohio!" Superb! Scan data from a "grocery/chain" market being extrapolated to an "independent heavy" market. That makes very little difference to somebody in the middle of Illinois!

Do a *relevancy* test to see if your data/message matters to your customer. The most unproductive habit on a sales call is to waste your time (and your customers') by sharing information he or she has no interest in hearing. Once more, I suggest you **ask first, present second.** Ask your customer how he or she wants the call to proceed. Most sales professionals lament the amount of time customers allocate for their sales calls. "It is way too short," they complain. Thus, you must make use of every second.

- **Stop over-analyzing** – look for trends that exist.

Let the data tell the story. Do not try to fit the data into *your* story. The last thing you want while sharing data is skepticism and mistrust. I recall many situations where salespeople tried to shape, mold, structure, and contour data to tell a certain story. It is not play-dough. You do not get to choose the shape. It is what it is!

One other thing: make sure your objective matches the data you are showing. If your objective is to sell in a new syrah, then do not show up with data on the white wine category (yes – it has happened).

- **Know how to interpret your data** – look at it beforehand.

When you present the data, make sure you have seen it before. You would be really surprised how many people show up never having gone through their presentations. You would be more surprised to know how many people show up with the wrong presentations or the right presentations but with the wrong customer name. Those meetings never end well.

Explain your points, and try to use the word "because." Years ago, a social psychologist named Ellen Langer did a study on the persuasion effects of using this word. Her study showed that there was a tremendous increase in cooperation when subjects used the word in their sales presentations. When you use the word "because," you are typically doing so to explain your position. "I think this makes sense because"…

Subjects in Langer's study felt that salespeople were doing a better job of explaining their positions. Try it, and you may see similar results!

- **Emphasize the first and last points.**

If you have multiple benefits for a product, make your first and last benefits the important ones. Many memory experts suggest that the first and last points are exactly the ones that your customers will likely remember. Take special care in picking out those points.

- **Use PowerPoint to your advantage.**

Be careful with the PowerPoint phenomenon. Too many distributor and supplier salespeople mistakenly assume that the customer wants the "dog and pony show!" PowerPoint presentations should be renamed *"power plays"* because of all the distributors and suppliers who show up and literally take over the room, dominating the time for their own propaganda shows. It is obnoxious and serves no one's purpose. Not to belabor the point, but the meeting is not designed to serve as a brag session and is not a time for proud salespeople to thump their chests out as if to say, "Look at all the great brands we have!"

In presentations big and small, slides are just there to support the presenters. I imagine you have all been in presentations where a presenter is monotonously reading slides. How motivating is that? Conversely, maybe you were not able to make the presentation, and the presenter said, "Let me just send you the slides!" If slides are detailed enough for someone who did not see the presentation to feel like he or she did, then your slides are way too detailed for members of your audience. You will lose them in a second.

Attention should be on you – the presenter. You are the one with the story to tell. You are the one with the unshakeable belief in your product or service. With all this said, though, members of your audience learn in different ways, so slides, if used effectively, can help get your message across.

Here are a few things to consider:

**-Use a customized opening graphic** – to make your customer feel that this presentation was created just for him or her. Sure, it only takes a second, and your customer knows that; however, to not do the *smallest of customization* will be a mistake.

**-Use a bumper slide** – with centered text. A bumper slide briefly tells the audience where you are in the presentation. According to Jerry Weissman (2008), author of *Presenting to Win*, a bumper slide "indicates closure of the outbound section and introduces the next section." It also gives your audience a break.

**-Titles should be in headline form** – much like a newspaper tries to attract readers with catchy words or phrases. Avoid complete sentences. After reading the title, your customer (or audience) should have some idea of where the slide is going and what point the slide will make. There is another important reason. As you prepare your deck, you should be able to follow along with the organization of your presentation just by *reading the titles*. The titles should tell a story.

**-Build your slides from left to right** – readers of many western countries (including ours) read from left to right. So if there is an object or word that is of particular importance, make sure it is left justified. That is how the eye moves across a page.

The idea here is for the audience to do as little work as possible. If sentences are too long, then the audiences' eyes have to move back and forth across the screen repeatedly. On a big screen several feet away that may be an arduous task to say the least.

**-Use just a few different styles** – A little color and variety will liven up your slide and add some visual stimulation. Colors should match your company's colors. The slides should have a consistent look and feel. There should only be a few different fonts, and the size should be no smaller than 24-28 points. It is not an eye chart, nor a ransom note!

Take some creative liberties, but remember, the attention should be on you, first, and the slides second. You are the *main* attraction.

**-Eliminate unnecessary information** – Remove unnecessary labels, titles, subtitles, legends, and other explanations that add little to a slide's information. Remember, the focus should be on you. The slides are just there to assist you. *Less is more.* Remove excess clutter. If there is too much information, the customer's (or audiences') attention will move away from you, the presenter.

Did I mention that you are the star of the show – not your slides? You are the one who believes so strongly in his or her product that you would sell it to your grandmother! Right?

**-Take special care with *numbers* slides** – The major point for slides with numbers is that some customers (or some in your audience) may see the meaning right away, and others may need more help. Take special care in designing slides of this type. If you are using a bar chart (or similar), make sure the visuals resemble that of a hockey stick, starting in the lower left corner and continuing on to the upper right corner. Most business charts are constructed this way, and doing it in the opposite manner may subconsciously bother your audience. Getting your customer to act is already an uphill battle – do not make it any harder.

**-Reduce the amount of bullets and animations** – Have only four points on a slide, and make each sentence four words or less. Also, if you do use PowerPoint presentations extensively, do not use seven different animations on each slide. Animations are the visual effects whereby information enters from the left and right, from the top and the bottom, and appears and dissolves with great fanfare like fireworks on the 4th of July. As they say about a football player who scores a touchdown and then celebrates (in the end zone) like a goofball, *"Act like you've been there before!"*

The big presentation is no time for your vaunted Steven Spielberg impersonation. Do not experiment with special effects. Be creative with the words on the slides but not the ways the words appear and disappear! Use the "fade and dissolve" animations if you like. Make sure your data comes in from the *left*, as that is how your audience will more comfortably read the slide.

## Part 2: How can I present more effectively?

- **Do not wing it** – and expect the customer to be motivated.

I always try to ask senior sales professionals in my audience if they used to "wing it" when they were younger. You know, show up for a call unprepared. "Of course!" The follow-up question is "does that work any more?" "No way!" Those days are long gone!

Ask a thought-provoking question. Be creative. Be prepared. Know the ins and outs of what you are selling, but most importantly, understand why in the world your customer would want your product, and be able to explain it concisely. The point is that, in the past, you may have had two opportunities to introduce this product, but now, because of the demands on your customer's time and yours, you may have less chances before the door closes.

- **Set an agenda** – this is no time for surprises.

Prepare an agenda, and, if time permits, send it to your customer in advance of the meeting. Bring the same copy to the meeting with another for your customer. List exactly what you want to cover and accomplish, which helps out greatly when you are face-to-face.

Set a start time, and do not be late! Set an end time; it shows you value your customer's time. Be reasonable about the topics you suggest and what you ask for – do not ask for too much. Suggesting more than two new products per visit will just serve to confuse your customers. The abundance of too many choices may even cause your customer to shut you out completely. Set reasonable goals on what you want to accomplish.

- **Remove distractions** – like your Blackberry.

Follow me on this one. You are right in the middle of your presentation. You have hit all your key points. Then your phone starts buzzing in your pocket. Sure, you turned it to vibrate, but you still heard it and felt it, and your customer heard it as well. There is a pause in the action. Your customer looks at you, wondering if you are going to answer your phone.

The momentum is gone. You, of course, are wondering who is trying to reach you, and that briefest of intrusions has allowed other thoughts to occupy your customer's mind. I say keep the phone in the car, but that is probably a discussion for another day. To be sure, there are many differing thoughts on this subject; however, at the very least, acknowledge the distraction that untimely interruptions can cause.

And what about your customer blabbing away on his or her cell phone? Recently, someone asked me what he could do about that. Well – really nothing. He or she is the customer and that is his or her prerogative. I do have two thoughts on the subject. First, control what you can control – and that is something over which you have no control. Use that time to review your notes or jot down a thought or two on what has transpired so far. Second, *do not show your displeasure!* Smile and wait patiently. If possible, go do something else in the account while you wait for your customer to complete his or her call.

- **Ease into the sales call naturally** – and take care of open business.

Many of you interact with the same individuals on a weekly basis. Even though you have great familiarity, it is still a nice touch to keep building the relationships. The following questions will help: "Has anything changed since our last meeting?" "Do you have any feedback on the sale, positioning, merchandising, display, etc., of XYZ product?" You could also say the following: "Before we get started, can I share with you what I got from our last meeting?" The benefit of this last statement is clarity, as it is always good to have key points reiterated!

When it comes time to move into the *sales* part of the presentation, do not lose the easy-going demeanor you (hopefully) had as the meeting began.

- **Conduct periodic reviews** – to help your audience comprehend what you have covered.

No matter how intelligent your customers are, they probably will not be able to keep up with you. Certainly not as fast as you are dishing it out. Take a pause. Let your customer know where you are at all times. If you see a confused look – slow down! Remember the old adage, "Tell them what you are going to tell them, tell them, and then tell them what you told them!"

This is particularly true when calling on culturally diverse customers. Many of you call on customers for which *English is a second language*. In these situations, make sure to *over-communicate*. You may need to ask questions in order to ascertain comprehension in certain situations. Far better to be safe than sorry. (For much more on improving cross-cultural communication – see Chapter 26)

- **Take notes** – so you remember important information.

It is said that 50% of what you hear or read you will ultimately forget in one minute or less. Do not fall prey to this. The human mind works at an amazing pace, and the brilliant and creative idea that you had just a few seconds ago might be lost forever if you fail to put pen to paper.

The other benefit of taking notes is that it suggests several things to your customers. First, it says that you are a professional, and you take your job seriously. Second, it says to the customer, "I must be saying something important because he or she is writing." What a great feeling for customers to have! Third, it provokes your customer to tell you more (to let his or her guard down), which leads to more selling opportunities. Finally, taking notes ensures that you will remember everything and gives you a platform to review key points with the customer. A bonus benefit is that your customer will have greater confidence in your ability to deliver.

- **Say it in English** – not fancy marketing/sales speak.

Your presentation is not the place for a vocabulary or knowledge contest. Use layman's terms. Respect the fact that your customers probably have different levels of experience and different levels of education.

Make your message understandable. I remember reading somewhere that Peter Lynch, a wildly successful fund manager for Fidelity Investments, used to suggest that individuals *invest in companies they understood.* After reading that, I bought a few shares in Bed, Bath and Beyond. (I should have bought more and laid off the tech stocks, but I digress.)

I understood (or thought I understood) their brand message. The stores were packed with inventory; my stores were packed with inventory. I understood the model: great inventory selection.

Use the same thought process when designing your presentations. Make sure you are conveying your message in a way that your customers will understand (comfortably) what you are saying. Clear, and not overly complex. Not too detailed and not too long. Never take for granted that people understand the mundane.

- **Share the important points** – humans can only process so much information at one time.

As I mentioned, make the first and last points the key takeaways. According to many memory experts, that is what people remember the most. Do not throw everything and the kitchen sink at your customer all at once.

Stick to the basic selling points – the variables that resonate and are important to your customer. Most likely, your customer wants facts that have to do with dollars and cents. How do you find such information – what your customer wants to see? ASK!

Your customer may be interested in any of the following variables: increased revenues, increased profitability, higher traffic counts, and improved store/bar/restaurant image among many other possibilities. Another important variable is excitement. Your customers are always looking for unique and exciting products to attract customers. As we discussed in Chapter 3, your customers are not **always** looking for items with the best prices. Many care just as much about having exciting and interesting items.

- **Be creative and confident** – to capture your customer's attention and share your unshakeable belief in your products.

Have a strong opening, much like a speaker strives to engage his audience when the speech starts. Take advantage of the first few minutes, as it is imperative to get your customer engaged. Look directly at your customer, straight in the eye. Not staring, that is a bit creepy, but letting your customer see the gleam in your eye. Be passionate and enthusiastic, even if the last thing you feel like is being passionate and enthusiastic. When you present your product, act "as if" it is the most precious item in the world. Your presentation does not need the ups and downs of a James Bond movie; however, it should be engaging.

Be realistic about what you are offering. Trust me on this one! Your customer would rather you commit to realistic timing than to a time frame that looks good but is unrealistic.

Look good and feel good. Dress appropriately for the selling environment. Be clean and groomed - no wrinkles (hey, I have taught myself how to iron, and if I can do it....). You know the drill: better safe than sorry. Your customer's place of business is no venue for a radical and extreme fashion statement. You do not want your customer to think, "*Some* village is missing its idiot!" Plus, when you look good, you will project more confidence, and that is really half the battle.

Understand that if you are speaking to someone new or someone that is not familiar with you, he or she may be uninformed about your product or service. He or she may also be skeptical or dubious or worse, firmly committed to the opposite position. Tell an effective business story. When you do so you will be perceived as being in command and deserving of the confidence of others.

- **Go from *I* and *me* to *YOU*.**

Back in the early 1970s, Yale University commissioned a study to identify the most persuasive words in the English language as a way to help businesses with their marketing. It should come as no surprise that the number one word was **"you."** My suggestion is that you incorporate the word **"you"** into your presentations in limited doses. If you do this, then you will remember to frame the benefits of carrying your products into your customer's terms. Why it is good for your customers to carry your products! Why it will help their businesses! Why it will attract customers and create excitement.

One last note on the word "you" in presentations. Make sure you are using it the right way. Check out the following examples:

**Good use:** *"You will see that consumers are responding quite favorably to our advertising and flocking to retailers to buy this product in droves."* (I know – it is a little hokey!)

**Bad use:** *"You have a terrible craft beer selection, and your business will surely fail if you don't buy our incredible product."* (A bit too incendiary?)

One statement is positive, and the other is purposely quite negative. The point is as follows: be careful! Using phrases like "you always" or "you should" gets too personal, accusatory, or condescending, and never ends well. A basic premise in selling is that your customers want to buy your product because they think it is a good idea, not because you told them to!

Other powerful words from the Yale University study were: money, save, new, results, health, easy, safety, love, discovery, proven, and guarantee. Also, there are a great many books available on the subject of great selling words. Pick one up *after* you finish this one!

One last point: any statement about you or your company should be changed to answer the question, "What is in it for my customer?" For example, saying, "I've been doing this for 30 years," means nothing to the customer. Instead, if you say, "I've been doing this for 30 years so I have seen how products like this one react in the marketplace. This product will do well because...," you are stating a benefit as to why having 30 years of experience will help your customers make better buying decisions.

- **Use confident words** – to appear, you know, confident.

Once again, from the book *Presenting to Win*, avoid words that seem wishy-washy. Avoid these problematic phrases:

  o   I believe
  o   I think
  o   I feel

The trouble with these phrases is that they each usher in a bit of uncertainty. Try these instead:

- o I am confident
- o I am convinced
- o I am optimistic
- o I expect

These phrases imply that you are a little surer of yourself.

While you are at it, avoid presenter-focused phrases like "now I'd like to." The audience (or your customer for that matter) does not care what you *would like to do.* Just do it. Use words that are less about you and more about your audience. Some examples:

- o Let's look at…
- o As you'll recall…
- o We discussed earlier…
- o As you know…

## Part 3: Other strategies for better sales calls.

- **Prepare!** Ask yourself – what materials do I need for this sales call? What information? Is my *sell sheet* current? Is my sell sheet laid out in a way that helps me get information quickly? If not – make a cheat sheet. What do I hope to accomplish? What might my customer ask me? Are there any unresolved issues? What is open from the last sales call? Anything open from last week, last month or last year? Are there any open inventory issues? *Are there any opportunities?*

- Practice, practice, practice. Say your presentation out loud. Practice the first thing you are going to say when the meeting begins. What is your interest gaining statement? That is what you should be concentrating on. You can reduce jitters by spending some quality time with your notes, but make sure to practice *out loud.*

- If your customer is talking a lot, that is actually a good thing. Keep your mouth closed, listen (really listen, do not fake it), and take good notes. Wait for the selling opportunities to roll off your customer's tongue.

- If there is more than one decision maker in the room, make sure to address everybody to make each individual feel included. The fact is that you will probably have to gain the approval of everybody (whether they say so or not) to make the sale. One way to keep people involved is to simply say, "How do you feel about (insert product or opportunity)?"

- If the competition is brought up, your job is to remain objective. As I have said in other parts of this book, disparaging the competition is bush league. Simply state, "They are an excellent company," and spend more time explaining why your customer should do more business with you, not why they should do less business with the guy down the street.

- If you really want to get the meeting off to a great start, send (fax or email) an agenda the night before. Chances are your customer will not have time to read it, but he or she will take note. Want maximum kudos? Mention an item languishing in inventory so your customer can sleep on the fact that you are actually coming to help.

- Always begin the presentation by thanking your customer for his or her time. It is a really nice touch, and even if you see the same person at the same time every week, he or she could still be doing something else.

- Act like it is your first time. Sometimes, I do the same three-hour workshop three times in a day, but I always try to present it in an upbeat manner. Do the same no matter how often you have to present the same new product. Yes, it may be the 37th time (for you), but for that customer, it is likely the first.

- Never overwhelm your customer by blabbing on and on about your products. Most people can only listen to three sentences before getting overwhelmed. Take some advice from the famous rock band The Eagles, and *take it easy.*

- Have some confidence and avoid debilitating self-talk. Think about it for a second. If you felt massive pangs of doubt driving up to make a sales call, did anything positive happen during the call? Did you have success? Probably not! You are not held back by lack of ability or opportunity but fear of rejection and the doubts that are triggered.

  Instead of worrying about the negatives, reflect on the positives. You are there because your company has faith in you, and in some cases, they have been doing this successfully for a long, long time. Anyway, something like 90% of what we worry about never happens.

- If your customer is giving you short and vague answers, then your job is to keep probing. Keep it interactive. Keep trying to find your customer's hot button issues.

- Take some chances. Famous hockey play Wayne Gretzky was known to say, "You miss 100% of the shots you don't take!"

- If you are new, just admit it. Everybody was new at one point or another. Be yourself; it is easier to remember for your visit.

- Bring coffee or a sandwich. Yes, I know – it is the oldest trick in the book, but the truth is when salespeople went out of their way to feed us (or help with our caffeine needs), we were usually in the midst of selling (or contemplating the sale) of their products. It was a very nice gesture.

- Try to **talk turkey** to people who can give you an order – the decision maker. Of course, I suggest you try to get to know as many people within an account as possible. Make everybody feel special; however, make sure you are spending enough time with the decision maker. Do not sell to lower levels because you are afraid to deal with more senior-level people or you cannot identify those people. Persevere and keep trying to identify those that can sign on the dotted line!

  Your goal is to match your message to the decision maker's interests. What is keeping him or her up at night? What concerns are front and center in his or her mind? If you can pin-point what your customers' desire, you will get their time and attention – and they will buy your products.

- If your customer seems busy, get to the point quickly. He or she will appreciate you for that.

- Be realistic. You cannot possibly have all the answers (although you should have many of them), and it is okay to get back to your customers – as long as you do so shortly.

- If there are difficult issues, raise those issues first. You are not going to be operating at your best until you get the news off your chest. (See Chapter 19 – Sharing Unpopular News for more on this topic.)

- Schedule appointments either early or late in the day. Try to avoid the commotion of the mid-day hours. I used to take appointments as early as 6 am in the morning. It was quiet and conducive to good meetings. The best salespeople do not sit in rush-hour traffic.

- Abort the meeting if it just does not feel right. Recently, I read an article in the local newspaper about planes aborting their landings just before touch down at O'Hare. Usually, the plane was not in imminent danger; however, the pilot did not feel right about landing the plane at that point. If your customer is not in the right frame of mind, better to pack up (abort) and come back another day.

- Create conviction: your customer must be drawn to the conclusion that your product is the one that will genuinely meet his or her needs. Can you imagine your customer saying "So what?" as the benefits roll of your tongue? If so, develop stronger points.

- Tell the truth even if it is not what you want the customer to hear. (Much more on the subject of trust and honor in Chapter 14.)

- Follow-through like you said you would. If you say you will call that day with information, make sure to do it. Did you promise to email some information in the upcoming week? Do it. As my friend who owns a small wine shop tells me, "Nothing is as irritating as begging a salesperson for information to sell his or her product!" Remember, people who break small commitments like, "I'll call you tomorrow!" will also break big commitments. Count on it.

  I got a great tip from a distributor out in California. *Keep a promise book* and write down every promise you make. Just this simple act will help you keep your commitments.

- When your customers say "YES," thank them and reassure them that they have made the right decision, but do not think for a second that the *hard part* is over. The hard part is just beginning. Over-communicate the next step. Do not be afraid to repeat the commitment. Immediately begin tracking what you have committed to do.

## Part 4: If the *call* could have gone better!

One last note: Hey, wake up!

What if the sales presentation is a disaster? Frances Cole Jones (2008), in the book *How to Wow,* suggests that you take it personally and that you not take it personally. How is that for a contradiction?

Do not take it personally. Maybe your customer had a death in the family. What if the bank just called? It is never good when the bank calls you! Perhaps the meeting after yours was to decide on the new warehouse-inventory-truck-routing logistics system! Could that be affecting your customer's attention span? The point is, you never know. The customer did not want your product on that day, and you will *probably* have another chance.

I say you will *probably* have another chance, but you may not. Maybe the customer wanted to buy, but you wrecked the deal. While not taking an unfortunate sales call personally, you do have to be a bit introspective. Did you do anything to jeopardize the deal? Be honest. Lying about it will not help a soul, especially you. Spend some time considering why you did not get the response you wanted? Were you setting forth value in your presentation? Did the value proposition get translated to the customer? If not, why? Ask for feedback so you can improve your effectiveness. No matter what, always try to end sales calls (even the unsuccessful ones) on a positive note. Invite a definitive action.

The simple truth is that many studies show nearly 80% to 90% of a buying decision is based upon how your customer feels about **you**, his or her salesperson. Are you doing a great job? That is wonderful; however, you still have to be prepared. You still have to design (and execute) a presentation that captures your customer's imagination while addressing his or her objectives. It is not about fancy graphics, scintillating data, and the shrewd handling of objections; it is about making a one-on-one connection with the person sitting on the other side of the table!

*That is just how it works!*

Taking notes (which says, "I am a professional and I have a job to do") is one of the best things you can do at a meeting!

Vending Machine man shows up with every report known to man. He is a pretender because he does not want to take the time to pre-pare more diligently. Your job, as partner, is to identify (hopefully, prior to the meeting) what information your customer needs to make a confident, sensible decision!

# Questions from the Field

**Q:** How can I be a better presenter when I speak (or sell) to a larger group of people?

**A: Here are some strategies to engage your audience for effective meetings and presentations,** no matter the size of the group. Many come from the world of professional speaking because being successful in public speaking and as a sales professional requires many of the same skills.

- **Determine if people are listening** - so you know how to proceed.

Some salespeople are deliberately tuned out, while others are simply overloaded. "Is either group listening?" According to a book by the Harvard Business School Press, *Presentations that Persuade and Motivate*, "As a rule, if they're crossing their legs, fidgeting, or looking around a lot, chances are you don't have their rapt attention." Keeping attention is critical for continued success.

- **Ask for input** – to get the audience involved.

Nobody wants to hear someone drone on and on about anything! One of the most important (and motivating) things you can say in a meeting is, "I don't know; what do you think?" Solicit opinions. Take extra steps to include everybody, especially the quiet, shy types. Ask questions and get people talking. Never embarrass people or take cheap shots. Never make others look foolish so you can look better.

- **Move around the room** – to keep everybody awake.

Did you ever sit in the back of a lecture hall in college and read the newspaper? I imagine we all did at one point or another because we knew the professor stayed up on the stage and would not catch us. Now, what if he or she moved around? Would you have been more attentive? Would you have kept the newspaper in your bag? Once you establish an unpredictable pattern of movement, your audience will have no choice but to watch your every more lest you appear in front of them and ask a question for which they are not prepared.

- **Tell a story** – to illustrate a point.

Paint a picture for your salespeople or audience. Do not rely as much on facts and figures but more on success stories. Did one of the salespeople place a new product in a fast growing grocery store? Show a picture and have the salesperson share how or why he or she was so successful. How did he do it? Did she learn anything from the experience? What were some of the obstacles? Anybody can refer to a successful placement and move on; however, to truly have your people learn from successes and failures, you have to be creative. More importantly, you have to share the story with the team.

- **Greet the audience as they arrive** – to get people on your side.

Something I do regularly and recommend wholeheartedly is the act of greeting audience members as they arrive for the meeting. That simple act is a great way to make friends and get people on your side. Obviously, it is not applicable in all cases; however, it makes a nice touch for larger groups.

- **Vary your presentation style** – to keep things interesting.

Sometimes, you can use different presenting aides to liven things up a bit. Try a dry erase board or a pad of paper on an easel for visual purposes. Sure, some people learn by listening, but others need to see key points for retention. Additionally, try varying your speech patterns. I talk fast, so if I slow down my rate of speech a bit, people take notice. Try varying your volume. Raise your voice for emphasis. Lower your voice to make a serious point. Repeat things. Be exciting and interesting to engage your audience. Take a few chances!

- **Let your audience win** – let them be the heroes!

Let your participants look good, and they will surely start paying attention. Offer praise and encouragement to the audience. Ask questions that the participants can answer. Ask for personal stories to help illustrate key points. Get people involved, and give them chances to shine. Give credit sincerely, and it will come back to you.

*That's just he way it works!*

# MAKING INVENTORY MANAGEMENT YOUR STRENGTH

If I close my eyes, I can imagine the scene right now.

It is a Friday morning, nearing 8 a.m. A sales team is sitting around a conference table. While not everyone is indulging in the breakfast fare (doughnuts and coffee), most are eagerly waiting for the morning announcement.

Did the team beat the XYZ product goal?

Finally, the announcement is made. The sales manager, a burly former minor league first baseman, approaches the lectern. He attempts a joke: "I have the news that everybody is waiting to hear. The company softball game has been rescheduled for next Tuesday night!"

A few people laugh, mostly out of courtesy.

"Just joking, folks," he chuckles. "Thanks to a last minute, on-premise push by Tom, Mary, Peter, and Paul, we made the goal by 125 cases! We're all going to the Bahamas for golf, sun, and relaxation. More details to follow. Great job, everybody!"

The room erupts in cheers. What a successful incentive program, right? Everybody is happy. The supplier is happy. The distributor's people are happy. The retailer is happy…

Wait a second, here. Is the retailer happy? How did the sales team reach the goal? Did they make promises about velocity and sell-through that may be hard to realize? Do the members of the sales team intend to honor the promotional promises they made that brought the goal within reach? Will the retailer be able to move through the product in a reasonable amount of time without the dreaded markdown? Do the **customers** feel good about the deals they struck to make the goal a reality? These questions will be answered in time, long after the lucky sales people have enjoyed ample amounts of sand, surf, and margaritas.

I may know what you are thinking.

Are you possibly naïve? Do you understand the complexities that grip the beverage business as we enter 2009? It used to be that there were many distributors, and many of those houses were local. Companies based in the United States owned the suppliers and brands, and things were less complicated. Relationships were more important back then, and a distributor was not likely to lose a line of brands unless something went terribly wrong.

Touché!

I remember when things started to change. One year, the biggest distributor in Chicago lost a major line of imported vodkas. They lost millions of dollars of profit in a New York minute. Shortly thereafter, they no longer existed, having been absorbed by another distributor in Chicago. Yes, things were changing.

Now, the people who own the popular brands are based in other countries. Goals are made almost in a vacuum (some would say), without any real knowledge of what is realistic in different markets. A buddy of mine likes to say that, in the beverage industry, we "worship at the altar of the shareholder," a statement with which I suspect many would agree. After all, many of the largest suppliers who still exist are public companies.

What is the result of all this change?

Distributors, the vaunted middle tier, are constantly squeezed by both of the groups they serve – the retailer and the supplier. The supplier wants improved distribution (read: more cases), and the retailer wants to buy fewer cases.

Lovely!

**Here are a few things to think about so you may use this situation as a strength instead of a weakness:**

- **Measure your success in terms of your customers' successes**

If you reached a goal (and, as a result, had a great golf vacation) by selling pallet loads of product, the promotion was successful *if and only if* your customers made money. On the other hand, if most of the inventory remains in your customer's warehouse, you have not been successful. Truth be told, in our family business, our biggest challenge was managing inventory. We were not so hot at saying "no," and as a result, we often suffered from a bloated inventory. I fear that the scene I imagined at the beginning of this chapter was replayed countless times in sales meeting rooms all over Chicago, due in no small part to our overbuying.

So, were there any successful purchases? Yes, of course. In some cases, we moved through the goods in a reasonable amount of time at a decent enough profit margin. (Though I am no longer a retailer, I still cannot admit that we made a good profit. I just cannot; it is just not in my DNA). There were many deals that afforded us new and exciting items for our customers. There is no doubt about that.

In other cases, things were not so good! The inventory did not move at the desired velocity, or, in some cases, any velocity at all. The goods clogged up our storage capacity, forced us to keep featuring items long after our customers lost interest, and in the end, we were forced to cut margins to create some sell-through.

But wait, there is more.

Our sales people grew tired of selling the same items over and over. Back in the day, one would just say, "You sell what I tell you to sell!" But that does not really work anymore. Come to think of it, I do not think it ever worked. The plain truth is that happy associates beget happy customers, and excessive inventory levels and the corresponding push to mediate those levels were not good for morale. A negative by-product, which was usually never considered, was that by discounting national brands, we were effectively cheapening those labels in the eyes of our customers.

The point is that, no matter how many incentive trips a team wins, no matter how successful a distributor becomes (financially) by moving through truckloads of items, *a purchase (deal) is only <u>a real success</u> if the customer considers it a success.*

- **Acknowledge the problem, and care about it!**

A young salesperson posed the following question to me recently. We were talking about the surplus of goods that distributors are expected to move, and he asked, *"Sometimes, don't you have to oversell because of the pressure placed by managers who have been told in no uncertain terms to move goods?"*

What if your job is on the line? Really, I know that my *principles* on inventory management will create superior relationships in the long term, but what about the short term? You cannot eat principles for dinner.

Ok, good point. I agree! You might one day be in a position where you have to oversell, not because of the glitzy golf vacation but to keep your job. Yes, but remember the following tidbit: your managers cannot limit the amount you **care** about the situation.

Show your customers you care!

Do more to help the situation. Do more tastings. Go there on a Sunday. Make some signs at home. Hand-sell a few bottles yourself. You could also educate the staff on how to sell the item – not product attributes but what to look for in customers who might enjoy the product. Give your customers weekly updates on your efforts to improve the sell-through. Do not turn your back on the situation.

Give it 100% plus one. A buddy of mine recently shared a strategy with me. He asks his people to give 100% but then do one or two additional actions so the effort is greater than what they originally thought was possible. What great ingenuity! The key, after all, is standing behind the products you sell to the customer. What, you did not sell *that* stuff? It was the last guy? Even better! You will emerge the hero!

- **Lose the "dump and go" selling mentality**

Nothing should be sold without first giving your customers a plan for selling those products. The best salespeople say, "I want you to buy this deal (promotion), but first, I want you to be comfortable with my plan for the successful sell-through of these products." Make sure the plan addresses the following: promotions, stackings, displays, signage, tastings, and other types of support. To accept an order without the plan is having a *dump and go* mentality. Such greed and ignorance is hard for a salesperson to overcome in the long run.

- **Withstand the urge to sell your customers products they do not need**

The pattern is very predictable. A salesperson oversells a customer, does not have a plan for sell-through, and, ultimately, the customer is angry with the salesperson and the company. Those situations never end well. Always ask yourself, "Would I make this purchase if this were my company?" Yes, put yourselves in your customer's shoes. If you would not make the purchase (i.e., if the shoe was on the other foot), then why should your customer?

Do not make the sale. Rework the program, and ask yourself again, "Would I do this if it were my business?" If the answer once again is no, do it again. What if you cannot come to the conclusion that it is right for your customer? You have two options. The first option: do not make the deal. That is right. Walk away. Ok, since *that* is not really going to happen, consider the other option. Be honest! Some customers may be determined to make a deal come heck or high water. Tell them you do not think it is in their best interests. Most likely, they will either follow through and do it anyway, or you and your customer may try to rework things yet again, together this time. One thing I can tell you is that your customer will appreciate your honesty.

Do not act like your customers should automatically carry your new items. There is a big difference between a placement and a sensible decision. Never act like getting *the hot new product* placed is a slam-dunk!

- ## **Do not turn your back on inventory already sold**

Instead, spend more time helping your customers sell what they already own. There have been numerous studies in this industry that show that way too much time is being spent on negative cash flow activities. By that, I mean the regular ordering or introduction of new products. Experts peg negative cash flow activities at 95% of the time spent selling. If my math is correct, that leaves a scant 5% to talk about the sale of inventory currently clogging up the aisles. Your customers simply cannot afford tying up big dollars in inventory.

Sure, if you sell in new items or process the weekly order, ultimately your customer will see the profit, but that takes time. You can take the following to the bank: spending more time and effort improving the sell through of existing inventory will set you apart from the competition in a positive way. Make it a regular part of your sales calls…hopefully, the first part.

- ## **Identify other areas where products can sell successfully**

Be creative. Find other areas of the store to place your goods. Create demand in an innovative way rather than just putting your product on a shelf and hoping it sells.

One of the topics in Chapter 20 is *observing*. In particular, try noticing other positions to place where they may sell more rapidly. It is critical to shake things up a bit. Displays must be rotated. The look and feel must change once in a while. If you feel that a certain product has stopped moving because the display is languishing, the onus is on you to say something.

Develop new on-premise promotions and exciting and different ways to use your products. Sometimes, all it takes is you stopping by the bar or restaurant to re-introduce a slow-moving product. If you do not do it, nobody else will. Your customer will appreciate you when you take an active interest in his or her basic business needs.

- **Keep your eye on the ball.**

Remember, when making buying decisions, your customer is taking a leap of faith, one that he or she will ultimately base upon the trust you have built up over the years. It is simply not worth putting a trusting relationship with a long-term partner at risk just to push another product through. Furthermore, when your customer knows that you are not going to throw things at him or her that do not fit his or her product mix, you gain credibility. So keep the following in mind: however great the product is, however great your bonus could be, nothing is as important as keeping that trust factor.

*That's just the way it works.*

Vending Machine Man turns his back on slow moving inventory and other problems he helped create. He is a pretender. Your job, as a partner, is to show up with a solid plan for moving forgotten products and not waiting until the cobwebs appear!

# Handling Objections Confidentially

Did we ever throw an objection at a salesperson just for fun?

Absolutely! We routinely threw objections out there for fun and to see if the salesperson was on the ball. We also did this to see if he or she had confidence in his or her products. In many cases, if we got a reasonable response to our objection, we would fold like a house of cards.

Objecting just for fun? That may have been my weird sense of humor!

I know most salespeople hate objections because they think the sale is lost. Do you feel that way? Do you cringe when your customers say, "But wait," or "I can't," or "How can we?" The important criterion for handling objections is to realize that resistance of this sort does not mean a sale is lost. It is merely an obstacle that should be dealt with calmly and professionally. But why would a customer object and then ultimately agree to buy the product? There are many reasons. Here are a few:

- to get a better price
- to get better terms
- to be sure that they are making the right decision
- to get more time to make the decision
- to gain clarification on a specific point or concern

So if you hear statements like...

- "Let me think it over."
- "Can you leave me some information?"
- "I have to talk it over with the owner."
- "I can't afford it."
- "I don't have the space."

...all might not be lost!

In some cases, your accounts may object because they do not want to feel like they are saying yes too quickly and want to slow things down a bit. "It's a defense mechanism," according to Tom Hopkins (2006), author of *How to Master the Art of Selling*. You know how it goes! Sometimes, you delay making a decision so you do not look impulsive. It happens all the time with your customers.

One more point: according to Gerhard Gschwandtner (2007), author of *The Ultimate Sales Training Workshop,* not getting an objection does not mean you are on your way to easy street. *"Until you hear an objection, you're strictly a visitor and an information giver."* Customers who fail to come up with objections either are not qualified to make the decision or do not have the money to make the purchase. If customers do not challenge you in one way or another, then they are not serious about buying. So, if you hear an objection, you now have a chance to make the sale!"

Here are some thoughts on handling objections smoothly and confidently:

- When you first hear an objection, hold your tongue until the customer has finished stating it. If you write down what the customer is saying, then it might help you remain quiet.

- After you hear the objection, pause for a few seconds.

Think about what was said even if you have heard it a thousand times before. Pausing lets your customer know that you are processing what has been said. This shows you are listening, and that is half the battle. Do not rush. That seems pushy. Hopefully, you will have a sense for what type of objection is coming, but if you did not foresee it, pausing will give you time to develop a thoughtful answer.

- **Try to postpone answering the objection until after the presentation**

There is a natural tendency to try to quell your customer's objection right away. Resist this urge. Acknowledge what has been said, but respectfully ask if you can address the concern at the end of the presentation. There are two benefits to using this strategy.

First, if you handle the objection right away, your momentum will be stalled, and your customer will be focusing on the issue at hand. Conversely, if you keep going, then you will bring your customer's attention right along with you. You may then have a chance to emphasize other benefits – factors that may help you overcome the objection. Second, as you proceed with the presentation, your customer may be able to overcome the objection in his or her head and may no longer consider it important.

- **Be prepared for the *normal (typical)* objections**

Most customers object over a handful of similar issues time after time, so there should be no reason why a salesperson is not prepared ahead of time to handle the most common objections. Hopefully, your sales team discusses common objections with each other, but if not, try the following exercise at your next meeting. Three or four days before the meeting, ask your sales team to come up with a list of common objections, those most frequently heard and most difficult to handle. The hard ones!

The purpose of this is to brainstorm better and more effective ways to respond to customer objections. List all the objections on a flip chart or whiteboard. Review the list. Determine if the objections listed are the real objections or if there is something else troubling your customers. For example, a simple response like *"I'm not sure that's a good idea for us"* is obviously shielding the real issue. The real reason could be, *"If I buy it, my boss will see my decision and explode!"* Now we are getting somewhere. What criteria does your boss use for making decisions? That could be your next question. Have your salespeople question each other to isolate the real reason for resisting the purchase.

Consider the emotional challenges involved in responding to customer objections. One part is your customers' feelings. The other part is your apprehension in handling the issue. Suggest ways to overcome these feelings. Learn from each other. If the team takes this exercise seriously, then you should come out of the session with a list of objections and time-tested ways for handling these issues.

- **Take your time when responding to an objection** There is nothing wrong with asking for some time.

In fact, it is far more desirable to take the time to answer an objection correctly than to simply make something up.

- Ask for clarification so that you will be clear on your customer's concerns, priorities, expectations, and requirements. "What I hear you saying is..."

- Feed the objection back.

Sometimes, the simple act of repeating what your customers have said will actually help them answer their own objection. They may realize that it is not such a big deal. Never question the concern. Avoid sarcasm, impatience, or any other mockery.

- **Address all objections with a well thought-out response**

For example, let us say the objection is "The price is very high!" A well thought-out response would be the following: "**You're right**. The price is high, and here is why. This beer is made using an extraordinary process. The process makes the beer taste very smooth. It also creates a layer of freshness so you can take the beer out of the refrigerator and re-refrigerate it on multiple occasions. The beer will stay fresh!"

- **Address all objections with sincere appreciation**

Your customer is giving you an opportunity. It should not be thought of as a negative. If it were a negative, the customer would not respond to your sales presentation – at all. He or she would just ignore it.

If there ever were the perfect time to have sincerity, empathy, and appreciation, this would be the time. The absence of such skills will spell disaster. Make sure to take your customer's objections seriously. The worst strategy is to minimize an objection and act like it is no big deal. It *is* a big deal to your customer; otherwise, he or she would not have mentioned it.

- **Do not rush.** You are not on the clock – *it's not the NFL draft.* (I know, I am repeating this point, but it is important!)

- **Be sold on your products** - or answering objections will pose a big challenge.

You must be the first person to be sold on your product. If you are not sold on the quality of your craft beer or chardonnay from Argentina, then why should your customer be interested in what you have to say? They will not be. You must like what you are selling!

Sometimes, all an objection means is that you have not sold your customers on the true benefits of your products. Keep at it! Keep pointing out what is different and unique about your items.

- **Do not argue.** No anger, sarcasm, or other forms of deal-killing heat.

- **Get your customer to say "yes"** to increase your chances of succeeding.

I read a study once where Encyclopedia Britannica brought together a group of psychologists to study the effects of saying "yes." The study showed that, each time a customer said "yes," he or she was that much closer to buying the product. Let us say your customer says, "Is that your best price?" Instead of replying, "Yes!" ask the customer, "Do you feel that I always give you my best price?" If you do (and your customer trusts you), he or she will answer, "Yes." You are closer to the sale. Ask, "Do I always give you a fair price?" If you do (and your customer trusts you), he or she will answer, "Yes."

See how this works? Get your customer to answer in the affirmative, and you will move closer to the sale.

- **Always try to walk in your customer's shoes.** See all objections from his or her perspective. (It is called empathy!)

Avoid the temptation to label your customers in any of the following ways: stupid, a jerk, lazy, pushy, crabby, or crazy. Yes, I realize that, in many cases, your customers *are* lazy, crabby, and crazy (and many other adjectives). Yes, they can be real jerks; however, the key is to avoid letting this negative filter distort your perception. Be careful how you react because there could be a reason for how they are acting. Maybe your offer is unclear. Maybe you are not clearly defining your value proposition. Maybe your customer is distracted.

Try to understand why your customer might be acting in a certain way. Yes, you are going to have these negative perceptions, but the key is *are you going to dwell on them?*

- **Do not leave without an explanation of vague objections**

One of the most common objections is "I want to think it over." At this, many salespeople would move on to the next item, but the goal here is to delve a little deeper so you fully understand the true meaning behind the objection. For example, you could say, "I understand that you want to think it over. Just for my knowledge, though, what is it that you need to think about?"

Your job is to uncover the real objection, so you can come up with an appropriate response. Realize that a negative or neutral comment may mean you have not given enough information for your customer to make a good decision.

- **Have a plan for handling indifference** to get the sale back on track.

Some examples of indifferent comments may be:

   o   "Maybe next month."
   o   "Not sure about that."
   o   "I'll think about that."

Indifference is hard to handle. Unprofessional salespeople keep *selling* and repeating themselves when they receive an indifferent reaction. The odds are that your customer heard you, so you do not need to restate benefits, etc. The key at this juncture is to keep questioning your customer to convey the value proposition.

- **After you address the objection, try to ascertain whether or not you have succeeded in easing your customer's doubts and concerns.** Ask questions like the following:

  o "Henry, does that answer your question?"
  o "Peter, how does that option sound to you?"
  o "Sally, do you like the sound of that?"
  o "Will that work for you?"
  o "How will that fly with your supervisor?"

- **If you feel that you have answered the objection, go ahead and ask for the sale again.**
- **No luck? Re-state the benefits. Ask more questions. Keep trying!**
- **If all else fails, thank your customer and use the experience to your benefit as you prepare for future sales calls.**

Sometimes, you are not going to make the sale. How you react will help pave the way for your next sales appointment. In a few chapters, we will talk about attitude, but in the meantime, here are a few things to think about.

Be flexible. Priorities can change in a second on a sales call, like they may have for many runners prior to the 2007 Chicago marathon, which was run on a really hot day. Temperatures were hitting 70 degrees at the start of the race and were in the mid to high 80s with humidity by mid-day. I have never run a marathon under such extreme conditions, although I once came close. I ran one in 1979 (as a naive 13 year old) when the mercury topped off at 84 degrees. I remember the challenges those conditions presented.

Many marathoners were probably eating their pasta the night before the race and worrying plenty about the race conditions. They were probably making decisions on how to run the following morning. What would you do in that situation? Would you back off your original racing plans or run as fast as you expected to run before they announced the weather? Would you observe the conditions and adjust your plans accordingly? I know what I would do, and, suffice to say, it is probably good that I was not running!

Those runners with flexible personalities probably changed their plans and aimed simply to survive the elements. The inflexible runners, those who stayed with plans they made prior to learning about the extreme conditions, likely had a pretty tough day! So what do you do when things change before, during, or after a sales call? Sometimes, you have to be flexible.

And what if your customer says *no*?

Do not take it personally. Maybe the customer is having a bad day. Maybe his or her business is suffering in a bad economy. Rejection comes in two forms: valid and invalid. If the rejection is valid, then you need to know what you may have done, said, or not said to dissuade your customer. His or her comments will form the basis for changes to your selling strategy. Do not avoid the situation or back off. Similarly, never counter-attack! Do not become more aggressive, and do not over-react. Such negative reactions will do more harm than good.

Some other reasons why salespeople take rejection too personally is because they feel that their customers are very important, so the idea that he or she may be rejecting them is too much to take. Other times, salespeople get emotionally involved, and thus, turn defensive in their behaviors when things do not go the way they planned.

As a way of wrapping up this chapter, here are some quick tips from the editors of *Selling Power Magazine*. They suggest you have "fun" with rejection. The following are examples of beliefs or thoughts for enjoying failure and being amused by rejection.

- I love rejection!
- Rejection turns me on! (I think you would agree that this one is a bit odd!)
- Negative feedback ignites energy!
- Hostile people amuse me!
- I attack my fears!

- Failure sharpens my objectivity!
- Adversity makes me resilient!
- Failure is a maturing process!
- I do better under pressure!
- Stress stimulates my creativity!

The fourth bullet above is the one I like the most. I once tried to set up a meeting with a distributor, and I got the following response: "I am NOT available to see you, and we are NOT interested in your workshops!" *Wow! Ya don't say! Good use of capital letters!* There was only one emotion I could feel here. Laughter!

So, stand tall and have confidence. Collaborate like a true professional. Welcome dialogue even in the face of potential rejection. Allow the customer time to evaluate your recommendations. Know that every "no" is not final. Your customer might ultimately have a need. Do not give up. Act as if it is impossible to fail. Your next sales call may result in your biggest sale of the month, but if you do not approach that account with a huge smile and tons of enthusiasm, you will never know.

*That's just the way it works!*

# Questions from the Field

**Q:** Recently, at a sales and service excellence seminar, I was asked about closing techniques. Specifically, a beverage professional asked me if there was one in particular that I found to be effective.

**A: Not really. (Want a more detailed answer?)**

I do not really believe in closing techniques. As a retailer, I experienced many different techniques (even the infamous "sending the goods in even though I did not say yes technique!") I have four reasons why I am not a big fan of these.

- I find closing techniques to be a bit manipulative.

- I believe that a large majority of successful selling hinges upon whether or not your customer likes and trusts you.

- I believe that, if you have conveyed your case confidently and convinced your customer, and they have a need for the benefits that your product provides, they will pull the trigger. They will show you by their spoken words or unspoken gestures. You just have to be observant enough to see them.

- I believe that closing (a sale) is more a continuation of a long-term relationship than a specific point in time.

That said, I understand the need for salespeople to take their customers' temperatures to gauge their levels of interest. There are many resources for salespeople to learn different closing techniques, but for the purposes of this book, I would like to talk about one useful tool.

Many experts call it the *trial close*.

The trial close is a way to determine how interested your customer is in what you are selling. The advantage of this technique is that it is not much more than checking your customer's interest much earlier in the sales process than you have probably been taught. It is not like traditional techniques that occur towards the completion of the sales process.

Here is what I like about the trial close:

- The trial close takes away the element of surprise, leaving no confusion as to why you are there and what you are trying to accomplish.

- The trial close helps you keep your mouth closed. For example, many salespeople keep talking after their customers have already made the decision to purchase. A trial close makes you less likely to talk your way out of a sale.

- The trial close is a great diagnostic tool. It helps you to see where you are in the sales process.

- The trial close prevents you from waiting too long to seek a commitment. Like a movie that takes forever to get to the point, if you wait too long, your customer's mind may have already moved on to something else. One caveat – if you ask for the sale too quickly, you may risk losing it.

So, make sure to keep things simple, and support your claims with facts and figures. Never sell beyond the limitations of your product. Answer all objections because unanswered objections just create more objections.

However you decide to do it, "Should I send in 15 or 20 cases?" or "Do you want delivery on Tuesday or Thursday?" just make sure to ask for the sale. You are not going to get the sale through mental telepathy.

*That's just the way it works!*

# QUESTIONS FROM THE FIELD

**Q:** When presenting a new product, if the customer says no, is it ok to re-present the same product at a later date?

**A: Of course it is. Your goal was getting a new product in the door. You were not successful. So what?** It took Thomas Edison over 100 tries to get a light bulb to work. Right? Nobody achieves all his or her goals on the first try. Often, it takes many attempts.

Try the following:

- **After the sales call (as soon as possible), try to determine what you could have done differently**

In other words, what went wrong? Why was the buyer unreceptive? Was there something in your approach? Were you prepared? Were you on time for the meeting? Did the buyer seem rushed or harried? What was your interest-gaining statement or approach?

This is some time for some soul-searching. Some salespeople will blame someone or something for their failure, anybody but himself or herself. Of course, it is always somebody else's fault. Do not fall prey to that unproductive thinking. Take the blame. Assume that you just did not get the job done.

- **Send a handwritten note**

Wait, a thank you note? And you expect it to be handwritten? But my customer did not do anything for me. They said *"NO!"*

That is not the right way to think about it. Did they give you an opportunity? If you do the proper soul searching from the paragraph above, you may see that he or she gave you information that will help you in future sales presentations.

The note should say similar to the following: *"Thank you for the opportunity to present XYZ Product. I will be back in the next few weeks with more benefits to demonstrate why XYZ Product will help your product selection."*

Do you catch my drift? Change the words if you like, but keep it brief and to the point. The objective is twofold. First, you want say thank you, and second, you want to let your customer know that you will be back to re-introduce the product. This way, he or she will not be surprised to see you again.

- After a short period of time, **feel free to re-present the product...**

...but not until you have come up with a creative way to get your customer excited about it. Remember: unless your product is the second coming of (insert any fantastically exceptional product introduced during the last 10 years), your customer probably would rather encounter the bubonic plague than sign a purchase order. How many selections can you have on the drinks menu? How high can their shelves go?

Put yourself in your customers' shoes. Step outside of the "my product is perfect" mentality! What would excite you? Be creative.

So, there you have it. It is not over until it is over. Keep asking for the sale. If you execute in a thoughtful and creative manner, your customer will appreciate your persistence. I know I always did.

*That's just the way it works!*

# MANAGING CUSTOMER RELATIONSHIPS

Years ago I participated in a triathlon in Central Florida. Long story short, I swam ½ mile out of my way in the choppy waters of Lake Clermont because I was not looking up. I was looking down. Unfortunately, Lake Clermont, unlike a swimming pool, has no line on the bottom to guide swimmers. Consequently, I was in for a long day *and* a long swim.

Welcome to the chapter on customer relationship management. Yes, I know – the whole book is on relationships; however, it is here in Chapter 13 that I will share exactly what your customers are probably thinking and what they are looking for.

The objective of this chapter is to understand why it is so important to continually monitor your customers, and why managing customer relationships is so critical to long-term success. Another objective is to give suggestions on how you can improve your relationships. and how to handle complaints or conflict along the way.

Often, you and your customers are in uncharted waters. There is no *line to follow* which is why you must always try to ascertain what is important to your customers.

**Consider the following:**

What is important to you and your company is not nearly as important to what is important to your customers!

**Also consider this:**

Do you measure your success by the level of your customer's success? If I went around the table at your year-end sales meeting and asked each person what he or she achieved, would anyone mention the word *customer* when laying out achievements? Sales people who win the customer loyalty marathon measure their success by the successes that their customers achieve.

**Ask yourself:**

Besides price, what really motivates your customer to pull the trigger and support certain vendors? Are the barriers between your customer and yourself getting smaller and smaller with each visit?

**Also ask this:**

If this were your business, what would you do?

**And this:**

Your goal is to achieve the status of 'preferred sales representative.' Are you considered a **trusted** partner, or a **self-serving** pretender?

**And this:**

Is there potential in this account? If you did something different in this account, might there be a different result? (You all know the one about doing things the same *over and over*, but expecting a different result!)

**Don't forget this:**

Your goal is to stay relevant and visible to **gain and keep distribution.** Your customers are mentioned on the web in local newspapers every day. Are you actively looking for those mentions and then sending a congratulatory note? The more times you reach out **without** the objective of selling something - the better.

**What is your customer thinking?**

Will my sales person ever ask **me** what is important to **me**?

**Is there anything really important that salespeople should know?**

Yes, your customer wants you to know that his or her feelings about *you* might often outweigh the facts about *your products.*

**Does you customer want you to know anything else?**

Yes, funny you should ask.

Your customers want you to realize that things that are good for you **should be better for them.**

Your customers want you to understand that they are a bit wary and cynical by nature. If they realize that an offer is *better for them than for you* they may be more willing to pull the trigger.

**Anything else?**

Yes! Do not ask for favors! I think I hear sales people groaning, "*We always ask for favors!*"

Try to eliminate that practice. *Here's how it works.* You ask your customer for a favor. They say *yes,* and then the dangerous part comes.

For the favor receiver (salesperson), the favor is really significant at first, then less significant. For the favor giver (customer), the favor is small at first, but then gains in significance as time goes on. It gets distorted. Then when you ask for a favor again, your customer thinks, *wait a minute - I just did you a huge favor!* Not a dynamic that ends well for sales people. Better to earn your orders with solid *benefits,* rather than favors.

**Could there be anything else?**

Your customers, at times, feel that their sales people lack a basic understanding of human interaction. Your customers want you to realize that before you sell them any products, you sell yourself. They want you to think through your first interaction with them. They want you to sell yourself on your products to build your own self-image and self-belief. They want you to know that the more confidence *you* have, the more courage *they* will have to pull the trigger to stock, support, and promote your products.

**There couldn't possibly be anything else (make it stop)?**

- Your customers want you to understand that the reason they said "no" may be because you failed to properly translate the value of your proposal – that you did not capture their attention.

- Your customers want you to appreciate that if you make it more about "them" and less about "your products" – you may have a better chance at succeeding.

- Your customers want you to know that every time you call or visit, you have a choice and opportunity to do by right by them.

- Your customers want you to make it easy to do business with you. They want you to work around their schedule. They want you to have materials ready. Nobody wants to see you shuffle through all your materials and/or dump your briefcase or purse on the table.

- Your customers want you to understand that the "truth" is much, much more than what you *"can get them to believe"* (Much more on this topic in Chapter 14.)

- **Your customers want you to give facts that back up your claims**

Everyone has had an experience where they see an interesting headline on the web and click on the link, only to find the wrong article. Claims in presentations should be backed up by concrete facts that support your position – and not something out of left field. Your customers should not have to assume, infer, deduce, surmise, or construe the support for your arguments.

- **Your customers want you to be engaged as you sell to them**

Your customers want you to realize that words like passion, enthusiasm, and attentiveness are not to be taken lightly. These words, when executed with sincerity, are the building blocks of successful relationships.

- **Your customers want you to know that getting them to say *"yes"* is sometimes the easy part**

For example, say you get the go-ahead to put up a display. That may have seemed like the hard part – but it was really the easy part. The hard part will be consistently maintaining the display so it always looks fresh, exciting, and inviting for consumers. Your customers want you to know that the less maintenance they have to do, the more likely the display will enjoy a long and fruitful life!

- **Your customers want you to understand that win-win negotiations and/or arrangements are much more convincing than the alternative**

If you have your customer's best interests at heart, your customer interaction will always go much more smoothly and end up in a better place. Long-term, high quality relationships should not be adversarial. Your customers want cooperation, not competition, and collaboration, not manipulation.

- **Your customers want you to know they understand conflict happens in every working relationship**

The ultimate test of a relationship is to disagree, but to respect the other person's opinion, agree to disagree, and move forward without bitterness. Your customers want you to understand that, while disagreements may occur, it is vital to always try to keep the relationship in working order.

- **Your customers want you to know that it's never good to be the smartest person in the room**

If you think that you are the brightest person in the room, you may be in trouble. The best sales person *operating individually* is no match for a team of individuals working *collaboratively* towards a solution. Further, it is a sign of respect when you solicit your customer's opinion by asking questions. It is flattering, and it shows sincerity and concern. The best part - it does not cost a dollar or any free goods because it is completely free!

On the other hand, your customers expect you to know your stuff. They realize when you have not done your homework.

- **Your customers want you to know that they understand you're busy**

We all have busy schedules, but you must take the time to make contact and nurture the relationship. Your goal is always to make your customer feel like the most important person in the world to you - and *that*, my friends, is a marathon, not a sprint.

## <u>To be successful:</u>

- **Help your customer gain a competitive advantage**

Show your customer how to use, position and market your products. Give them good reasons to get behind your products. Demonstrate how your items will help the them gain a competitive advantage?

Help your customer by sharing the best competitive practices. Does the competition have similar offerings? How are they similar? How are they different? How does the competition display the product? What is their merchandising strategy? Are they seeing better results? Why? The best salespeople take an active interest in their customer's success. They educate. They help customers understand the why's and how's of profiting from the sale of their wines, beers and spirits.

- **Educate everybody, not just the buyer**

Everybody in each and every account wants to feel important. Follow the words of mega-successful entrepreneur Mary Kay Ash, "Everybody has a sign on their head that says *make me feel important!"*

- **Learn names so everybody feels valued**

You never know who will be calling the shots tomorrow, and it makes people feel good to hear their name. Revisit Chapter 8 for some suggestions on remembering people's names.

- **Be cognizant of competitive sales trends**

Do your homework so you know what is happening in your industry so you can inform your customers.

- **Be aware of your customer's culture and values** – especially for the increasing number of multi-cultural customers. (Much more on this topic in Chapter 26!)

- **Learn about your customers** – find what you have in common. Know more about their businesses.

Try to learn the answers to the following questions – and then some. Find the time to know this type of information about all your customers.

- o What are your customer's children's names and ages?
- o What is your customer's spouse's name?
- o What is your customer's hometown?
- o Where was your customer born?
- o What are your customer's favorite sports teams?
- o What is your customer's favorite wine, beer or spirit?
- o What are your customer's favorite charities?
- o What is your customer's biggest challenge?
- o What is your customer's biggest business fear? What keeps him or her up at night?
- o What is your customer's biggest opportunity?
- o What is your customer most proud of having achieved?
- o Where did your customer go to high school or college?
- o Where did his or her children go to college?
- o What is the last new product your customer purchased from your company?
- o How is that product is doing **(in your customer's eyes)?**

Of course, there are many others and my goal here is just to give you an example of the types of things you should know. The point is, if your customer has a passion or a raison d'etre (reason to be), you better know what it is!

- • **Be your customer's advocate in all areas of business,** not just when it concerns the products you are selling.

In an earlier chapter I mentioned that a salesperson once mentioned a new advertising approach, something that was new to me. It was a new avenue that worked out very nicely. He showed that he wanted our business to do well and his reach extended beyond those traditional boundaries. I appreciated the initiative.

- • **Learn how decisions are made within your customer's organization**
- • **Ascertain your customer's strengths, weaknesses, opportunities and threats**

Be willing to take a chance. I recently read an interview with Mel Lagomasino, the former CEO of JP Morgan. He suggests that if you want to win your customer's trust, you have to be willing to lose and lose big. You must be willing to lose the relationship by telling your customers facts that they might not necessarily want to hear.

- **Make people look good** – make allies!

  o Help them get raises and promotions.
  o Help them achieve higher status in their companies.
  o Help them make a difference. Help them add value.
  o Help them by bringing sunshine in to their lives.

- **Understand what motivates your customers**

Some customers think outside the box and want you to be creative with them and some do not. What appeals to some, will not appeal to others. Try to identify as many possible motivators as possible. Remove your ego and self-interest from the equation. Make sure you hear from your customers exactly what they need, rather than what you want to give them. In other words, what is most important to your customers?

You may be thinking – we are asking a lot of invasive type questions, how do we get this information? Good question. The trust you need to obtain this type of information is built over time. You have to put first things first. Develop a reputation for returning phone calls and emails promptly. Make sure your company is making deliveries on time and that your customer's beverage department is stocked and merchandised properly. Continue to add value in ways that make your customers more profitable.

Once you have established a reputation for trustworthiness (for operating with impeccable integrity), the barriers between your company and theirs will begin to drop. The goal is to become the partner they turn to for help, the partner in which they place the most trust.

- **Resolve to improve relationships** – if they are in need of repair.

Take the initiative to improve relationships that are not going so smoothly. Simply approach your customer and say, *"I value your busi-*

*ness and would like to work with you to get our relationship back on the right track.*" It never hurts to try, and I think you will be happy with the results.

## What happens when things don't go as planned?

Here is a newsflash! News you can use! Despite all your best efforts, there will be situations and circumstances that really test your relationship. There will be kinks in the armor, so to speak.

When your customers are unhappy, they will likely respond in one of three ways. First, they will keep their unhappiness inside and resist the urge to share their feelings. Second, they will complain and give you a chance to remedy the situation. Third, they will complain and will do so in a heated fashion. It cannot be emphasized enough – the more successfully you handle these potentially negative situations - the better your relationships will be. The truth is that you can engender a much, much higher sense of loyalty by handling adverse situations favorably than you had before the problem occurred. Let us go through these scenarios.

## When customers don't complain:

In most other businesses, customers do not complain, they simply vote with their feet and take their business elsewhere. If customers are leaving a business, the proprietor usually does not see it until his transaction counts start to slide, or his sales start to falter. But, in the wholesale wine, beer and spirit business, your customers do not have the luxury of shopping elsewhere; nevertheless, it still makes a great deal of sense to know how to handle customer complaints. **Despite the fact that your customers' choices are limited, you can still achieve a much higher sense of loyalty, by handling problems quickly and compassionately.**

Before we go through some steps designed to help you resolve complaints, while preserving relationships, let us understand why customers are hesitant to complain.

- **They think you don't care** - *show them you do care.*

Head off customer complaints at the pass. Make it easy! Customers who take the time and effort to let their feelings be known are actually saying, sometimes, SHOUTING, "I want to be your customer. Do something!" They are giving you an opportunity to show how great you can really be! Show them that their opinions will not fall upon deaf ears.

- **They're afraid of a confrontation** - *handle things professionally.*

**Never argue with your customers.** Arguing with a customer is a situation that typically ends with two losers: (1) they will lose face if you embarrass them, especially in front of others, and (2) you will lose a customer (or at least they will not want to do business with you any longer). Keep your cool! Yes, it is *simple but not easy.* Simple to get into heated discussions with customers, but not easy to take the high road and steer clear of such situations. Do not go there.

Robert Bacal (2005) makes a great point in his book *Perfect Phrases for Customer Service.* "The goal in (heated) situations is to find agreement points. Sometimes, a simple "You're right!" will help diffuse the situation." That approach surprises an angry customer. Often, they will be at a loss for what to say next, which allows you to equitably handle the situation.

- **They think you do not want to hear feedback** - *ask for it.*

Show your customers you want their feedback by asking for it. A simple statement like "How can we improve our service?" will work wonders with your customer base and you already know my two favorite questions: *What could we do better?* And *what are we doing well?*

Ken Blanchard (2004) in *Customer Mania* suggests the following simple questions: "How can we make the experience better?" and "What can we do to provide better service?" The goal is to encourage customers to be specific and to get them to start talking! Poll your customers about the top three to five things they would like to see changed or fixed, and act upon the list immediately. Let your customers know that, with their input, you will be able to provide them with better service.

- **They do not think you will do anything about it** - *show them that this is not the case.*

No matter how you ask for your customer's feedback, make sure that you are sincere and that you act upon what they tell you. If your master plan is to be insincere and to let the feedback go in one ear and out the other, then it may be better just to keep your mouth shut.

Your challenge is to act immediately, and to develop strategies to counteract this perception. Once customers see some action, they will happily give you their honest feedback.

## So what do you do when a customer complains?

Complaint resolution is tricky business because egos and personalities are involved.

- **Let the customer explain the situation** – *let them vent.*

This first step is *crucial.* The fact is that the customer placed trust and confidence in you and your company and was failed. Does this sound harsh? Probably, but this is how customers feel when we let them down. Part of the process of repairing the relationship is to let the customer explain the situation. Let customers vent. Let them speak their feelings. Let them use their own words. It is simple in theory, but not easy to actually sit there and listen. It has been my experience in a lifetime of customer interactions that if we do not listen to the venting, no amount of goodwill will help the customer forgive us for our error. It will hurt the relationship in the long run.

Whether you speak in person or over the phone, make sure to use visual and verbal clues so the customer knows that you are listening. Let the customer speak. Do not interrupt. Resist the urge to jump in and start defending yourself. Do not think about what you are going to say when your turn rolls around. Concentrate and just let the customer get the problem off his or her chest.

- **Respond with empathy** – *show that you care.*

Apologize, and do it in a timely fashion. Do it "quickly," in 2 or 3 hours or days -- not weeks. If you wait too long, the customer will develop a grudge, which will be much harder to diffuse.

When customers complain, we have the opportunity to turn a negative into a huge positive. Unfortunately, most people fail to understand the opportunity. Instead they become difficult to deal with and feel threatened. Respond with empathy and maintain your professionalism. **It is always vital to maintain your professionalism under pressure.**

• **Ask how you can make the situation right**

This is a tough one in the beverage business, but a vital part of the equation. I realize that many of you operate in states with various rules about free goods. If not, I am sure your company has some pretty comprehensive rules on this type of activity. Nevertheless, it is important to ask the question – *how can we make the situation right?* Often the customer might just want an invoice fixed, or the proper price or something inconsequential (and allowable) in the scheme of things.

To do nothing will ring hollow. At the very least, do what you were supposed to do in the first place.

• **Validate the quality of your operation**, but *admit your mistakes.*

This is the step that is usually forgotten. Immediately note how unusual this is (the error you made) and state *that it will never happen again.* A friend of mine owns a chain of wine stores. Years ago, he felt that a distributor hadn't dealt with him fairly on a highly allocated wine. He was upset, and hurt. Instead of lying or making something up, the sales manager admitted the oversight. He took full responsibility and made the situation right – but not before sharing how infrequently the problem occurs in actuality. Do not be defensive, but simply reinforce the systems you have in place so your customer leaves the conversation having some confidence that the problem will not happen again.

## So what if things get hot?

How do you communicate when situations become difficult? Handling difficult situations reminds me of the holidays in the beverage business. While the holidays bring in elevated numbers, they also usher in elevated stress levels. No question – things with customers can get heated in a hurry.

Disagreements are bound to happen. How you handle these situations will go a long way toward maintaining a cohesive relationship with your customer. Here are a few things to keep in mind.

- Be flexible and adapt to your surroundings – have a plan, but remember that the plan should not be the same for every account and manager on your route.

- Ask for feedback – so you can fix what is broken in a sincere and professional way. Ask what went wrong and how you can avoid the same situation happening again.

- Exercise patience, never add anger – do not feed into negativity, and never do anything to exasperate the situation.

- Keep your tone as calm as possible when hearing about a problem. You remaining calm may help your customer remain calm!

- Never leave the conversation without coming to some kind of mutual agreement – do not allow things to fester.

- Reply with a heartfelt, sincere "thank you" – it disarms an upset customer. Besides, you should be happy to learn of problems so you can fix them.

- Take a step back and put yourself in your customer's shoes – try to see what they see. How would you handle it if it were your business?

- Let negative comments run off your back – remain calm and do not let the criticism get the best of you. Learn from it.

- Get over it; apologize and affirm your operating philosophy when mistakes are made. Take the blame; preserve the relationship.

- Excuse yourself from the situation – if things get out of control. Leave and return to sell another day instead of saying something you will later regret.

In summary, managing customer relationships is a full time job. Never get too high, or too low with customers. Never let the success with a customer go your head because that causes arrogance and complacency. Let the negativity run off your back. Take the blame, even when you know it was not your fault. Give the credit to your customer even if the idea was yours. Do everything in your power to create an environment where your customer does business with you – not because they <u>have</u> to but, because they <u>want</u> to.

Listen to the thoughts of Tim Sanders (2006) from his book, *The Likeability Factor.* Tim suggests that, *"ultimately, people believe what they want to believe and they tend to believe you more if they like you."* Makes perfect sense in my world!

Handle conflict compassionately. Recognize and appreciate that your customer probably has a completely different take on the exact same scenario. React properly, when things go wrong, and you will solidify your place in that account.

*That's just the way it works!*

# Questions from the Field

**Q:** I get along with most of my customers. Why do I have such trouble seeing eye to eye with customers who are different from me?

**A: You already get along with most people, so whatever you do subconsciously and easily to get along with your friends and others just takes more thought as you interact with your customers.**

The truth is that when we do not get along with people, we usually concentrate on what makes us different, rather than what makes us similar. Success in communication centers on finding common ground. Think about it this way: Do we easily communicate with people who seem to be different, or against us? Probably not! It is more likely that your attitude is *"you're either for me or against me!"* and your behavior and mannerisms back up that idea.

Try finding some common ground. Many sales people talk to me about diversity. They suggest that they do not know how to talk to people from different ethnic groups. So I say, "What do you talk to them about?" and they say, "I don't know. We are so different." Well, do you have a family? Do you have a favorite sports team? Do you enjoy a favorite beverage? Do you have a particular skill or hobby? Start with one of these topics.

This is a simplification I realize, but getting along with different people is simple, but not easy. Simple (so simple) to say we are so different, but not easy to say we are very different but we are also very similar, and to put forth the effort to find those similarities. The good news is that once you purposely blend with that person in some manner as if to say *I'm with you – I'm not the enemy* - it will be far easier to find common ground on other, more difficult topics.

*That's just the way it works!*

# Motivating Sales People on Day 1

I have been traveling the country helping distributors and suppliers achieve sales and service excellence. At each stop I've asked an upper level manager, company president or business owner to share the words he or she uses to motivate and inspire his or her team to achieve greatness.

Since you have spent the last 100+ pages listening to me, I thought it might be a nice change of pace (here at the halfway point) to hear how the leaders of your company and (companies like yours) responded to the following question:

### *What do you tell a new sales person on the first day?*

For the sake of consistency and because I excel at beating a theme into the ground, I present to you – **26.2 thoughts for Day 1:**

> *"If we all did what was outlined in our job description, nothing would get done. Pitch in and help out even if it is not in your job description and you will enjoy benefits seen in this industry but no other!"*

> Dina – Glen Rock, New Jersey

*"No one person is responsible for our success. It is a collective effort of everyone working together that has made our company successful and will continue to be a determining factor in our future"*

Terrence – San Jose, California

*"Welcome! There is a consensus that you can be a valuable player on this team and we are glad you have accepted the position. We believe you can make a contribution to the success of this organization. My door is open, and I expect to hear from you, and hear about you.*

John – Hammond, Indiana

*"Ladies and Gentlemen, this is the easiest business in the world in which to make promises and one of the toughest in which to keep them. Take notes and record all of your promises in a small, memo-style 'promise book' and cross them off only as each task is completed. Your Retailers will quickly learn that they may place their trust in you and will begin to rely on you as their category consultant and consummate professional."*

Ed – Tustin, California

*"Your word is all you have in the beginning. Be organized so you can fulfill all of the promises that you make to your customers. In the future, it will not matter what your sales pitch is if your customers don't believe in you!"*

Tom – Green Bay, Wisconsin

*"Always be on time. Always respond to your customers email, text, or phone call within 24 hours. Be diligent in your follow up. The quickest way to lose credibility in an account is to not honor your commitments. Be honest in your communication even when it is bad news. Be part of the positive solution not part of the negative problem."*

Daniel – Oklahoma City, Oklahoma

*"If you were looking for a* <u>job</u> *do not even start today, but if you are looking for a career then you found the right place because we are all passionate about what we do. Work hard and the industry will treat you like a king!"*

Paul – Omaha, Nebraska

*"1) Be prepared 2) Listen and 3) Be customer service oriented. The three things you can expect from us in return are 1) Constructive feedback 2) Performance based analysis and 3) The tools and resources to compete and do the very three things we'll ask you to do each day. Don't be afraid to make mistakes because if you're not making mistakes you're not working hard enough."*

Arnie – Jersey City, New Jersey

*"The bottom line is whether or not you can sell wine. You are responsible for generating sales on day one and will need to make an immediate impact. Everyone in our company, from ownership to sales team, from marketing and customer service and from warehouse and delivery, is in some way involved in sales and available for support. Our salespeople are responsible for running their territories like independent small businesses. Those most successful have the right combination of wine knowledge and passion, a strong work ethic, impeccable professionalism and keen business acumen. We are in the wine business. And it is just that, a business. Hobbyists should build a wine cellar or work for another company."*

Andy – Chicago, Illinois

*"Welcome and thanks for joining the team. Have fun, make friends, have a plan, smile, ask thoughtful questions, under promise and over deliver. You will ROAR! If I can be of any service to you or any of your customers, please reach out. Roar on!"*

Vail – Dayton, Ohio

*Many of our staunchest supporters today were some of our most difficult customers in the past. More often than not, the so-called difficult customers are merely more passionate about their*

155

*own business. And if you show them that you care about their business through attentive service (especially follow up), they will passionately support your business.*

Brookes – St. Augustine, Florida

*"Welcome aboard! We are glad to have you as part of the team. Focus on the big picture, which is servicing our customers and suppliers. Please let me know if there is anything I can do to help."*

Ted – Omaha, Nebraska

*"Realize that first impressions will set the stage for your entire career and always tell the truth."*

Chris – Chicago, Illinois

*"Be a member of the CIA - Communication, Initiative and Accountability. If you can do these three things well, you will be successful in our industry. Also, do the right thing and trust your internal judgment"*

Kurt – Houston, Texas

*"Under promise and over deliver to meet and exceed retailers' expectations!"*

Tom – Chicago, Illinois

*"Working in this industry is a life style and you must understand that when you are selling as well as servicing each account. As a Sales Consultant your day is never done, nor is the business of making friends over when you close your sales call. It is just the beginning of your journey."*

Ron – Dayton, Ohio

*"Selling is simple but not easy. See your accounts, follow through with what you say you will do and you'll be ahead of 90% of all sales professionals!"*

Mike – Reading, Pennsylvania

*"Make sure you act professionally and you know what you are talking about before you say something. You sell the way you dress. If you dress sloppy you will sell sloppy."*

Kevin – Kearny, New Jersey

*"Whatever you say to anyone in the beer business, expect it to be repeated – especially if you ask for confidentiality. If you're the right fit for the beer business it will be fun, fast paced, and rewarding and days will pass in minutes. If you're counting those minutes you're probably not the right fit."*

Jon – Arlington Heights, Illinois

*"Welcome to the team. Always remember, you don't have to be the smartest person in the room. I have a lot of confidence in your supervisor and if you have any questions or want to talk about anything, my door is always open."*

Paul – Detroit, Michigan

*"You know you are in the right business if you start liking Mondays!"*

Tom – Markham, Illinois

*"Remember, when you are in your company uniform, you are representing not only the brands we sell but more importantly, the reputation of the company that employs you"*

Ken – Melville, New York

*"Do not promise anything that you can not deliver."*

Mike – Arlington Heights, Illinois

*"This is truly an industry where you get back what you put in and if you take care of your customers, they will take care of you."*

Scott – San Antonio, Texas

*"This is a relationship business, and there are a number of competitive reps that will have the advantage of having had years or months more time than you. As a new rep, our expectations for developing relationships surpass the expectations for sales. We*

*understand that reps have various talent levels and skills and what is most important is that you give us your best effort. Be prepared to the best of your ability and be on top of all the basics. Be organized and follow through."*

Steven – Niles, Illinois

*"Give "Plus One" service. Give excellent customer service. Be on time, be polite, listen tentatively, answer questions and be positive and always give your customers that one percent more than you yourself would be "wowed" by. Follow-up, send personal notes and give more options than just one single answer, or product for them to chose from. That's the "Plus One" service I am looking for my reps and managers to provide for our customers."*

Keith – Dallas, Texas

## The Final Straightaway

Our final quote comes from my buddy Steven Hirsch, President and owner of Heritage Wine Cellars in suburban Chicago. Steven, along with his late father Gerry Hirsch, goes way back with my father and I in the beverage business. He truly summed it up with his quote:

**"Appreciate what is special and unique about our business. There is nothing like it, and we are fortunate to be in it!"**

You are correct, Steven, we are fortunate to be in the beverage business and I am fortunate to speak, write, coach and motivate professionals, both young and old, to deliver great service and create better relationships. I will continue to do so until I am too old to make it around to engage the people in the back row.

*That's just the way it works!*

# DEMONSTRATE TRUST, HONOR
## AND INTEGRITY

Did you follow the saga of Major League pitchers Roger Clemens and Andy Petitte? Both have been accused of putting steroids and other drugs into their bodies. They have been teammates, neighbors and friends of each other for years, but their handling of these allegations is as different as night and day. Clemens has steadfastly denied any involvement, while Petitte has been honest and clear about his use for the entire world to hear.

What is left for these two pitchers? They probably have earned enough money for their families many times over so the only thing left of value is the Hall of Fame, and of course each player's reputation. Unfortunately for Clemens, every time he opened his mouth, he moved farther away from induction into the hallowed halls of Cooperstown. His reputation really took a hit *(pun intended)*. On the other hand, Petitte took a giant step towards repairing his reputation with the attitude he displayed in his first public appearance after the news broke. He took responsibility. He accepted the blame. He apologized, and most importantly, he made no excuses. One can learn so much about trust, honor and integrity just by watching this pathetic saga.

What does this have to do with you? As we discussed in Chapter 1, you win the customer loyalty marathon one relationship at a time, one gesture at a time and one customer at a time. As a result of every action you take, you either move closer to the finish line, or farther away from it. There is no such thing as status quo. All your actions have reactions. Nothing goes unnoticed.

It might take months or even years to earn your customer's trust but just one careless, stupid (or worse) action to throw it all away. Reminds me of riding a bike up a long, steep hill. Takes forever, but the descent is over *just like that*. The great news is that once you have trust, you can move forward faster and it will be more likely that your message will be positively received.

This may be the most important chapter in this book.

Do you understand the importance of trust and integrity in the selling process? Do you know the one thing that follows you everywhere you go? Yes, your reputation and being honest and ethical is a major part of the equation. Read the following quote about trust and its effect on business relationships.

**"Trust impacts us 24/7, 365 days a year. It undergirds and affects the quality of every relationship, every communication, every work project, every business venture, and every effort in which we are engaged. It changes the quality of every present moment and alters the trajectory and outcome of every future moment of our lives – both personally and professionally."**

**The Speed of Trust – Stephen M.R. Covey**

Not a subject to be taken lightly as trust and integrity form the foundation for everything in a business relationship.

Keep the following in mind:

Make sure your actions are always moving you closer to the finish line. Always ask yourself, am I being candid? Am I a straight shooter? Do I call things the way they are or do people have to guess whether or not I am telling the truth. The challenging point about integrity is the perceptions that your customers already have about honor and trust. Your customers are skeptical from the start. The unfortunate reality is, before you even open your mouth, they wonder *is this person telling me the truth? Do I need to know the expression "buyer beware"? Can I trust this person?*

Ever wonder why your customers want to trust you? I recently read a new book from Jeffrey Gitomer. His latest book *The Little Teal Book of Trust,* is a great little read on the subject of trust. According to the author – there are several reasons why your customers want to trust you.

- Your customer wants to trust you so he or she can believe what you told him or her is true.

- Your customer wants to trust you because he or she has most likely confided in you and wants the specifics of his or her business kept confidential.

- Your customer wants to trust you because he or she has most likely asked you to do something and is counting on you.

- Your customer wants to trust you because he or she wants help determining what is in his or her best interest.

- Your customer wants to trust you because you have given your word and he or she wants to think that your word is your bond.

Before we get into the meat of the chapter, first a small exercise: Whom do you trust? Why do you trust these individuals? Is it because he or she is reputable or dependable? Because he or she can keep a secret? Who trusts you? Why? Is it because you always do what you said you would do? Is it because they can always rely on you to do your job to the best of your ability?

Assuming that you carry out your duties with honor and trust, what can you do to ensure that your customers see these virtues in you? Consider the following:

- **Be candid, open and transparent**

Ask yourself: am I withholding information that I should be sharing with my customer? Am I projecting the right amount of sell-thru? Of course, projections often would be better suited for toilet paper, but are you being totally honest? Are you taking some liberties with the facts? Do you know someone who plays hard and loose with the facts? I imagine it is no treat to deal with (or depend) on that person.

- **Follow through and keep your word** – make commitments carefully and keep them.

Do what you said you would do, when you said you would do it. Great trust builder!

- **Consciously try to increase your integrity**

Genuinely try to be honest in all your interactions with others. Walk your talk. Have congruence between your intent and your behavior. No gaps. Be clear on your values and be willing to stand up for said values. Be open to re-thinking issues. Be able to consistently make and keep commitments to yourself and others.

- **Be upfront when problems occur**

When do you usually tell your customer there is a problem? Do you wait until the last minute? If you do, you are not alone. There will be a better outcome when your customers have more time. Having more time allows more options for resolving problems in a satisfactory manner. Address the tough stuff directly and acknowledge what people are afraid to say.

- **Admit your mistakes** – hold yourself accountable.

Take responsibility. Why did it happen? The chances are you made a choice and the violation was clearly an extension of that choice. Acknowledge how the effected party may be feeling. Understand, after you have made a mistake and violated the trust placed in you, that it is not about you and how you are feeling or what you are going through. It is about what your customer is feeling.

Maybe you know that I am from Illinois (The Land of Lincoln). Lately, though, Illinois is more known as The Land of the Disgraced Governor. Yes, as I type, Rod Blagojevich is still the Governor of Illinois. About ten days after he was arrested, he made his first public remarks. Here is the some local reaction to his speech.

*"During his 445-word speech, including a long passage of poetry, the governor used 44 first person singular pronouns such as "I" or "me" or "my." In other words, an astounding ten percent of every word in that speech was*

*a pronoun referring to himself. Add the "you" words in the Kipling excerpt, which the governor obviously believes are about him, and we're up to 52 first person pronouns. Almost every single sentence of the governor's defiant speech referred to himself. Just one tiny section was addressed to the people of Illinois, but even that was a self-centered plea to the citizenry to allow him the same "presumption of innocence" rights that they, themselves enjoy. Nowhere did he apologize to the people of Illinois for dragging our state through the mud. Nowhere did he express regret for the coarse language and the extreme cynicism on the federal surveillance tapes, or try to explain that snippets of conversations might not tell the entire story."*

Why the people elected him to a second term (with the *Feds* swirling) is a subject for another book! When a sales person betrays a bond of trust, it is no longer about the sales person. It is about salvaging (and re-building) a fractured relationship. The first time you err, you may get the *benefit of the doubt.* After the 2nd or 3rd time – you will likely never get it back.

- **Avoid words that can seem insincere** – so nobody is confused.

Once in a while I say one of the following words or phrases: *I mean, truthfully, honestly and quite frankly.* I try to catch myself because I hate the way those words sound. Try to eliminate these words and phrases from your vocabulary. Think about it this way. Why should an *honest* person have to preface a statement with a word or phrase that purports to prove his or her *honesty?* Just a little thing but winning your customer's loyalty is all about doing the little things.

- **Don't hide behind ambiguity and call it truthfulness**

Years ago I asked a sales person if any other wine & spirit retailers had bought a certain product. My mistake was asking a vague question. I should have asked if any of a *select* group of retailers had pulled the trigger yet. He answered affirmatively (of course) and I went ahead and purchased a pallet. He was being honest in the fact that he had sold some of the product (locally) but the real truth was that none of my direct competitors were carrying the item. Only a few really small accounts several miles away.

Wait, you say, *is he supposed to read your mind?* No, but I *had* asked him the question many times before and he knew exactly what I was after. He relied upon a technicality, and I later learned that he had bonus money on the line. Do like it says in Dell Inc.'s Code of Conduct: "What we say is true and forthcoming – not just technically correct."

- **Build trust through your actions**

As noted author Jeffrey Gitomer echoes repeatedly in his books, *"Give trust first, and that will lead to trust."* Also, build your competence and skills because that leads to trust. Teaching others and helping others leads to trust. Giving accurate advice leads to trust. And random acts of kindness lead to trust. The point is you often have to get the ball rolling to build trust. It does not always happen automatically.

- **Always adhere to your customer's best interests**

The worst of all sales people in this industry let their customers buy products when they know a mistake is being made. They look the other way and just wait for the commission check. You may win the battle but you will never win the war with that mentality.

According to the author of the book, *You, Inc.* (Harry Beckwith), customers *don't buy goods and services, they by you.* They *buy* people with integrity because people with integrity do what they say they will do. "Like Maytag washing machines, people with integrity can be relied upon." In every business relationship, your customer hopes that you are looking out for him or her. Create an environment where your customers can rely upon you, and you will truly reap the benefits.

- **Demonstrate respect** - genuinely care for others.

Certain points bear repeating. Treat everybody with respect, even those who cannot do anything for you. Do not fake caring for someone. Show kindness. Speak about people as if they were present. Help the people who cannot help themselves.

- **Have great character**

According to John C Maxwell, author of many great books on relationships and leadership, character is comes from who we are, not what we have accomplished. Character isn't judged by the titles you hold or the position you have earned, it based on how you conduct yourself <u>now</u> and going forward. Credentials are transient and look to past accomplishments. Character is permanent and sets forward your legacy for the future.

## • **Be authentic**

In Chapter 2, I asked you to consider *what your customers think of you.* Invariably, when I bring this up in a program or workshop, a sales person will want to delve deeper into the subject of building authenticity. The dictionary defines *authentic* as *not false or copied. Genuine.* The word genuine means *real and pure.*

The truth is that most people are not authentic, real or genuine. Most people are like most people.

What is your reputation in your market or your industry? How are you standing out? How are you building your individual credibility in the industry? Do you have a reputation?

Many experts suggest you *google* your name to see what comes up. If you google your name – what happens? If you google *Darryl Rosen* you get many listings for a disgraced Sacramento, California police officer who has been *as my children say, "a very bad man!"* I promise, that is not me. Scroll down and you will find the various articles I have written to highlight critical issues in the industry.

What about you? Do you have a website with your name? <u>www. yourname.com</u>. Do you send a weekly email to your customers with tips or suggestions for building their businesses? Do you have a web site with information for your customers? Does your company?

These are all actions that build authenticity (and trust) in the minds of your customers.

## • **Let the truth out quickly, not slowly**

My favorite presidential press secretary, because he worked for a successful president during the *oddest* of times, was Mike McCurry. He was Bill Clinton's press person during the Monica Lewinsky/White House intern days. His most famous quote came during the Lewinsky scandal when he was being bombarded with hostile questions. He suggested that he was "telling the truth - but slowly."

Beverage professionals do not have that luxury. *Don't run away from the truth.* Lose your customer's trust and you will go nowhere near the finish line. You might as well start the race over!

### Take the credibility test:

How credible are you? How consistent are your actions? Consider the following:

- **How well do I treat people if I gain nothing?**

In our retail stores, sales people had to pass by our cashiers to get to the offices. Believe it or not, one thing I looked for was whether or not they said hello to our cashiers. Whether or not they acknowledged those individuals. If they said hello, I knew I would enjoy working with this individual. If the sales person breezed right by with nary a nod (which happened quite frequently), we had a problem. It really bothered me, as I wanted every member of our company to feel like he or she was *on the team*.

- **Am I the same person outside the office as I am in the office? In other words, are my actions consistent?**

I had a sales person that was quite cordial when he visited our offices but quite another story in other venues. I remember very vividly a lunch we had together. That poor waitress: he yelled for the entire world to hear because the salad dressing *did not come on the side.*

Check please!

If you are gentle and nurturing in front of customers but quick tempered, abrasive, abusive, vindictive and hostile to your teammates and other individuals at your company – there is a problem!

- **When I have a complaint or criticism, do I speak directly to the individual or about the individual behind his back?**

I developed so much respect for a sales person who thought one of our sales associates was not giving his products the proper amount of care and attention. What sealed the deal was that he requested a meeting, not only with me but also with our associate. He aired his feelings;

we cleared the air and **the three of us** lived to fight another day together. It was so refreshing that he did not go behind the associate's back. If you have something negative to say to someone, or about someone, make sure he or she is there to hear it firsthand.

We always used to say *sticks and stones will break my bones but names will never hurt me*. Not so true. Criticism must be given and handled in the proper way.

- **Am I likeable?**

Have you ever sought advice from someone trustworthy that you really *cannot stand*? Probably not! Usually, the only way we get to a place where we feel comfortable seeking council is if we have some sort of friendship or relationship with that individual. Being likeable leads to believability, confidence and, over time, trust. Yes, always be professional, and while you are at it – be likeable.

- **Am I honest with myself?**

For you golfers out there, have you ever posted an 85 that was really a 90? Being honest with yourself takes tremendous courage because it means doing the right thing when no one is watching.

- **Do I put people ahead of my personal agenda?**

About 10 years ago, I had the pleasure of having a sales person who always made **and kept** 2 promises to me. One, that he would always call me back the same day and two, that he would tell me if it was not in my best interest to buy something. He kept both those promises until the day he retired.

- **Do I admit wrongdoing without being forced to?**

You may know that Silver Oak Cabernet Sauvignon is a highly allocated item in the wine business. Years ago, I noticed a discrepancy in our allocation as compared to our nearest competitor. I called the sales person one evening and asked him about the difference. He admitted right away that there had been an error. He did not play games. He did not hide behind a spreadsheet calculation error or an inexperienced associate. I respected him and his business with us increased immediately.

- **Do I ask for trust?**

How many times has someone you barely know said, "Trust me on this one?" Trust is earned. It is not the result of a request. Of course, you may ask for it, but if the other person does not consider you worthy, you are not going to get it. Reminds me of going to the pool and sticking your toe in the pool to see if you should take the plunge. Often, as your customers get to know you, they approach the decision to trust you the same exact way.

Think about a customer who trusts you. When did the trust begin? Can you point to a specific day? Chances are you will not know when the real trust began. It will have just evolved over time.

### Integrity is about the small things

Integrity, in my book, is what you do when nobody is watching. Integrity is what you do when you stand to gain nothing by doing something. In our flagship store, my office overlooked the beer department. I could see what was going on below but if you were in the beer department, then you could not see me. Once in a while, after a busy weekend, I would witness a beer driver picking up the empty beer carton of a *rival* beer company and throwing it away. Few things told me more about a driver (and his company) than that simple gesture. That was a real measure of integrity.

Integrity is **earning** your business – not **buying** it! Chances are that if you are reading this book, it is because you want to earn your customer's business the right way, not with cash and cases that magically appear in your customer's pockets and backroom. I remember, back in the day, we had a receiver oddly nicknamed *Houndog*. For a while, (until we cracked down) he made the decisions (at the back door) and whoever wanted to *line his pockets* came out ahead.

Apparently a few slimy sales people were on the mind of George Washington when he said, *"few men have the virtue to withstand the highest bidder."* Using cash and other shenanigans is a very, very slippery slope. Try stopping the practice and you will see what I mean!

For more on this topic – see the *question from the field* at the end of this chapter.

Integrity, as author Dan Kennedy suggests, is *showing up on time for your first meeting*. I often tell the story about a sales person who showed up 90 minutes late for our first meeting. He had agreed to meet me at high noon. If he was late for that first meeting (read: he could not keep his word), then why would I be inclined to listen to anything else he said?

Integrity is the act of wanting to do more. Integrity is the act of genuinely wanting to help your customers because you feel an obligation to do so. Not because you <u>have</u> to but because you <u>want</u> to.

One last point: integrity is about the small things. It is a full time endeavor and not a trait you can use when you feel like it. Lying is lying, no matter how small the lie. As 19th century clergyman Philips Brooks maintained, "Character (and integrity) is made up of the small moments in our lives." Integrity is not based on circumstances.

## Don't be a con artist

I recently came across a list of the common characteristics of a con artist in Gerhard Gschwandtner's (2007) great book, *The Essential Sales Management Handbook*. These behaviors and characteristics are considered by sales experts to be telltale red flags for unsavory characters. Have a look at the list.

- Calmness in anxiety-producing situations
- Inability to display deep emotion
- Little respect for people's feelings
- Highly skilled at establishing exploitative relationships (great ability to charm, flatter and persuade)
- Nearly flawless image *(that rules me out!)*
- Appearance of perfect psychological health *(I'm out, again!)*
- Unfazed by punishment
- Irrational belief of being treated unfairly in the past
- Distorted view of the world (everybody does it)
- Savvy and quick with schemes and tricks

I have shared this list with you because I feel so strongly about the need for sales people to have an impeccable reputation and to always carry themselves above reproach.

*The truth is that an untruth is an untruth. Omissions, lying because it is for your customer's own good, fudging the truth and hiding facts are all considered lying. It is actually pretty black and white.*

Almost done with this chapter. I promise.

In closing, according to renowned expert, Fred Reichheld, author of many books and articles on the subject of customer loyalty, "Without trust, there can be no loyalty, and without loyalty, there can be no growth." The simple truth is that trust means confidence. When your customers trust you, it means that they have confidence in you. It means that when you make claims during the selling process, they are inclined to believe you and that, my friends, is what it is all about.

*That's just the way it works!*

# Questions from the Field

**Q**: My competitor consistently undercuts me by giving away hats, lights, and glasses not to mention cutting a few pennies off a case here or there. Cases seem to fall off the truck at random and miraculously end up in the customer's stock room. What do we do? Do we cross over to the dark side? We want to run a legitimate (and lawful) business but find it hard to compete.

**A: Good choice on the decision to stay above that nonsense.** It is a very slippery slope and once you start giving away the kitchen sink, the house cannot be far behind. You are not going to eradicate that behavior; you can only continue to demonstrate and relate your positives to your customers through your words and actions.

I suggest the following: Get your team together and pose the following question: What do we do really well here at XYZ Distributor? Why should people buy from us? What are our positives? What might motivate our customers to do business with us because they <u>want</u> to, not because they <u>have</u> to?

You might come up with some of the following answers:

- Our customers enjoy our flexible delivery policies
- Our customers enjoy the ease in ordering product
- Our customers value that we are constantly sharing relevant product knowledge
- Our customers appreciate that we teach them how to sell premium products
- Our customers see that we maintain their displays, coolers, etc. better than the other guys
- Our customers appreciate that we make more calls than anybody else
- Our customers acknowledge that our sales people are the most responsive in the market
- Our customers have unfettered access to our company's leadership

The CEO from a beer distributor in Illinois suggested that his most educated customers (in terms of understanding the dynamics and attributes of a successful business relationship) are the most likely to be turned off by the kind of back door selling described above. If that is the case in your market, your challenge is to make sure that more of your customers understand what you bring to the table. I am sure your team can come up a list just like the one above, so whatever you excel in, always make sure to let your customers know. Sometimes you have to help your customers understand how you are helping them.

*That's just the way it works!*

Vending Machine Man earns his business "the good old fashioned way." He's lazy and slimy. A true pretender! Your philosophy, as a partner, on the matter should be quite simple: Don't go there!

Vending Machine Man is always looking over his shoulder. He's untrustworthy and devoid of integrity. A pretender and a true con man! Your charge, as a partner, is to hold yourself to the highest standards so your customers feel comfortable doing business with you!

# Understanding Sincerity, Empathy and Appreciation

Finally, what you have all been waiting for: A chapter on soft skills! Soft skills (as defined on Wikipedia) is a sociological term for a person's "EQ" (Emotional Intelligence Quotient), which refers to the cluster of personality traits, social graces, communication, ability with language, personal habits, friendliness, and optimism that mark people to varying degrees. Soft skills complement hard skills - which handle the technical requirements of a job.

It has been suggested that in a number of professions, soft skills are more important over the long term than technical skills. For success with customers in the alcohol beverage environment, I agree wholeheartedly.

For our purposes, we will concentrate on the soft skills of sincerity, empathy and appreciation.

### Sincerity

The dictionary defines **Sincerity** as…

1. An earnest feeling

2. The quality of being open and truthful; not deceitful or hypocritical

3. Freedom from deceit, hypocrisy, or duplicity; probity in intention or in communicating; earnestness.

Sincerity is not the same as truthfulness, a topic we covered in the last chapter. Sincerity is something that emanates from the heart. The most successful people in the beverage business understand the trait of sincerity. I have had way too many people tell me they were looking out for me only to find out they were taking me for an emotional ride and did not care a lick about me. That was the absolute worst! Notice, I am not calling them liars; instead, I feel there are certain people who just do not mean what they say.

### Here are some practical suggestions:

- Learn to deal with people you do not care for or respect without having to resort to phony, insincere behavior just to get something done. Give people the benefit of the doubt.

- Pick your pack more carefully – surround yourself with people that elicit warm, *sincere* feelings instead of those who bring out the worst in you.

- Compliment someone only if you really mean it. Customers (and friends, family and colleagues) can spot phoniness a mile away.

- Think how good it feels to be sincere. Consider the following – if I told you something (but did not mean it) and you found out – not only would I be embarrassed, but you also would be hurt. Nobody, anywhere, likes that feeling.

- Just do it! If you see somebody as sincere, simply say, "I can also become sincere." Just remember, though, there is a great difference between saying "I can" and "I have become!"

### Cheer for your customers:

Lead with a compliment and cheer for others to get your relationships and your sales calls, off on the right foot. Ever watch a marathon in person? Spectators openly cheer for people they have never met. The spectators feel good giving the cheers, but not as good as the runners who receive those cheers. It is a sincere act that you should try with your customers.

No, I'm not suggesting you yell, "The finish is right around the corner!" but there are some parallels. The next time you enter an account find something different (in a positive way) and mention it to your customer. Your comment should have nothing do with your products for that is insincerity at its best. Look harder; there are improvements all over the place. Could be renovations and new touches. Maybe the floors were redone. Maybe there is another section of wine or beer. Perhaps a new display that integrates wine and cheese in a clever way. It does not matter. Find something positive, mention it and watch your customer's face brighten. You have made his or her day and your sales call and relationship will go much more smoothly.

### When you make a mistake:

It is these situations that bring out the best or worst in people. If you screw up, apologize with feeling to be taken seriously. If you say *"It was just a slip of the tongue. I don't know why **you're** so upset!"* do not expect a positive result. That makes it worse because you are suggesting that it is his or her problem. That the other person is overreacting! Instead, say, *"I was out of line. I apologize"* or *"I don't blame you for being angry. I would be angry too."* As Lynn Johnston (famous comic strip author) said, "An apology is the super glue of life. It can repair just about anything!" Just make sure it is sincere.

## Empathy

The dictionary defines **Empathy** as…

The action of understanding, being aware of, being sensitive to, and vicariously experiencing the feelings, thoughts, and experiences of another person without having the feelings, thoughts, and experiences fully communicated to you in an objectively explicit manner. My take: understanding and recognizing (how your customer may be feeling) without having to be told. Reading social cues!

### Consider the following:

The history of empathy in the workplace is quite interesting. In the old days, we were taught to leave all our heartfelt emotions and spontaneity at the door. There was simply no room for personal emotions on the job. Today, that dynamic is shifting. It is now understood that friendly service-orientated people often outsell an impersonal sales team. Is there any scientific research you ask? Yes, Princeton University studied this phenomenon in an attempt to scientifically prove that the thoughts you think can influence another person's impressions and emotions – even from a distance.

**The result: Yes, it was proved that your
thoughts could indeed negatively affect another
person's impressions and emotions.**

**<u>Try this on for size:</u>**

Before, during or after any business encounter, it is best to maintain a positive attitude toward your customers. If not, your negative thoughts and emotions will influence and color the customer's experience. All things considered, people would clearly prefer to do business with those they know and trust, but mostly, with people they like. If you consciously shift your thinking away from **you** to the welfare of your customers, you will be more compassionate.

**<u>How about something practical:</u>**

- **Remember, it's all in your mind** - even warm-hearted people have to practice to consciously be empathetic at all times.

It is simple, but not easy. It is simple to want to act (and feel) a certain way, but not easy to actually do it on a consistent basis - to wake up every morning and execute with positive thoughts and feelings.

- **Maximize the last moment** – often, this is what your customers remember.

Back in the day I knew many sales people who ran out of our store as if somebody was chasing them (no one was). Try another approach - shake hands warmly, throw your other hand over his or her hand (a very warm handshake), look your customer (partner) in the eye and tell him or her that you appreciate the business he or she does with you. Everybody wants to feel valued.

- **Accept somebody** – without judging him or her.

Unfortunately, we all "judge" from time to time, but some of us are perpetually stuck in judgment mode. When we judge, it is very difficult to see others' points of view, which is the very basis of empathy. Make sure to "walk a few feet in their moccasins" (as the expression goes) before judging other people. If you do, you might see where they are coming from and what they are thinking and feeling. Tell yourself, *"I accept this person!"* and you will give the relationship *a fighting chance.*

- **Do not minimize your customer's feelings** – and display true empathy.

Sales people should not decide how important an issue maybe to the customer. Back in my retail days, for example, from time to time a case of wine or beer would be left off the truck and we would have to call our customer (the consumer) to explain that we could not fill the order as promised. Naturally, we would be upset, and occasionally the sales person (who failed to send the case in) would tell <u>us</u> to *calm down* or to stop *over-reacting*.

That was always the worst thing they could say since little or no effort was being made by them to *walk in our shoes.* The last thing we wanted to do was deliver that news to our customer but our sales person did not understand that because he or she refused to see our perspective. Those exchanges never ended up well (for the sales person). Empathy is saying, *"I understand that you're upset and I will make sure it never happens again."*

- **Be open-minded** - have patience and be accepting of all views no matter how dissimilar to your own.

Each person's opinions are his or her own, and like it or not, having an open mind is important in business. Also, holding another person back because his or her views are different (from your views) is wrong and bad for business. Try to see the world as they see the world!

Vending Machine Man is most interested in the person he sees in the reflection and not much else.  He is a pretender. The true sense of empathy (and how a partner acts) is caring what is best for the other person - not yourself.

## Appreciation

The dictionary defines **Appreciation** as…

Gratefulness, a statement of thanks, a statement of praise.

### Consider the following:

According to the father of modern psychology, William James, the need to feel appreciated is our most basic human emotion. The act of giving thanks reminds me of a quote I once read in the local paper. A basketball coach, fresh off a loss in the state tournament lamented, "*We knew they were going to crash the boards, but knowing it and doing something about it are two different things!*" **Knowing** how vital appreciation is and **applying** it on a daily basis are two different things. It takes practice and a deep desire to sincerely let your customer know how you feel. To let your customers know that you value them!

### Ask yourself:

When was the last time I truly showed my appreciation? When was the last time I should have showed more (some) appreciation but did not show any? Do I take my customers for granted?

### How about something easy to remember?

Sure thing! Try this: *Thank your customers big and small for orders big and small!*

### My favorite story of appreciation:

Last year I received a thank you note from a well-known beer supplier whose name goes back almost as far as the earliest suppliers in the business. It was a handwritten note thanking me for my book, and it took me completely by surprise.

This is what happened that prompted the note. I had just attended The Beer Summit in San Diego. There were 300 big hitters (and some little hitters: me) in attendance and as I scrutinized this gentleman's nametag, I realized that I had sold quite a few thousand cases of his beer over the years. I unsuccessfully tried to get him alone to say hello, but as a last resort, I stuffed my book and some literature in an envelope and gave it to him.

That was the last I heard until I got his wonderful handwritten note in the mail. It reminded me of the role appreciation plays in business, and also reminds me of the story Jay Leno tells about his trip to the local supermarket. (That Jay goes shopping by himself (or at all) is a bit surprising, but I guess his biggest question is which car to take.)

He noticed that the girl at the register was not smiling or saying anything. She was throwing everyone's purchases in bags without a care in the world. Probably putting the eggs on the bottom! When Jay approached he asked, "Would it kill you to say *thank you*?" She looked at him and without batting an eyelash said, *"It's printed on the receipt!"*

A funny story to say the least, but showing appreciation in business is far from a laughing matter. The note from the beer supplier really touched me. Salespeople who put themselves in their customers' shoes and are sensitive to their needs (especially for appreciation) win their customers' loyalty more times than not.

### <u>Ways to say thank you for a nominal value:</u>

- **Send a holiday card** - $3 tops – it does not have to be that elaborate.
- **Send flowers** – Great after an initial order for a new store, bar or restaurant.
- **Give a compliment** – be sincere; customers can sniff out insincerity a mile away. The truth is that your customers, for the most part, are probably insecure. Help them gain confidence while you make them feel appreciated.
- **Stop by an account unannounced** – and help out.
- **Bring back shopping carts** – so the retailer's associates can help consumers.
- **Shop with your customers** – spend money in their businesses to show appreciation.
- **Help out on a busy Saturday** – a great way to sell your products.
- **Help out on a slow Saturday** – a great way to sell more of your products than the next guy, who is probably at home watching college football.
- **Clip an article** – on your customer's favorite hobby and sent it to him or her.

### What are some reasons to say *thank you?*

Say *thank you* for all the business you earned this year…and you may earn as much business next year!

Say *thank you* for all the sales presentations you were allowed to make this year…and you may be welcomed in to make more next year!

Say *thank you* for all the tastings and promotions you did this year…and you may do more tastings and promotions next year!

Say *thank you* for the times your customers overlooked your mistakes this year…and they may be as kind to you next year!

Say *thank you* for all the feedback customers gave you this year… and you may get more feedback next year so that you can improve your skills!

Say *thank you* for taking in new products this year…and you may have the chance to introduce more new products next year!

Say *thank you* for the fact that your customers supported you this year…and they may support you next year!

Say *thank you* for placing your products at the end of the power aisle this year…and they may give you the power aisle *and* eye level next year!

Say *thank you* for suggesting your products to their guests and patrons this year…and they may sing the praises of what you sell next year!

Remember, sometimes an ounce of appreciation is worth more than a pound of everything else in business. Say *thank you* to customers *big and small* for orders *big and small* today, tomorrow and every other day this year and your customers will enjoy the experience of doing business with you.

Someone asked me once, *"Why should I say thank you, nobody ever says thank you to me?"* I understand completely and it bothers me to no end when people do not show their appreciation. I remember as a business owner how I would give sports tickets in appreciation for a job well done and the recipient would not show his or her appreciation or acknowledge the gift. My office mate, Stefania, used to tell me not to expect gratitude for my gratitude. I guess that was her version of (my favorite expression) *that's just the way it works.* She was right!

I wanted appreciation like everybody else. Reminds me of a quote by 1920's era psychologist named George Crane. He said, *"The world is starving for appreciation. It is hungry for compliments but somebody must start the ball rolling by speaking first and saying a nice thing to his (or her) companion."* Be the one that gets the ball rolling and your customers will love you.

*That's just the way it works!*

Sometimes an ounce of appreciation (a simple "thank you") can be worth so much more to your customers than several pounds of everything else!

# SHOWING RESPECT FOR ALL

Many years ago we had a spirit expert who was "top shelf!" He worked for our retail wine and spirit company for several years before we literally gift-wrapped him and handed him over to our closest and fiercest competitor.

The guy that lured him away from us related this story to me. What was the major reason for his leaving? **Our General Manager would walk right by him without saying "hello".** Could something so simple really have driven him away? Yes, there were many facets to their working relationship but this bothered him the most. Unfortunately, no amount of fence mending from my father and I could prevent his departure.

The General Manager showed this man very little respect. Does *respect* matter? Is it part of the sales equation? Certainly! Many *respect* others for what they have accomplished but fewer understand that you can show *respect* for others with thoughtful actions. Of course, there are many variables which determine the success of a business relationship but I dare you to find a success story that exists without the parties treating each other with respect. The simple fact is that the preponderance of thoughtful actions can forge many a win-win sales relationship.

As author Truman Capote puts it…

*"Simply pay attention to another person as it they were the only person on earth. Do this consistently, day in and day out, and regardless of the other obstacles in the relationship, you will find yourself united with that person*

Keep the following thoughts in mind and your customers will notice:

- **Do not forget the little people** – I could tell a ton about a sales person long before he entered my office.

In our store, sales people had to walk past our cashiers to get to the offices. Many sales people would visit our account multiple days a week. Some would say **hello** to the cashiers (critical components to our operation) and some would brush right by with nary a nod. In many cases, the lack of this simple gesture told me everything I needed to know about this sales person. (Yes, I repeat this story multiple times in this book. That's how important it is!)

Do not forget the little people that make the engine go. They have names, dreams and children to put through college just like you and I. Do not forget: when you acknowledge your customer's front line people, then they may enjoy their jobs more. Anything you can do to help your customers retain good people the better.

- **Be candid** – have the hard conversations.

Tell people when they are making a mistake. Do not beat around the bush. Be direct and honest. From time to time a sales person would tell us we where making a mistake. It could have been a purchase or an advertising approach and whatever it was – we appreciated the honesty.

- **Learn more** – about other people.

Sometimes the simple thoughtful act of asking your customers how they got their start in business or asking them to share their proudest accomplishment can get a sales relationship off to a great start.

- **Believe in people** – because they probably do not believe in themselves as much as they should.

Why should you believe in people? Because most people do not believe in themselves and unfortunately, *what you think you are not* really holds you back in life and business. Most people will do anything within their power to embrace someone's belief in them. Make a pledge to spend more time believing in people than trying to get them to believe in you.

- **Consider the value in what others do** – to understand that difference between menial and major.

My buddy runs a chain of great beverage stores and he once told me a story about an act he witnessed that really threw him for a loop. A "stock guy" loaded a heavy keg of beer into a customer's car, smiled warmly and proceeded to stop and pick up a piece of trash before heading back to the store. Here was somebody with tasks most would classify as menial, yet this business owner was truly amazed by what he saw and how he felt. For a moment, the planets were out of alignment.

Did this young man really have a menial job? The dictionary defines *menial* as *unskilled*. Was this a job that required no skills? Not whatsoever, he thought to himself. After all, the last person this keg customer saw was the "stock guy". When the customer thinks back upon his experience, he may remember the warm smile he received. The next customer may note how clean the parking lot appears because there is less trash on the ground. Did this individual really have a job that was less important than others?

Here is the point. Stop every once in a while and re-examine things. Leave time for reflection. Be honest with yourself. As he sat in his car near the edge of the parking lot, my buddy questioned whether or not he really knew his business. Did he know the *menial* from the *major*? Did he know what was truly important? A bit overly dramatic? Probably, but there are lessons to be learned from watching how other people within your company do their jobs.

- **Raise people up** – instead of bringing them down.

I recently had a conversation with a prominent supplier. He mentioned that there are "two types of sales representatives in this business. Ones you have to do business with and ones you want to do business with." Much of this has to do with how people perceive you.

Before entering an account, I always suggest that one should pause and take stock of himself or herself. What kind of mood are you in? What kind of aura do you have about yourself today? Try to determine what your customers think of you because I guarantee, your customers are making snap impressions of you every time they see you.

- **Be punctual** – so you do not waste your customer's time.

A big pet peeve for retailers is sales people that show up late for meetings. Be punctual. Showing up on time is thoughtful, smart and does not cost a few extra dollars a case. Stephanie Palmer (2008), author of the book *Good in a Room* suggests you arrive early and if possible leave early. Schedule more time than you need so when you conclude the meeting early your customer will feel like she has been given a gift. The gift of time! Make sure you realize the importance of respecting one's time.

- **Listen with calm compassion** – throughout the meeting, not just the beginning.

Sales people usually begin meetings with some social interaction but then, after a while, stop listening with empathy and begin selling in a manipulative way. The problem with this is it counteracts everything for which you have worked thus far to gain: a solid bond with your customer.

Make sure to focus on being a sincere listener to ensure that your customer feels acknowledged and well served. The person you are meeting with has a driving need to satisfy. Your job is to sit back, listen, and draw that need out so you can satisfy it. Engage beyond the product you are selling. When the meeting comes to an end, focus on the person as someone you would like to see again. Continue your warmth so that person feels valued as a friend and not just from a business point of view.

- **Be formal** – until you are told to be less formal.

One of biggest deal breakers is addressing someone informally before the time is right! Some people try to create instant relationships by using a nickname or something less formal. Deal-breaker! Let your customer suggest taking the relationship to the next level. Another mistake is suggesting that the customer knows who you are before you are formally introduced. When I meet distributors for the first time (even though they have granted me an appointment), I always assume that they have no recollection as to why they agreed to see me.

- **Praise often** – support your teammates.

Just like runners need positive reinforcement, especially during the middle miles, associates need the same treatment to give great service. The opportunities to *pat* your teammates on the back are endless. Have your managers read, *The One-Minute Manager*, by Kenneth H. Blanchard and Spencer Johnson (1982). Managers should always be trying to "catch their associates *doing something right.*" Upon witnessing positive behaviors; the authors suggest immediate praise and specific feedback.

- **Stop talking** – keep meetings brief.

Remember the Gettysburg address? This historic speech was less than 250 words and your meetings and sales presentations do not need to drag on forever. Once you have made your point, stop talking. Author Michael Staver noted (in an interview with Investor's Business Daily) that droning on is common. "You know your droning when you can feel yourself wandering around in a dense forest of communication." Help yourself get to the point by summarizing your message (to yourself) before the meeting starts.

- **Let the customer be the star** – so they feel good about the meeting.

Let the customer show off. Let the customer feel good about his or her accomplishments. Ask the customer what he or she thinks. That is very motivating as your customers (and anybody else you come into contact with) probably love sharing their thoughts. Be a good listener. Look into your customer's eyes.

- **Share only what is necessary** – and avoid information over-load.

This is not a conversation about how much data you give during a presentation; this is about the information you give that nobody wants to hear. You know, personal stuff! There are few bigger ways to show a lack of respect than sharing too much personal information, which will cause your customers to feel uncomfortable. Steer clear of sex, religion, politics and finances. Further, resist making any observations (comments) about how much money your customers may or may not have.

- **Keep your opinions to yourself** – if they are of a personal nature about your customers.

I remember once asking a sales person to buy me a soda. He replied; "I thought all millionaires had a ton of dough in their wallets!" I did not have a ton of dough in my pocket and all of that was none of his business. He did not know my situation, much like I had no idea about his situation. It was a careless comment and, as a result, his business suffered. Was that fair of me? Probably not but *that's just the way it works*. He should have bought me the soda and kept his mouth shut.

Leave disrespectful perceptions of your customers (and their finances or other personal business) in your car before entering accounts.

- **Take ownership of problems** – and your customer will thank you.

Many sales people simply say, "*That's not my problem!*" They separate themselves from the situation and steer clear of everybody involved. Mentally, they jump ship and when things blow over, they act like nothing happened. This is the worst way to handle problems.

- **Practice humility** – and be more in touch.

Do not over-estimate your value. I remember working with a guy who wanted to make a lot more money than he was making. He told me once that, *"He knew his value!"* That was his first mistake. People with an inflated view of themselves and their accomplishments are generally perceived as out of touch with reality and are not liked.

What is the moral of all of this?

Be thoughtful and compassionate, clear and concise. Always consider how your actions affect other people. Keep in mind that despite all the mergers, consolidations and other craziness that goes on in this business, at the end of the day, it is still people selling to other people and your customers will *always* choose to do business and buy the brands of people they like and trust and those who treat them the right way.

*That's just the way it works!*

# Questions from the Field

Q: My customer is very strong-willed. How can I get through to him?

**A: There are commonly thought to be 4 distinct personality types. Your customer sounds like a "driver"...**

Drivers are often thought to be dominant and have very strong personalities. They demand respect and like to initiate control. Many are hardworking and results-orientated. Drivers are often direct and to the point when dealing with others.

Here are a few ways you can approach these types of individuals:
* Be specific and to the point. Do not beat around the bush
* Be factual but do not overwhelm your customer with logic
* Show respect and attention but avoid being submissive as it important to keep your footing!
* Provide options in the form of well thought-out ideas
* Summarize your content quickly
* Let your customer make the decision by the options you have given

If you are expressive and demonstrative, make sure to back up your enthusiasm with actual results. Demonstrate that your ideas work. If your personality is more amiable in nature, make sure to be business-like. Exhibit professionalism. Most importantly, let your customer make a good decision based upon the options you've provided. *Drivers* will feel a lot more comfortable with this approach and will do more business with you.

*That's just the way it works!*

# Adding Value before Asking for Value

Recently I was asked the following two questions about my experiences as a wine, beer and spirit retailer:

1. Did you ever hide from a sales person?
2. What would make you hide from a sales person?

Yes, of course I hid from sales people and I remember exactly where I hid. In the warehouse, most likely, right behind a pallet of vodka or something similar. The *why* part is a little more complex.

Why would I hide from somebody just trying to do his or her job? What would cause me to go to such great lengths? What type of sales person would I hide from?

The sales people that I hid from were the ones who always asked me for something. The ones who always wanted value from me but conveniently forgot to give me any value. The variety who failed to read the social cues and never offered to help me in some way out of the goodness of their heart, not always for the benefit of their wallet. The people that always expected me to reach in my pocket each and every time they stopped by.

You know the type. They got the order and quickly moved on to the next nameless, faceless notch on the way to their year-end bonus.

The self-serving pretenders; sales people who do not add any value to the process. Sales people who resemble a vending machine.

Not the valued partners.

Do not get me wrong. I understand that sales people have to sell. That is a given and how they put food on the table. I am simply suggesting that sales people do not have to sell every time they stop in an account. That builds resentment. That builds the perception that the sales person is just out for himself or herself and, unfortunately, perception is reality. Sometimes, your customers need a breather.

The worst label a sales person can earn is that he or she is only out for the immediate sale.

Last fall I asked my readers to share how they *add value without asking for value.* The response and contributions were incredible and the following list is a compilation of the thoughts from beverage professionals located throughout the country! Here is what they had to say:

### 26.2 ways to add value without asking for value:

- "While walking the account make sure and remember as many people's names as possible all the way down to the sacker or maintenance people. It makes them feel as though you care about them and their business and creates a relationship with all employees, which can be advantageous to you, your company, and the account." *Todd*

- "I use off scheduled days to take product around for customers to taste. I visit and educate. It is usually too tight of a schedule to do this during normal call days for both of us. I find most customers enjoy and look forward to my visits. I also help stock and dust and do whatever else needs to be done while we visit." *Terri*

- "Visit the retailer's website and comment on it via email. Shop at the establishment." *Juan*

- "I appreciate when a distributor will take time to brain storm on creating an event that will be a win-win activity…such as bringing a winemaker to the store or hosting a themed wine tasting. I really appreciate when they actually **follow up** with information that I have requested in a timely manner without me having to nag at them to receive the information I need to sell their products!" *Jan* (retailer)

- "Prior to a big holiday, I call to see if the customer is comfortable with our preparation and then follow back up after the fact to ensure that he or she was satisfied." *Kelley*

- "In this day of data driven business reviews too many sales teams have forgotten that we are still selling to PEOPLE and that not everyone is fact driven. You have to know what motivates the person you are selling to. The data is the justification of the end result. It is much more productive to reward a partnership than it is to buy your business. If you start with buying it you will always buy it and finally it has been my proven understanding that a relationship will override hard facts 90 percent of the time. That is why I set aside days just for getting to know my customers." *Kelley*

- "One thing that I have always done to bring value to an account without asking for the sale is to clean and service wine and dinner menus on a random visit. It takes 20 minutes and it's always appreciated. It seems to be one of those tasks that doesn't get the attention that it deserves." *Edwin*

- "How about trying to understand my business needs (i.e. ask me what my customers are buying, how much they are willing to spend, how the business is changing due to recent economic trends) and then bring in products/services that match those needs." *Kathy* (retailer)

- "Stop by the account at a random time (not the usual call time/day) and just offer up some help. Spend some time/money and shop/eat/drink there during your free time. Show the customer you are interested in his or her business not just as a sales person, but also as a friend. Help with bar promotion nights. Offer hand selling or in-store or account tastings (if allowed) to educate consumers." *Ryan*

- "You need to sell yourself before you start selling. Earn your customers trust and you can sell anything you want. Show up every week, fill the cooler and displays and make sure your signs are up. Have a conversation with the manager or owner every time you are in the store. Even if they're not buying - show persistence and they will start asking you what is selling and what to buy." *Robert*

- "Find out their interests outside of the workplace. You may find out that you and the retailer have a lot in common, thus building an outside relationship. Becoming their friend instead of just their salesman." *Michael*

- "Clean (wipe/dust) bottles and shelves. Bring in POS (rail mats, napkin caddies, permanent signs, etc.) Bring in table tents/shelf POS for brands placed prior to help them sell. Bring in breakfast or lunch for all employees in the account (donuts in the morning go a long way). Just stop by to ask about business, and what you can do for them." *Irwin*

- "Once in a while I like to go to an account just to make small talk and bring the account a sandwich or snack. A lot of the owners work from open to close, and can't leave for lunch. While you are there, fill the shelves and cooler and they will be very appreciative!" *Bob*

- "I have found on a weekend or holiday it is very advantageous to visit the customer. They always need help during the busy times. Making a second visit to an account has a great impact even if just for a few minutes. I always remember that a manager once told me, if you visit an account, make sure you say hi so they see your face." *Dan*

- "Share best practices from other accounts in the area." *Dave*

- "Ask questions of the buyer: *'I'm not here to get an order, I just wanted to know your thoughts on how I can better serve your account to help your business grow.'* Help with sell-thru of existing product: *'I'm not here to sell you anything today, but I have some great ideas on how you can sell...'* " *Wesley*

- "These are valuable things that I do, which increase my value and my company's value with my accounts. Staff seminars, product training for existing brands. I deliver swag and server information cards. Create staff incentive programs for sales contests. Not only maintain displays, but also create NEW displays monthly to showcase brands. Drink & dine in accounts to support their business. Sometimes I literally visit accounts, with nothing to sell. I just talk with my buyers, owners, managers, bartenders, and servers just to build rapport and strengthen my relationship with the account. Actually, I plan that into my day. Cross-promote with social groups, provide leads for sales for my accounts." *Shyla*

- "Customers do not enjoy being hounded all the time with us asking for sets and or specials. Just take the time to find out what they like and make your relationship stronger. So far this has worked well for both the retailer and myself in selling more of our products in and through the account. The retailer benefits by not having lots of the inventory sitting in the back room. He is able to get a faster return on his investment, which gives him the flexibility to invest his profit in other areas of his business." *Robert*

- "Here is what I try to communicate to my reps: The fastest way to gain someone's respect is to work hard for them and show them you care about their business, for example: circle back on Friday or Saturday, after you have already made a sales call earlier in the week to the account, and help them in any way shape or form. You can hand sell, help with stocking or bring them lunch or just a snack to get them through the day, etc. Spend time merchandising non-alcoholic products that seem to always go bad or look tattered on the shelf. Nothing deters sales worse than bad looking mixers and nothing can improve sales like a section where the mixers look fresh, are in date and are neat and easily shopped. I encourage my reps to always pick up old stock (personal pet peeve) and replace with fresh good-looking stock." *Robert*

- "Added value to an account is when a frantic phone call comes from the account on a Friday at 4pm that they just ran out of a product and you run back to the warehouse to put a case in your trunk and run it out to his store." *Kevin*

- "Identifying consumer profiles and habits to help bring your customer the best-suited items." *Barry*

- "On the retail side, it is important to rotate stock and update POS and ratings for current vintages. A salesperson can spend a lot of time making notes on current vintages in the store and doing research on ratings and awards when they get home." *Chuck*

- "When we see our customer in the newspaper or magazine, we laminate the article and send it to the customer with a congratulatory note!" *Anna Maria*

- "Face all products. Take a picture of the door and save it to use for future presentations. Sell a new reset to another retailer based on the success of that store's sales!" *Eileen*

- "Without naming the competition, create a list of products that you know consumers are buying at your customer's nearby competitors, that your customer does not carry or feature. Put some items on the list that you do not sell to add credibility." *Mark*

- "Take care of breakage!" *Theresa*

### Other things to do from my perspective:

- Stop by just for the purpose of checking inventory
- Stop by just for the purpose of seeing if your customer needs assistance
- Stop by with a plan to sell inventory your customer already owns
- Stop by and teach sales people how to sell your products
- Stop by and share some timely information
- Stop by and help consumers find the right wines, beers & spirits
- Stop by and help fill the shelves
- Stop by and say thank you for all the business you get on a regular basis

Are there benefits to going above and beyond for your accounts? Of course! Seasoned sales people tell me that their customers are more willing to spend time with them because they do not always see a sales pitch coming. They are even more receptive because they remember all the times you helped make their businesses more successful.

Try it! Stop by, drop a sincere compliment about positive changes you noticed lately and resist the urge to introduce a new product or ask for an order. You will not have to play hide and seek much longer.

*That's just the way it works!*

Stop by to *maintain* your products and share something nutritious to help your customers *maintain* their health!

# GETTING THE CONVERSATION *FLOWING*

We were there to be had, and sometimes, all someone had to do was ask. While helping customers in my family's wine stores in Chicago back in the day, I often noticed that salespeople would come in, hang a few shelf-talkers, and head for the exits like the place was on fire. I almost wanted to yell, "WAIT! SELL ME SOMETHING."

Presumably, there were sales managers all over town wondering why their training programs were going to waste because the salespeople refused to use even a smidge of the sales methods they had learned. Here is the point, sales professionals: you are not there to hang a few signs and a beach volleyball poster. You are there to sell your products and to build, cultivate, and maintain long-term, mutually beneficial relationships.

Strike up a conversation, and see where it leads you. It could go one of two ways.

One possibility is to the bank. That is, you will start uncovering needs, doing more business, and cashing bigger paychecks. The second possibility is that you may uncover issues or concerns that have been bothering your customer, and you can quickly mend the relationship and keep it strong. At the very least, the person you are talking with will enjoy being asked for his or her opinion.

Here is how this works. Imagine asking your customer the following question:

## Q: Any aspect of your beverage business surprising you lately?

## A: Yes, we are seeing an increase in our customers asking for the grape *Mouvedre*.

Wow, what a coincidence. You happen to have to have a new Mouvedre that just won a famous tasting competition in Provence, the home of Mouvedre. Everyone knows that Mouvedre is a sparsely planted variety found predominantly in the southern Rhone, Provence, and elsewhere near the Mediterranean coast. Right?

Anyway, that is a great question! Not too intrusive but just gamey enough to get news you can use! (Pun very much intended on the "gamey" reference. Mouvedre is great with wild game.)

But wait, you say, they do not make purchasing decisions at the store/restaurant/bar level, so why in the world would I ask the question. My answer: You never know! Maybe policies have changed. Maybe the district manager is stopping by that afternoon. Maybe they have a small, discretionary budget just handed down from corporate. The truth is *you never know*, and if you do not make a sale, you can always move on to the next spot. The important part is if you do not ask the questions, you will never get the answer.

Do you need another reason to ask questions? Well, at the beginning of this book, I told you about a UCLA professor, Dr. Jeffrey Schwartz. Dr. Schwartz talks about how hard it actually is to get customers' attention. You may think that, just because you have their eyes and ears, you have their undivided attention. Not exactly! You see, gaining your customer's motivated attention (and illuminating his or her mind) is not enough. You must engage them.

Here is how it works. You must get the brain going, most specifically the area behind your forehead called the *prefrontal cortex*. I bet you knew that. Anyway, according to Professor Schwartz, this is the part of the brain that does the heavy lifting. To engage your customer, you must reach the prefrontal cortex. Unfortunately, it is not as easy as it sounds. Customers are bombarded with a whole host of distractions, and you must be one of the few things on which he or she focuses his or her attention.

How do you accomplish this seemingly impossible task?

By asking questions that light up the brain and get your customer thinking! Power questions! Questions that will grab your customers' attention and make them stop and think. It is that easy!

Here is a list of 26.2 questions you can ask while visiting accounts, instead of just hanging a shelf talker. Please do not misunderstand me. Maintaining POS and like activities is important, and I am just suggesting that salespeople should not be afraid to ask the questions that might lead to sales. One final caveat: stay away from questions for which you can easily get the answer yourself. That is just wasting your customer's time.

- How is business?

Be prepared for an answer you might not want to hear, but listen for clues on how you can add value and help the situation. Some customers may consider this to be a lazy question. The important question, in my view, is the follow-up question. You *should* be able to ask a more detailed question based upon your customer's answer.

- What is selling well? Why?

Not your stuff – other people's stuff. This way you can compare to how your products are faring. Trends can be so powerful.

- What is not selling well? Why?
- What trends are you noticing from your customers?
- What trends are you noticing in the beverage business?
- What trends are you noticing with our products?

If the overall trend is good but your sales are not, then you may have identified a problem. By the way, I love the practice of asking questions about trends. The word makes people think, and that is what you want!

- How are your customers' tastes changing?
- Any aspect of your business surprising you lately?
- Any aspect of your beverage business surprising you lately?

- Any aspect of our business with you surprising you lately?

- How can our company meet your needs better?

- What is selling well on tap or by the glass?

- Why do you feel that (insert product that is selling very well) is selling well in the cold case or at the bar or by the glass?

- What is your take on (choose a recent news story)?

Choose a story that actually affects the customer, not the latest gossip on Britney Spears or her sister.

- What are the biggest challenges your company faces?

- At one point, you mentioned that (insert what is important) is most important to you in a beverage partner. Has that changed?

- How did you decide to do that? (If you notice something unique, new, or different about your customers' premises.)

This is a concept called "cheering for others." In a marathon, people cheer for random people they do not know. Do the same by complimenting someone for making a good decision. It is a great way to start a sales call! Never, however, compliment your customer if the unique, new, or different item has to do with the purchase of your products. That is ridiculously shallow!

- What do you think of (choose a competitor's new product, and always remain positive about somebody else's products)?

- How did you get your start in the business?

Remember, people love to talk about themselves. When you ask this type of question, you are saying to your customer, "You may be important to me!" When you remember the answer, you are saying to your customer, "You are important to me!"

- What part of your (wine, beer, or spirit) business is strong right now?

- What is one part of your (wine, beer, or spirit) selection you would most like to improve upon right now?

- What price range of (wine, beer, or spirit) products would you like to improve upon the most?

Maybe your customer is looking for a product in a specific price range. Areas where your customer wants to improve are areas of need for your customer. Your job is to find those places.

- What are your customers asking for these days?
- What do you look for when you select a new product?
- What (wine, beer, or spirit) are your employees and co-workers drinking these days?

They will more likely sell what they like to drink. You know that!

- If you could have any bottle of (insert wine, beer, or spirit) tonight, which would you have and why?

This question will uncover what product he or she is particularly fond of, and it is always good to know the decision-maker's favorite!

## The Final Straightaway

Take careful notes on what you glean from your customers. Do not be shy and recognize the inherent boundaries that exist between you and your customers. Be respectful and tread very carefully when it comes to questions of a personal nature.

Take the opportunities when they present themselves. Everybody who knows me understands that I am a diehard Chicago Cubs baseball fan. In my old office were at least 50 pictures taken at Cubs games, including many photos from my August 2003 trip to Wrigley Field. Yes, the Cubs lost that day, but before the game, my wife and my two older sons had the opportunity to meet some players in the dugout. In those days, my boys were into the Cubbies – for 15 minutes anyway. They got off that train to nowhere, leaving just me, but I digress.

Anyway, everybody who visited my office knew about my weakness for the Cubbies, including Frank, a salesperson whose business never went very far with us. He never tried to connect. One day, I saw him at a Cubs game, and my jaw hit the floor. Frank was dressed in Cubbie blue from head to toe. All I could say was, "Frank, why didn't you tell me?" I was shocked. The point is that Frank never said anything about our mutual passion, and his sales would surely have been better had we made that connection sooner.

Use every opportunity to get to know your customers better and to get the conversation flowing. Do whatever you can to learn more about your customers' needs to help them solve their problems. In this case, the customer may have been looking to add more depth in the *Mouvedre* aisle, and you might never had known had you not asked a simple, yet powerful question. Choose a few of the above questions or create your own. However you do it, stick around and learn something about your customer. You will be happy you did!

*That's just the way it works!*

# Questions from the Field

**Q:** I just received a list of new accounts. What should I be learning about these accounts to get the relationships off on the right foot? What questions should I be asking?

**A: While good salespeople relish the chance to cultivate new customers, even the most seasoned would probably admit to a little trepidation before entering a new account for the first time. The great thing is that you have a fresh start! Here are a few ideas to keep in mind:**

First, move immediately toward a face-to-face meeting, not necessarily so you can sell something, but so you can introduce yourself properly. Your objective at this juncture is to ask important questions to determine a) how you can be successful in this account, and b) how you can help the account be more successful. For example:

- What is the opinion of my company and my products?
- How does this organization make decisions?
- What qualities does this customer like most in a salesperson?
- What qualities does this customer like least in a salesperson?
- What does the customer want the most from his or her salesperson?

Second, try to determine the answers to questions that you probably will not be able to ask the decision-maker directly. Who can you ask? Employees of the account and other salespeople (and their managers) who have called on the account are good sources. Some questions are as follows:

- How does my product (or mix of products) help meet a need in the account?
- What are the benefits of carrying my products?
- Who are the salespeople that I am competing against?
- How strong are my competitors as salespeople?

- What is his or her relationship with the customer?
- What companies am I competing against?

The more information you can gather before the first sales call, the better. Do as much work as possible ahead of time. This will make the first meeting go much more smoothly. If you fail to ask these specific, personal questions, you will be poorly equipped to know precisely how and precisely when to proceed.

One caveat to always remember: come on softly! I am sure you have seen it a thousand times. A sales professional, more like a car salesman, swoops in and covers the customer like a bad toupee. Give it time, especially when it comes to issues of trust. Let the relationship grow naturally. It is not going to happen any other way.

*That's just the way it works.*

# SHARING UNPOPULAR NEWS

"I've got good news and bad news." Ever heard that one before? It does not matter what type of business you are in; everyone has to say no, and usually, say it frequently. Maybe you are contemplating a price increase. Maybe you are out-of-stock on the hot new beer. Whatever the case, delivering bad news is painful and stressful. To avoid pain, we become professionals at the game of hemming and hawing. We delay the inevitable and use little tricks like, "I've got good news and bad news," to make it easier.

Does that really help? No, it just makes it worse.

Being compassionate, but firm, is the key. Here are some tips to keep in mind when you have to deliver bad news.

- **Reduce stress** – for the person receiving the bad news.

What happens when you have bad news to deliver? You wait. You delay, and you procrastinate. Perhaps you are waiting for the situation to change and improve, but it never does. The waiting and uncertainty creates stress for you, but more importantly, for the other person who is waiting for you to get to the point. The other person's stress and anxiety rise because he or she, in most cases, perceives what you do not want to tell him or her – bad news.

Because of the heightened level of awareness, the recipient's first re-action may be some type of knee-jerk reaction. To avoid this scenario, act quickly and decisively. Keep the delays to a minimum, and get the bad news off your chest as quickly as possible.

- **Use some tact** – for better results.

Sharing bad news quickly does not mean that you should do it without the requisite compassion. Donald Trump may be able to look into the camera and say, "You're fired!" but that is not *nearly* as effective in real life. Similarly, on *American Idol*, Simon Cowell bemoans a performer's qualities (or lack thereof), and viewers all over America get a laugh, but that only works in reality TV.

Be direct, but do not be mean. Do not make it personal. Maybe you need to shoot down a silly idea from one of your salespeople. Let people down gently. Always remember, "What goes around comes around." Treat people with dignity. Never belittle. Your customers and colleagues have hopes, dreams, bills to pay, worries, grandchildren, and children to put through college, just as you do. Similarly, they also want to feel good about what they do.

- **Get to the point** – because they know it is coming.

So you finally muster up the courage and call the big account for a meeting bright and early Monday morning. Do not beat around the bush. Ask how the weekend went, but resist the urge, stall and delay the real reason you asked for the meeting. To be sure, you know that building and maintaining rapport is essential for long lasting relationships, but in this case, it just exacerbates the situation.

Once you get better at delivering bad news, you will see that there will be ample opportunity for chitchat after the difficult part is over. Remember, the person may have an idea that difficult news is on the way, and if not, you should let the other party know the subject matter in advance. When the day comes, do not delay and stretch things out with fake conversation.

- **Do not be afraid** – to tell the boss when he or she is wrong.

Many of you report to a boss or supervisor. Telling the boss he is wrong is one of the hardest jobs in the country, whether you work on Wall Street or Main Street, the corner grocery or a Fortune 500 company. Look at how many American presidents have gone wrong because people too scared to speak up surrounded them.

The key again (as in most things) is not *what* you say but *how* you say it. Never ambush your boss or supervisor with bad news. Never share that information in a manner that will demean him or her. Make sure to analyze his or her receptivity. Go in with a plan. What might your boss or supervisor say? What might his or her concerns be? Try leading him or her to the point by asking questions, those that get at the heart of his or her greatest concerns or problems. If done correctly, you will lead this person to the *right* answer, and your job will be a great deal easier.

- **Learn to handle** - those who disagree with you.

It is essential that you know how to emphatically handle those who disagree with you. Empathy, by definition, is the ability to understand the feelings of others, to "walk in their moccasins," as the expression goes. Make certain that his or her voice is heard and that he or she is given ample opportunity to present his or her position. And make certain that his or her questions have been answered or addressed.

Remember, you are not necessarily after agreement but acceptance. Do not change your decision to avoid confrontation, as that is a sign of weakness. Practice listening and responding, and your delivery will be smoother. Think about the potential responses, and know how to handle them. Listen with the intent to understand, and over time, assuming the decision is a good one, he or she will come to accept it.

- **Respect the opinions** – of others.

There are no bad opinions. There are no right or wrong opinions. There are no right or wrong recommendations, and while you may not decide to use one's idea, always remember the spirit with which it was most likely given. For example, a young salesperson may share an idea for which you see no merit. To discount or mock such input will ensure that you never get input from this person again. Additionally, the same can be said if you do not take his or her opinion seriously. Always be sure to be respectful of the time and effort others take to provide you with their opinions. Say no when you have to but do so nicely.

What about when your customer is wrong? Talk about sharing unpopular news! How do you handle those situations?

Recently, I had the following experience.

Usually, I rent cars from Hertz. On a recent trip to Detroit, my preferred car rental company was out of cars. So instead, I rented from Thrifty Rent-A-Car. I rented a GPS device, but unfortunately, the navigation unit's charger cable was bent, and the unit worked (sort of) with great irregularity. I mentioned this fact to the attendant when I returned the car.

As I rode the packed shuttle to the terminal, the following conversation took place.

A voice came over shuttle's radio: "Is there a Darryl Rosen on the bus?"

Me: "Yes."

Driver: "Yes."

Voice over radio: "Tell him the navigation unit works. He wasn't putting the cable in properly. You have to push the two buttons in to insert the plug. He must not have been doing that. He went to the following addresses…"

Thankfully, my stop arrived, and I slinked off the bus wondering the purpose of that call. Why did that individual feel the need to tell me I was wrong? Why did she feel the need to do so for the whole shuttle to hear? To make me feel stupid, a task usually carried out by my children. I was not asking for any money back. I just wanted to alert them of the problem so they could fix it for the next customer. Was her goal to embarrass me? To prove that she was right, and I was wrong?

How do you handle situations when you know your customer is wrong? We are taught that the customer is always right, but that is not necessarily true. How do you get your point across without demeaning your customer? Without harming a relationship? Without embarrassing him or her for making a mistake?

This much is true – in the heat of the battle, difficult exchanges occur. Here are a few things to keep in mind:

- **Do not say it** – if it does not need to be said.

There was no logical reason for that call to have taken place. If you know your customers are wrong, and it does not involve a life or death situation or someone's safety, or you are not likely to see the person again, just eat it and move on. Keep it to yourself.

- **Preserve dignity** – so your customer can feel good.

The art of customer service is about how one communicates with customers in a way that produces the most positive outcome for everyone. In the wine business, customers often bring back *bad* bottles of wine. I once had a manager who would give customers returning a bad bottle of wine the third degree, right in front of everybody. He would call over a wine guru to take a quick taste of the bottle. Sometimes, the wine was actually corked (in other words, defective), and other times, the customer was simply mistaken or not used to the taste.

How do you think they felt during this Spanish Inquisition? Humiliated? They probably felt violated on many levels. Trying the wine in front of the customer was tantamount to saying, "You don't know how this wine should taste, and we know it!" Those exchanges never ended well.

- **Never make it personal** – that leads to big problems.

Never insinuate that your customer is stupid, moronic, dimwitted, unknowledgeable, uneducated, naïve, gullible, or possesses any other intellectual deficiency. Use facts – not opinions. Try saying, "This is wrong," instead of "You're wrong." Never make someone feel small or inconsequential just because he or she made a mistake. So your customer thought the chardonnay tasted like the zinfandel? Who cares? Treat it like a learning experience.

- **Understand human nature** – and get it right more often.

Help people grow and learn from the words in Richard Gallagher's book, *Great Human Connections*. "People hate being corrected, but they like being taught new skills. They hate looking bad in front of others, but like being helped in need. They hate being disrespected, but they like having the potential to grow and improve. Finally, they hate having their faults catalogued, but like having their potential recognized." The key is to make people feel good. Telling them they are wrong is not always necessary, and if you have to, you should do it with great caution.

- **Take blame** – and let your customer save face.

Customers are not always right. In fact, sometimes they are dead wrong. It may seem enticing to embarrass and humiliate people for making mistakes, but that is the last thing you should do. What if your customer orders the wrong case of beer? You could handle the situation in at least 2 different ways.

You could say, "You ordered the wrong beer!" That is *not* the preferred way. The more preferred way is to say something akin to the following: "A mistake has been made, so let me see what we can do to get you the beer you need!" You could also add the following sentence: "This happens all the time with many beers being so similar." If the customer insists that it is your fault, go ahead and take responsibility. It is ok. The goal is for the customer to feel good about the outcome.

Remember, the goal for distributors and suppliers is to have your customers do business with you – not because they *have* to, but because they *want* to. Ask yourself: "What part did I play in creating this problem?" Showing the proper courtesy when customers are wrong is a great part of this equation.

- **Do not defend** – say it, and then keep your mouth closed.

Resist the urge to defend yourself. Do not go on and on about why you needed to take a certain action. If you believe you made the right decision, *state your reasoning and be done.* Do not keep talking and justifying to soften the blow. Often, your goal may be to not look mean, and delaying just makes you look unsure of yourself.

Avoid the temptation to rush through this process. Allow time to talk it over. Use good listening skills. It has been my experience in 25 years of interacting with thousands of people that, often, the outcome is not as important as the way the news is conveyed.

*That's just the way it works!*

Oh yeah, I began this piece with the expression, "I have good news and bad news." That never works. Customers only remember the good news, and often, you have to deliver the bad news again. I am now done with this chapter, and I cannot help but wonder. Is this good news or bad news?

# LISTENING, CONVERSING AND OBSERVING

Did you think we were done with the soft skills? Not yet. We have one more chapter to go. In a way, this entire book is about the *soft skills,* but this chapter is pretty soft. The *hard skills* (in business) constitute the technical expertise you need to get the job done, according to noted author Peggy Klaus. *The soft skills are* competencies that go from self-awareness to one's attitude to managing one's career to handling critics, and not taking things personally, taking risks, getting along with people, and many, many more.

Here are more suggestions for improving your soft skills.

In my view, listening, conversing (building rapport), and observing are as soft as they get. Unfortunately, young people do not learn *listening* skills in school, nor do our youth learn how to build rapport in a formal setting. Sure, children learn to observe and build rapport, such as on the playground, but they never get the formal help they need in these areas. Conversely, we have plenty of math and science courses, and when companies hire sales professionals they are often more interested in what school they attended than whether or not they can carry on a conversation or make someone feel important. Trade math is important, but possessing other skills may be more important to a successful life in business.

Did I say that *softly* enough? Here are some thoughts on listening, conversing and observing.

## <u>Listening</u>

The dictionary defines *listening* as both the *act of hearing* and *making a conscious* effort to hear. Specifically, hearing is the faculty or sense by which sound is perceived, the nuts and bolts of how we hear sounds and people talking. Listening is hearing someone with the intent to understand them

The afternoon duo on the local sports radio station (here in Chicago) is very entertaining. Sometimes a caller will phone in and allege that the hosts said something outrageous about their favorite team. The hosts, having said nothing of the sort, will ask if the caller has been listening to an *imaginary radio* again. If the caller stubbornly continues, the hosts may quickly hang up, but only after shouting, *"Listening is a skill."* (I wish the imaginary radio would play a CUBS World Series game!)

The comment *listening is a skill* is very true. Good listening skills are a valuable tool, one that can help you connect with your customers. When your customers see you really listening, they will likely be more receptive to your point of view. Further, when you speak, you are only commanding a portion of your customer's attention; however, when you customer speaks, he is much more engaged. How are your listening skills? Be honest! Do you actively listen during conversations, or does your mind wander?

Are you thinking of what to say when your turn rolls around? Are you constantly interrupting your conversation partner? Winning the customer loyalty marathon requires that you have great listening skills, and that you ask the right questions and listen attentively to the answers.

Ask yourself: am I signaling to the other person (through my actions) that I am listening? Consider what your customer may be thinking. He or she may be thinking: *I hope that when I present a problem or an opportunity, my sales person is listening and not be thinking about next week's golf outing. Is my sales person going to hear me out, or jump to a conclusion before I am done speaking? Will he hold his fire?* Keep the following in mind for better listening skills:

- **Maintain eye contact** – and keep your eyes fixed on your partner.

Try not to let your gaze wander. Your conversation partner needs that reinforcement. Does your spouse ever ask "Are you listening to me?" while you are staring at your computer screen? Just ask my wife: without the proper eye contact, it is hard to know if someone is listening. Keeping the focus on your conversation partner is a great start towards being a better listener.

- **Incorporate gestures** – use facial gestures to show you are listening.

Nod your head when appropriate. Naturally! Not like a puppet, with someone else at the controls. The person talking wants to be heard. Proper gestures can help show that you are listening.

- **Remove distractions** - put your Blackberry in your pocket and leave it there.

Here we go with this one again. Remember Chapter 10? Admittedly, I am getting better at this, but it has been a long road. Nothing is so urgent that you must answer your phone every time it rings. I remember once my wife calling me during a meeting. I valiantly tried to explain that I would be able to talk in a few minutes. There was a brief pause, and then my wife, not to be deterred asked, *"Do you want grilled zucchini for dinner?"* Anyway, my phone of choice is not a Blackberry; it is an IPhone! A super cool device, even if I waited 9 hours at the Apple store the day it came out.

If it is really important - like that night's dinner menu - you will get a call back. If you are expecting important calls, make a different ring tone so you know when the call comes in. Always let your conversation partner know you are expecting an important call. That way, when it happens, it will be less an interruption.

- **Do not interrupt** - let other people finish their sentences.

Nothing is more irritating for both customers and colleagues than having someone else finish *their* sentences. It is intimidating for cus-

219

tomers when they are reporting a problem, especially something they consider serious. Let people vent. Let them complete their sentences.

- **Concentrate** – on what your customers are saying, *not* what you are going to say.

A common flaw while conversing with customers is not listening to their complete thought. For example, a customer may be asking a two-part question; however, because you are formulating your answer to the first part, you do not hear the second part. The customer must repeat the question, which is frustrating. It wastes their time and shows a lack of respect.

- **Ask clarifying questions** – to get a better understanding.

Sometimes you do not believe or understand what you are hearing. Ask questions! Besides gaining clarification, there will be other benefits to help you ascertain your customer's wants and needs. For example, you can get the proper meaning. You can identify areas of information where you are not strong and gain extra time to get that information. You can increase your buyer's receptiveness by expressing your interest. You can identify opportunities, and you can prevent mistakes by clarifying when you genuinely did not hear what was said.

What happens if you fail to listen? Great question, I hear you loud and clear on that one! Well, you will certainly fail to learn what is important to your customers. Your customers may stop communicating with you. Most importantly, if you listen you may hear *what isn't being said* and as the old Cherokee saying goes, *"Listen to the whispers and you won't have to hear the shouts."*

Let your customer do the talking, so you do
the walking (with an order)

## <u>Conversing</u>

The dictionary defines *conversing* as engaging in a spoken exchange of thoughts, ideas, or feelings; in other words, talk. Sounds a bit like rapport, which should not be a surprise as one of the main goals of conversing is building rapport.

Consider the following: successful relationships are heartfelt. Before your customers will make an emotional investment in a relationship with you, they are going to have to know you, like you, and trust you. That process takes time. The good news is that your customers will tend to listen, show interest in, and like or dislike you to the same degree you do for them. People are naturally conditioned to respond in kind. If you are friendly with them, they will likely be friendly back to you.

Ask yourself: when I first meet a new customer or a new associate within a customer's organization, do I take the proper amount of time to have that individual know me, like me, and trust me? I hope so, because the more rapport you build, the more you will enjoy calling on your accounts. If you rush through an interaction with a customer, your customer is probably thinking: *"I wish this sales person would take the time to get to know me before asking me to give them an order"*

## <u>To be successful</u>

- Learn how to keep a conversation going with certain expressions:
  - o Tell me more!
  - o I'm not sure I understand!
  - o Could we go over that again?
  - o I see what you mean!
  - o Are there other factors?
  - o What are you doing to keep?
  - o How do you determine?
  - o I understand how you feel! Why do you think that happened?

- Adopt some feel-good questions to learn more about your customers. Bob Burg (2006) author of *Endless Referrals* suggests questions similar to the following:

  o How did you get your start in the beverage business?
  o What do you enjoy most about the beverage business?
  o What is your biggest challenge in the beverage business?
  o What are the most significant changes you've seen take place in the beverage business?
  o What one sentence would you like people to use to describe the way you do business?

Please note: these questions are not meant to be intrusive or threatening. Of course, if you ask them in a row (all five of them), then you will not get the desired result of learning how your customer thinks. Instead, you may be asked to leave. The point is to encourage your customers to talk about themselves. The most interesting person in the world is oneself. Make your customer the most interesting person in the world!

- Understand the wonderful effects of enthusiasm:
  o Enthusiasm is the priceless ingredient in every relationship
  o Enthusiasm creates energy
  o Enthusiasm is contagious
  o Enthusiasm is the cause of success, not the result of it
- Keep up on current events – you may not care about global warming, but others probably do.
- Take notes: not only will you remember more, but also, your customers may tell you more because they see you writing it down. Taking notes is a huge sign of professionalism.
- Make the other person feel like a star by showing genuine interest in them.

Be approachable – make it easy to build a relationship with you. Build rapport by concentrating on your customer. Do not attempt to build rapport by ripping on your competitors. Never fall prey to the notion that talking *badly* about other distributors will make your customer want to spend more (or any!) money with your company or you.

## Observing

The dictionary defines *observing* as the following: *to see, watch, perceive, or notice.* Another definition is *to watch, view, or note for a scientific, official, or other special purpose.* I will refer to these definitions as Meaning One and Meaning Two. I know, pretty original! Anyway, in Meaning One, I want pay particular attention to the word *perceive.*

Many sales people fail to note, observe, or *perceive* that certain situations may not the right time to be selling something. For example, if the customer is doing any of the following it may not be a good time, and yes, these are all situations that I have been involved in or witnessed where a sales person kept trying to sell products.

**Instead of selling - what can you do in the following situations?**

- If your customer is busy helping a consumer – **help a consumer too!** Note: if you are helping a customer, resist the urge to only sell your products and never, never, never steer consumers away from your competitors' products.
- If your customer is busy unpacking a box – **help unpack a box, also!**
- If your customer is busy cleaning the cooler glass – **grab a rag and some Windex!**
- If your customer is busy carrying out purchases for a consumer – **grab a hand truck and help!**
- If your customer is busy serving food or drinks – **put an apron on!**
- If your customer is arguing with a consumer - **get out of the way so your customer saves face.**
- If your customer is arguing with an associate - **get out of the way so your customer saves face.**
- If your customer is busy chasing a robber – **don't do anything stupid!**

Even if I had all the time in the world, it would take me forever to tell you how many times a sales professional continued trying to sell while in the midst of bizarre (sometimes dangerous) circumstances. If your customer is running around like a chicken with no head, either help or get out of the way. It may not be an environment conducive to selling. Be perceptive!

Being observant to the specific situation and knowing when to put down the item book is critical if you intend to use your *observing* skills to your benefit.

The second meaning of the word *observing* (Meaning Two) is *to watch or view for a special purpose*. For this part, I would like to concentrate on *observing*, with the intent of identifying opportunities in on-and-off premise accounts. Some call this the act of *surveying*, and both words describe the act of thoroughly *checking out* the account to see where you can achieve additional placements and opportunities for growth.

A Trusted Partner notices what is happening in an account. As part of a sales call, the sales person "walks" the account with a keen eye for any changes or trends. The prepared sales person scouts all areas of a customer's premises for opportunities.

**Walk the entire account!**

Practice tip: go to your local grocery store with a clipboard. Make a list of everything you notice. Go back 2 weeks later and prepare a list the same way you did the first time. Compare the lists. What did you notice? Did anything change? Choose any product category like soda pop or ice cream. Who are the players? What brands are standing out for you? You may see the strong brands positioned by the door handle. Are those same brands placed anywhere else? That may be where you want your brands - in similar positions in your customer's businesses.

Observe customers: which aisles do they avoid? Which direction do they go when they enter the store? If they are holding a basket, is it in their right hand or left hand? As most people are right-handed, customers will typically hold the basket in their left hand and reach out with their right hand, which suggests that you should place your products to the *right* of where the customer may be standing. Observe and do your own research. Where do customers typically go when they enter an account?

Why a grocery store? Grocery stores are a great way to learn how large manufacturers/suppliers and large retailers operate. Plus, there is a lot of action and change on a daily basis. Many of you call on grocery stores as part of your normal routine, but for those of you that have other types of accounts, a grocery store may be a good way to learn the valuable skill of *surveying* and *observing* a retail account.

Try to observe the following in both on-premise and off-premise businesses.

### On-Premise

- **Review the wine list.** Is it as you remembered it or have there been changes?

What changes have been made? Is there a different balance of red and white wines? Is there a different allocation between price ranges? This could be an indication that the account's clientele is changing, or that drink trends, in general, are changing at that location.

- **Take a look at the back bar.** Has anything changed? Are all your important brands represented?

- **Look for new drinks.** See anything in the account from the latest celebrity mixologists? You know you have to keep up with that stuff! Stop by the local bookstore and scan the latest drink book. Do your bars make all the new drinks? What about the drinks that are *back in fashion?* How about all the drinks that use your spirit items? Anytime you can suggest a new drink, one that your bar or restaurant does not make, you have successfully added some value.

- **Observe the tabletops.** Is the account using the promotional materials you left on your last visit?

If not, why are they not using the materials you left for them? Are there any improvements that can be made? Do the promotional materials mention any upcoming events you have at the account? Do you have any upcoming events? Are you suggesting innovative and creative ways to get consumers in the door? Is another distributor getting more sponsorship opportunities?

- **See what the bartender recommending?** Spend some time at the bar observing the bartender and watching the patrons to see what brands they are routinely asking for.

- **Familiarize yourself with the by-the-glass program.** Have there been any changes?

- **See anything going wrong?** Your customers in the bar or restaurant business can die a *death by a thousand little cuts*. Word travels fast in the on-premise world (among patrons) so always be on the lookout for ways to help your customers. For example, if you stop by your account for a drink and it takes forever, you may want to say something to the manager.

Are there suggestions you can make that might improve the account's profitability?

### Off-Premise

- **Look at the shelves.** Have enough shelf-talkers?

Is there a way you could add more value by providing better POS materials? Are all your items priced? *No price generally means no sale!* Consumers will not take the time to ask the price. What about the labels on the display items? Are the labels clean or are they dirty and torn? Consumers do not buy bottles with ripped labels. Instead of reaching down, they will typically move on to another product. Are you adequately represented at eye level? If your bottles are on the bottom shelf, is there a way to have them moved to the top shelf?

If things have changed, do you know why changes have taken place? Are your products being filled, faced, dusted, and merchandised as well as your competitor's products? If not, there may be a problem somewhere. Maybe you need to spend some extra time with the staff as there must be a reason why the team is caring for other items, and not yours.

- **Watch the shoppers.** Suppose you notice that shoppers are avoiding aisle nine like the plague.

Is there a reason? In our main store in Chicago there were certain aisles with seemingly uncorrectable lighting problems. It was really dark in those aisles. The savvy salespeople suggested other places to keep their products.

- **Monitor the displays**. Is another company getting display opportunities that you are not being offered?

If that is the case – try to determine why. Has the sell-thru for one of your displays slowed down? Why? You may want to suggest other places to keep your products. How do your displays look? A great way to impress retailers is through well-managed displays.

Well-managed displays let consumers know that the product is available and stimulate a consumer's impulse to buy. If the signage is appealing, then it may attract attention from consumers. Good signage is like a *silent salesperson*! Further, a well-stocked display may result in less *out-of-stocks*, and nothing is more irritating (to both retailers and consumers) than out-of-stocks.

- **Ask what the staff is recommending**. Try to get a handle on what the staff likes.

Are they recommending your items? If not, maybe you have to spend some extra time educating, as they may not feel comfortable selling your products. Are there other reasons why your items are not receiving the best treatment? Is it something personal? Do some fence mending and do it quickly!

- **Evaluate cross-merchandising opportunities.** Are there any food (or glassware or accessory) products that you can place your products by? Combinations that might increase your sales and help the account become more profitable?

While on your *survey*, constantly be on the lookout for opportunities, whether or not they are in the beverage department.

When you notice changes, ask a question to determine what happened. Be careful, though, so you do not sound accusatory. Saying, "*I noticed my stacking of xyz beer is over by the wall, not where it was the last time I visited.*" is far better than, "*Why did you move my display to*

*Timbucktoo?"* Also, do not forget to monitor your tone and expression. Remember the famous phrase, *It's not what you say; it's how you say it!*

In this chapter we talked about the *soft skills* of listening, conversing, and observing. I can tell you one thing: if you master these skills, it will lead to one thing that is not soft. Cold, *hard* cash.

*That's just the way it works!*

Vending Machine man observes all right! Instead of observing ways to help his customers, he counts his facings as soon as he walks in. He's a pretender. Your job, as a partner, is to add value and (after you have done that over and over) then you can count your facings until the cows come home!

# SEEING THE FINISH LINE

Many years (and pounds) ago, I was a marathon runner (hence all the marathon analogies). Anyway, I had serious difficulties finishing marathons (i.e., dropping out left and right). Thankfully, I finally got over the hump in the 1997 Chicago Marathon.

I accomplished this long-standing goal by *seeing the finish line!*

Here is what happened:

I had taken several years off from running, but my 30s were *upon me*, and beer and fast food were *upon me*. It was time to get back in shape, so I started training. I ran all summer, and by the time the leaves fell, I was strong enough to give it a shot. I knew, though, that I had to make a few changes. It was time to wake up and smell the Gatorade.

In my previous attempts at the marathon distance, I had done the same things in training and during the race. Do you ever do the same thing over and over and expect a different result? Do not answer that; I know it happens all the time. Well, anyway, that is what I was doing. I knew I had to shake things up a bit.

The day before the race, I went to the finish line. If you have ever been near the finish line of a major marathon, it is a pretty cool scene. The day before the race, workers are busy setting up all the viewing stands, and there are tents, balloons, and people all over the place (guess you had to be there!). It is a very motivating place, and since I had not been to a marathon finish line since my first marathon (as a 13 year old), I decided to go down and check out the festivities.

The odd part is that I wore my race clothing! Yes, the day before the race, I went down to Grant Park in my hat, shades, running shirt, shorts (that were probably a bit too short), and my running shoes. I even put my number on for good measure! I stood at the finish line. I looked up, down, and around. The place was spectacular. I threw my arms up in the air much like the winner does on race day.

My wife took a picture – and that picture is hanging in our living room.

Just kidding!

But we did develop the picture at the 1-hour photo shop, and that night, as I lay down to sleep, I had visions of crossing the finish line.

I could see the finish line.

I knew what it felt like to stand there. I could feel it. I became *one* with the finish line. (Ok, maybe a bit too much, but you get the picture!)

The next day, I finished the marathon!

To cross the finish line in a marathon or with your customers, you have to find a way to survive the middle miles. The middle miles are the part of the race where the excitement of the start has faded, but you cannot yet imagine the taste of the finish line. Do you ever feel like you are in the middle miles? Maybe you are thinking, *"Don't throw that running stuff at me! There is no such thing as the middle miles in business."* Wrong! The truth is that, with any goal worth trying, worth having, worth accomplishing, you have to be able to survive the middle miles.

That is where the real race starts, and to succeed in anything (especially the beverage business), you have to know what it means to *see the finish line!*

So, what does it mean to see the finish line?

- *Seeing the finish line* means that you realize customers judge you in the first four seconds…or the first 20 seconds. Many studies differ on the exact amount, but the message is clear, and it really does not matter. You simply do not get a second chance to make a first impression. Seeing the finish line means that you greet customers sincerely, like you would your grandparents or your favorite friend.

- ***Seeing the finish line*** means you realize that delivering exceptional customer service is simple, but not easy. It is simple to *want* to provide great service each and every day, but it is not easy to wake up every morning with the drive, desire, determination, and discipline to (in the words of my old running coach) *make things happen* every day.

- ***Seeing the finish line*** means you have a solid plan and that you prioritize. Seeing the finish line means that you keep the "the main thing the main thing!" It means that you plan out your days the night before. Seeing the finish line means you realize that the simple act of spending 10 minutes planning your day will yield dividends beyond your imagination.

- ***Seeing the finish line*** means your underlying thought should always be, "How am I going to make my customers want to do business with me?" It means that you realize that your opportunity is in having your customers do business with you because they want to, not because they have to.

- ***Seeing the finish line*** means you separate what is in your control from what is not in your control. If you work for a large distributor, wholesaler, or supplier, you accept that certain decisions may be made without your input. Seeing the finish line suggests that you concentrate on what is in your control – the experience your customer has with **you**, each and every day.

- ***Seeing the finish line*** means you realize that if you do not want to take care of your customers, you do not have to worry. Someone else will, and they will see their business increase – at your expense.

- ***Seeing the finish line*** means that you realize you are in a growing industry with lots of customers, cool people, and cool products, but there is no such thing as an overnight success. Seeing the finish line means that when you start to enjoy some success, you resist buying into your own PR.

- ***Seeing the finish line*** means you resist the urge to complain to your customers, and you realize the huge cost of negativity. It means that you resist the urge to take shots at the competition. Seeing the finish line means you realize that everybody has strengths.

- ***Seeing the finish line*** means that, from time to time, customers will get angry with you, even when you have not done anything wrong. And, from time to time, you will put your heart and soul into a customer interaction, and it will not be good enough. Seeing the finish line means that, from time to time, you will have to take the blame when it may not be your fault.

- ***Seeing the finish line*** means that you may be hampered by the fear of failure, but instead, you must use your creative powers to make the most of every customer opportunity.

- ***Seeing the finish line*** means that you make every effort to learn as much about your customers as possible.

- ***Seeing the finish line*** means that you "cheer for others" and take the time to recognize the improvements in your customers' operations, especially when those changes have nothing to do with your products. Seeing the finish line means you understand that those comments help build your customer confidence.

- ***Seeing the finish line*** means that you find as many ways (and opportunities) as possible to say "Thank you."

- ***Seeing the finish line*** means that you call your customers back when you say you will and hopefully the same day or no more than 24 hours later.

- ***Seeing the finish line*** *means* you realize that initiative lays the groundwork for getting what you want, when you want it. It means that you will be much more likely to succeed when you have consistently gone above and beyond to help your customers be more successful.

- *Seeing the finish line* means you rely less on email and more on written correspondence. It means that you understand the difference between communication and correspondence and that you pick up the phone more often.

- *Seeing the finish line* means you handle customer complaints with the proper amount of empathy. You find points of agreement, and you do everything you can to make your customers happy. Seeing the finish line means that you understand that, when you handle a complaint properly, you gain a higher level of loyalty.

- *Seeing the finish line* means you realize that your customers need help. Your customers' businesses are growing, and their head counts are shrinking. Seeing the finish line means you make the extra visit, the extra call. It also means that you start your day a half-hour earlier and that you make sure your customers never run out of your products.

- *Seeing the finish line* means you develop an unshakeable belief in what you do. For most of you, that means selling alcoholic beverages! Could it get any better?

- *Seeing the finish line* means that you never "confuse activity for accomplishment." Cliché, I know; however, the reason everyone says it is because it is true.

- *Seeing the finish line* means you realize that sometimes you and your customers are swimming together in *uncharted water*, and the only way to ascertain what is important to your customers is to ask them.

- *Seeing the finish line* means you contact (communicate) with your customers as frequently as possible. That you stay visible. That you stay relevant. That you bring your customers information and ideas that help them increase their profits.

- ***Seeing the finish line*** means you understand great customer service is providing the customer with a subtle mix of product knowledge and personalized care.

- ***Seeing the finish line*** means that you uncover your customer's hidden needs and desires and that you ask for the sale. That you do more in your accounts than hang shelf talkers. Seeing the finish line means you never leave an account without first trying to sell something!

- ***Seeing the finish line*** means you look for ways to make your customers more successful. Seeing the finish line means you take more pride in your customers' successes than your own. It means that you do not count something as a success unless it is a success for your customers.

- ***Seeing the finish line*** *means* when somebody says no, you keep going. That you make the next call, the next visit, or the next presentation with a smile on your face. Seeing the finish line means you treat every customer like you are right on the verge of losing him or her.

## The Final Straightaway

Seeing the finish line means you realize that it is what you do every day, every mile that counts. It means you realize that perseverance is the key, and that, on that special day that your customer has chosen your company, that you have the drive, determination, desire, and discipline to show your customers that you genuinely value them.

When you see the finish line in all you do, you will be successful. *That's just the way it works!*

# Having a Glass-Half-Full Attitude

Do you believe attitude plays a big role in your potential for success?

Come on, *everybody* knows the importance of a good attitude, but do you know how it is *directly* related to your sales success? Although there are many reasons why attitude is so important, for the purposes of this chapter, we will concentrate on two of the main reasons. First, you simply cannot do a good job as a sales professional in this industry (or any other) without a positive mental attitude. There are just too many ups and downs in the sales world. Second, if your attitude is lacking, then your customers will probably have no interest in doing business with you. Simply put, if you cannot put a smile on your face, and back it up with sincere actions, your customers will not want you around. Dialog with your customers will dry up like an overcooked turkey on Thanksgiving, and if you stop conversing with your customers, your business will suffer.

*That's just the way it works!*

Most of the chapters in this book begin with a story or anecdote. This chapter is no exception; however, I have borrowed a story from my first book, *Surviving the Middle Miles*. I have done so because I think my trip to Florida in 2006 *still* provides a great backdrop for a discussion on the role your mind (and attitude) play in your sales success.

In December 2006, my family and I took our first-ever trip during the Christmas season. Since I was always in the wine business and working long hours during December we could never get away. Usually, we enjoyed Chicago's lovely weather in December instead of relaxing by a pool in the hot Florida sun (wearing SPF 1000, of course). This year was going to be different and we were all very excited to get things started. During the plane ride down I read a great book on positive thinking. Little did I know how quickly it would come in handy!

We were not accustomed to the throng of warm weather seekers, as we had never traveled in December. The line at the car rental counter seemed longer than the Mississippi River. We waited patiently, sort of, for 45 minutes, only to learn that we were at the wrong place! Have you ever made a bone-headed move like that? Done something that left you scratching your head? Typically, this would have thrown me for a complete loop; however, I was able to draw upon my new, positive mental attitude to save the day!

*"Good news and bad news,"* I told my family. *"The bad news: we're at the wrong car rental place! The good news is that we have another funny family story to laugh about for generations to come."*

The children were not impressed.

Neither was the wife, come to think of it!

Situations in life can either be positive or negative, happy or sad. You have all heard the expression, "When life gives you lemons, make lemonade." I believe that; do you? It is your frame of reference that makes the difference. Had I chosen to be upset by this fiasco, it would have been *my choice*! Having taken the car rental bus from the airport, we were caught in no-man's-land. I had two choices: take the bus back to the airport, or hoof it a mile to the right place. I hoofed it! (Yes, just a mile; however, I'm not in marathon shape any more. The other day I stepped on our talking scale, and it told me to come back when I was alone!).

Look at the bright side. At least I got in a work out!

Unfortunately, that line was just as long. The lady behind me was making all these frustrated noises, muttering under her breath about the long wait. She was not happy. Inside, I was chuckling because I had chosen not to let the situation get the best of me.

Positive mental attitude is vital for sales. If you think your customers are a pain, an intrusion and an interruption, you will treat them like a pain, an intrusion and an interruption. However, if you place them (and your efforts to help them) in a positive light, it can make all the difference in the world.

The objective of this chapter is to explain the importance of a *glass half-full attitude* and what you can do to keep a positive frame of mind. Please understand that I am not like a traditional motivational speaker who says, "You can achieve anything you set your mind to!" Not exactly. I believe there are certain limitations. For example, I am clearly on the wrong side of 6 feet in height, and I was never going to be in the NBA, no matter how much I wanted it to come true or how often I dribbled with my left hand.

Taking action is imperative. Doing something instead of talking about what you are going to do is vital. Having the inner drive and desire to get the job done. To be sure, I understand that one may not be able to achieve all of his or her dreams; however, you are going to get lot farther with a positive attitude than with a negative attitude. You will clearly accomplish more with a positive frame of mind.

Why does attitude relate so closely to success with your customers?

Well, it has been my experience that a large percentage of your sales success hinges on whether or not your customer likes you and wants to be around you. In fact, I believe that every time your customer sees you, he or she makes a silent decision as to whether or not he wants to be around you. Further, you sell yourself first, your company second and your products third. Selling yourself requires a positive attitude.

There is just no way to build, cultivate and maintain long lasting, healthy, profitable, mutually beneficial relationships if your customers have no interest being around you.

Your attitude is *always* front and center in this effort. Here are several ideas to think about:

- **Be an optimist** – control your inner dialog.

Have justified optimism - not wild-eyed blue-sky optimism. According to Martin Seligman's 20-year study and book called *Learned Optimism,* there are four criteria of optimistic people.

> o Optimistic people look for the good in every situation
> o Optimistic people seek a lesson in every setback or difficulty
> o Optimistic people look for a solution to every problem
> o Optimistic people think and talk confidentially about their goals

- **Understand that attitude** - like most skills can improve with practice.

Having a good attitude takes practice. It does not happen overnight and requires a conscious effort in order to have positive thoughts. Many experts who study the mind have learned that the mind can only have one thought at a time. That is, you can only be thinking of one thing at a time. Further, have you ever heard of a book called *Psycho Cybernetics?* This phenomenon, introduced in the 1970's, suggests that we *"react to the picture of us that we have in our brain."* So, if you are going to have one thought, why not make it a positive one? If you are going to have one vision of yourself, why not make it a positive vision?

- **Make the extra call** - visit the extra account.

I once heard a story about a great sales person. Seems this gentleman was asked for his secrets to success. Why was he the top producer at his company? He shared that every night as he prepared to leave the office, after he had put on his coat, he made one more call. And he never left without first making *that last call.*

The more often you show your face, the more often you check in, the more often you inquire to see if there is anything else you can do, the more successful you will be. *That's just the way it works.*

- **Develop an unshakeable belief** - in the importance of what you do and your products.

Have confidence so that your customers have confidence. That is half the battle in my book. If you answer every question with, *"Gee, I don't know!"* you are not going to instill much confidence in your customers. If you do not love your products, your customers will see that.

Your customers will say *"no"* from time to time. That is part of the business. If you fail to develop and maintain an unshakeable belief in your products, you will take that feeling of rejection into your next sales call. Instead, you must realize that your products are great and that it just was not the right day and time for that customer to buy your product.

- **Have a sense of urgency** – a sense of purpose.

Yes, I repeat this in many places because I believe in it so strongly. It is just so important to move with a sense of purpose. Moving with purpose builds your customers' confidence in you so you best pick up the pace a little.

- **Keep your problems to yourself** – avoiding complaining to your customers.

Many times sales people have come singing the following tune. "My company sucks! My boss sucks! My brands suck! My pay sucks! My bonus sucked!" That type of company bad mouthing is very detrimental and accomplishes a few unintended goals. First, the customer loses respect for the company. That is just what happens whether it is right or wrong. Second, the customer loses respect for the sales person. Third, the customer is made to feel uncomfortable. Finally, the customer can only feel, even though the sales person may just be venting, that his or her position is uncertain at the company. The truth is your business will suffer with this type of behavior because nobody likes uncertainty.

The Moral: vent to your wife, husband, mother, father, children, friends, softball buddies or the family dog but never complain and reveal private facts about your company to your customers. Some things are better left unsaid. When you feel bad emotionally (depressed, angry, bored – just plain negative) and you hit your customer with this, they will not want to do business with you. *That's just the way it works!*

- **Trust yourself** – do not be wishy-washy.

Be decisive. Going back and forth about a decision sets one up for failure. Former auto executive, Leo Iacocca, was asked once what he looked for most in an assistant or valued lieutenant. His answer: decisiveness!

- **Pick your pack** – hang out with the right people.

Is there anybody within your organization or on your sales team whom you envy? Is there a professional in your organization who has the skills that *you* think *you* need to be successful? What about an individual making the money you want to make or achieving the growth within the company (or industry) that you want to aspire to? Can you identify these individuals?

When you were younger, you did not choose your friends and the people you associated with; your parents probably did. Now, you have choices. Take the initiative to *pick your pack.*

Who do you hang out with in your personal life? If you hang out with people of nominal integrity, you will lie and cheat just like them. Instead, hang out with people who place emphasis on time and you will do the same. Associate with busy, effective people and you will be busy and effective, just like them.

Get to know the people who are doing great things in your company or industry. Study them. Interact with them. Question them. Befriend them. Do what they do and the same might happen to you. What are they doing that you are not doing? The point is that every professional can make a choice about whom he or she will be surrounded by. You can either surround yourself with the successful people at your company or the ones whose next stop is the unemployment line. It is your choice. Choose the internal relationships that will help you in the long run.

- **Top off your mental tank** – get better, continuously improve.

Prior to marathons, runners eat a big pasta dinner. The reason is that pasta (and carbohydrates) build muscle glycogen in your legs (and body). This act of eating all the pasta is meant to fill a runner's tank so that the next day he or she has the muscle reserves to make it to the finish line.

The same principle works with self-development. Spend time filling *your* mental tank and you will have more success and a better attitude. There are so many great resources (books, articles, tapes, CD's, etc) out there for sales professionals to improve their skills. It just takes a little effort to set aside a few minutes each day or each week for some extra learning. Listening to books on tape or audio CD's in your car is a great way to get in some extra learning.

Remember the following: What you know one year from today will only be what you know today – plus anything you expose yourself to over the next year. If your company does not adequately train you, train yourself. After all, you are the CEO of your personal brand. Be your own training department.

- **Plant the seeds** – and be patient.

Have you ever started a jogging routine in an effort to loose weight? What did you do when you got home after your first 3 mile run? I always ask the question in my workshops and the answers range from *had a beer or ate some ice cream* to the inevitable: *looked in the mirror or stepped on the scale!* Nobody gets a smaller stomach after his or her first 3-mile run and no one loses weight after one jaunt around the neighborhood. It just does not work that way. Typically, (remember, I used to be a runner) the body does not even realize you are exercising - for up to 2 weeks. It *may* even take up to 6 weeks to see meaningful change.

The customer loyalty marathon is won one act at a time, one gesture at a time, and one visit to your customer's place of business at a time. It does not happen overnight. By doing many of the small things that I mention in this book, you are effectively *planting the seeds*. Keep interacting with your customers in a positive manner and you will soon see the difference in your numbers!

- **Understand that nobody** - is perfect.

At one point Babe Ruth led the majors in homers and strikeouts and he was one of the greatest baseball hitters of all time. Even the

Major League hitter who wins the batting title each year only gets one hit every three times to the plate. The truth is that you are not going to close every sale and make everybody happy. The key when you do not succeed is to ask why. Why was I not able to convey the value in my proposition to my customer?

While at times you may run into a customer who really had no interest in your sales proposition, there are probably many other times when something in your approach turned him or her off. Learning something from the experience is the important part. Reminds me of a line in a great song by Jason Mraz ("I'm Yours"), *I win some and learn some.* Notice the tweak of the famous phrase, *Win some and lose some?*

Sales professionals with positive attitudes always try to learn something in the process.

- **Set goals** – commit your objectives to paper.

There are so many great resources on goal setting so I am not going to spend a lot of time on the subject; however, I do want to share one thought. Successful people set goals. Study after study has clearly shown that those who take the time to write down their aspirations have a much greater shot of realizing their aspirations.

Think about it this way. It is said that 5% of the people have 95% of the wealth in this country. Combine that with the fact that 90-95% of people *do not* set goals. Could it be that the ones with the money are the ones setting the goals? Do the math for yourself.

- **Never accept mediocrity or laziness** – and try to make a difference with everything you do.

Always go the extra mile for your customers. Retailers abhor laziness, as they typically have enough lazy associates of their own! Find ways to differentiate yourself and stand out with your accounts. Study other great salespeople from within your company (and industry) and from other vocations. Read sales books. Pick up ways to stand out and use those methods to show initiative with your customers. Remember, *there are no roadblocks or traffic jams on the extra mile.* Not sure where to attribute that quote but it really rings true for me. Does it ring true for you? Doing extra is a great way to stand out!

- **Resist the need** - to "*alibi*" away your lack of success.

Eric Hoffer (1951), author of the legendary *Thoughts on the Nature of Mass Movements,* said, "There are many who find a good alibi far more attractive than achievement." When one has an alibi, it gets easier. If I had better brands! If I had more support from management! From suppliers! If we had better customers! This thought process gets you nowhere and should be avoided at all costs.

- **Do for others** - what they cannot do themselves.

I remember a new, shy sales person who was afraid to make my acquaintance. A professional from a competing house made the introduction for him, something he was unable to on his own. I gained so much respect for the "introducer" that day. Her business increased because I loved the gesture.

On a personal note – I am so sorry I was not able to witness the following story. My youngest son Ben is 6 years old. One afternoon as the children assembled in the gym to take the bus home from school, Ben was having a bit of a *meltdown* because he couldn't get all his stuff in his backpack. Danny, my 11 year old happened upon the bus line and saw Ben in all his glory. He asked his brother what was wrong and proceeded to carry half of Ben's possessions home in his backpack. Oh to be a fly on the way when the big brother takes care of the little brother. The point is that he recognized Ben's need and did for Ben – what he was unable to do for himself.

- **Never say** – "*They don't pay me enough to do this!*"

Saying this phrase will ensure that nobody ever pays you very much to do anything at your current company or any other company.

- **Be Tenacious** – and determined.

Truly motivated sales professionals know that it is an honor that their customers call them. Never rely on anybody else to do your work. Give it your best; it is not up to anybody else to make you give your best and it has to come from within. No task as you take care of customers should be beneath you. As a beverage professional – your goal should be simple: to help your customers run the most successful wine, beer and spirit business in town. Strive for this every day of your professional life.

You may not accomplish your goals right away. You may not accomplish anything right away, but with a big dose of tenacity, you will. Consider the words of Benjamin Franklin – *"I haven't failed. I've had 10,000 ideas that didn't work."*

- **Be Real** – from the inside out.

The most effective leaders and sales professionals are perceived as real from the inside out. They conduct themselves in a consistent manner by always spot-checking their attitudes for the right behaviors. Always be transparent. Be honest and ethical in everything you do. Keep your promises. Show great character and be credible. Unfortunately, most people do not believe what they hear, so credibility is crucial. Be self-assured, but check your arrogance at the door. The truth is that if your competitor has a similar products and pricing, positive attitude will win out every time.

- **Rise above** – the pettiness of people.

You can either get bogged down in the minutiae of interpersonal relationships or you can give energy to the important tasks. The choice is yours.

- **Understand the theory of constraint**

The theory of constraint states that every organization has - at any given point in time - at least one constraint that limits the system's performance relative to its goal. There is one area that causes a bottleneck. Management experts have adopted this concept to suggest that most individuals have constraints that hold them back as well.

Typically, it is a skill that a sales person does not readily have and he or she blames the absence of that skill for his or her lack of success. Is anything holding you back? The point is to be aware of that weakness and to try each day to remedy the situation. My weakness is making sales calls, over the phone, so I try to make a few each day.

The key is how are you going to get from where you are today to where you want to be?  If the lack of a particular skill is holding you back – figure out what it is and how to fix it.

- **Show Initiative** – by identifying opportunities to stand out.

*"We need that wine here by lunchtime!"*

That was all we needed to say and poof, the wine would appear, usually from the back of a salesperson's SUV.  We did not care what it took; we just wanted to see results.  The salespeople who earned most of our business showed great initiative.  They identified, and more importantly, acted upon opportunities to *roll their sleeves up* and make a difference to their customers – us!

There are many ways to show initiative.  Some offered to make deliveries for us.  Others helped customers when they noticed we were a bit short handed.  One time, a helpful salesperson ran over to Kinko's for us when we were in a bind.  Other ways of helping included putting stock up, pricing items and helping us devise new and creative ways to market their products.  It was not necessarily what they did, but the fact that they genuinely wanted to help.

- **Understand the reality** – that there are no free lunches.

Many sales people feel a sense of entitlement.  They think they are owed something.  They think they should have something.  I see it especially in the case of new product introductions.  A *hot new* product will be introduced and your sales person will act like you have *no choice* but to automatically stock the new item.  You will *actually* get more placements if you pretend your customer may say *no.* The chances are you will try harder.

- **Do not create labels** – and go farther in life and business.

Resist the subliminal urge to erect boundaries on what you can or cannot achieve.  These labels, and other forms of self-defeating self-talk are terrible for your self-esteem.  The worst one is *I'm not a good sales person.*  The trouble is that if you think this subconsciously, then your actions will resemble the inept actions of a terrible sales person.  Do not create these types of artificial barriers on your achievement ceiling.

- **Be committed** – to working hard enough for success.

We often use the terms "amateur" and "professional" to describe sales people. Typically, what helps sales people move beyond "amateur" status (to "professional" status) is commitment - a sincere and heartfelt commitment to getting the job done and achieving success.

Reminds me of a story from my youth. While in high school I ran track and cross-country. You know, the glamour sports! Anyway, I was a true under-achiever. I was never going to light the world on fire (with my running acumen), but I could have achieved much more than I did. Adversity (the tough times during a race) and me hardly saw eye-to-eye. Dr. Paul Stoltz (a leading expert on measuring and strengthening human resilience) talks about a trait he calls the *adversity quotient.* According to his research, there are quitters, campers, and climbers. Quitters give up – never give any effort. Not me; I worked extremely hard in practice. Climbers are resilient, tenacious and persistent. That is a better description of me *now,* but not back then.

I was the camper. I would go only so far because I became *weary from the climb.* Here was my typical race week. I would compete in a meet (under-achieve) and promise myself that I would try harder and do better in the next race. Between the meets, I would wake up every morning and tell myself I would try harder and do better in the next race - up until the morning of the race. *That morning,* I would get out of bed and tell myself, "*Nah!*" That afternoon - you guessed it - I would under-achieve. This was the consistent – up until the 2-mile at Maine East Invitational.

That morning (and during the entire day) I deliberated mightily. Should I run hard? Should I dog it? This went on right up until I toed the line. That day, the light bulb went on. I ran my guts out, literally - as evidenced by my quick after-race sprint to the trackside wastebasket (sorry for all the detail, but it is part of the story).

Anyway, that day I gave it my all, and I was rewarded. I committed myself to excellence, at the last possible moment, and it worked out in the end as I ran my fastest 2-mile time ever.

That exemplifies the race day commitment we all need to be successful. Here in Illinois, York High School has won 26 state cross-country titles. I saw the powerhouse team win the state meet several years ago. Each of their seven runners were lying on the ground after the race. They gave it their all. They were committed, and as a result, they were successful. Betcha those guys had positive attitudes!

In summary, there are many reasons besides winning races to have a positive attitude. Many studies show that having a positive attitude will help you live a longer and happier life, one with better, more fulfilling relationships. Not accumulating more stuff. I am not talking about that – I'm talking about success. Anyway, you cannot have everything because, as comedian Steven Wright puts it, *"Where would you put it?"*

For the purpose of selling, we have examined two reasons to have a positive attitude. One, because you will likely be more successful, and two, so your customers will want to be around you. Both will lead to success and remarkably, you have a choice each day as to what your attitude should be.

You guessed it, the choice is yours – but you have to make the sacrifices.

*That's just the way it works!*

Your glass is either half empty or
half full.  The choice is yours!

# Being a Good Teammate

And the first pick in the 2008 NBA draft goes to…

The Chicago Bulls have a great new point guard. In the summer of 2008, at the NBA draft lottery, the Bulls defied the odds and somehow won the first pick in the upcoming draft. A pretty odd occurrence since the Bulls have lost far more than they have won lately! It was the best thing to happen in the Chicago basketball scene since Michael Jordan was propelling the team to numerous championships in the 1990's.

Those were the days!

The Bulls selected a product of Chicago, Derrick Rose, and he is turning heads all around the NBA with his dynamic play. Despite the fact that he is the youngest and newest player on the team, he is by far the best player on the squad. Unfortunately for Bulls fans, the rest of the team is terrible – and that leads to a very important question.

Will Derrick Rose lead the Bulls back to the *promised land*?

Uh, probably not! Not until management surrounds him with some real players and they start playing like a team. I remember when Michael Jordan entered the league. He quickly emerged as a dominant force, pumping in 40 points a night. Sometimes, he put down 50 or more points, but the funny thing is the Bulls always lost those games.

*The Bulls didn't start winning until they started playing like a team.*

Is there a team atmosphere at your company? Or is it every person for themselves? Are your teammates interested in your success, or are they silently rooting against you so they will look better in the eyes of management?

To be sure, there is probably a star on your team. Someone with the biggest and best accounts - someone who has been in the market for ages. Someone who seems to know where all the skeletons are buried. A polished individual. A true performer.

*But what about the rest of the team?*

Most likely, the majority of the team consists of role players - sales professionals out there day-in and day-out winning some and losing some but giving it their all. The truth is that the more the team works together in a cohesive fashion, the more the company will thrive. The more individuals put their teammates and their interests before their own, the better the company will perform. Brands will thrive and careers will thrive.

That's just the way it works! The funny part is that the skills that help a sales professional blossom with his or her team are the same skills required to be good with customers.

Here are a few things to keep in mind to make sure that you are a team player and your team is acting like a team:

- **Be committed**

Committed individuals are rock solid all the time. Committed individuals thrive in the face of adversity. These individuals ask *what is best for the team?* As George Halas, the legendary coach of the Chicago Bears, put it, *"Nobody who ever gave his best regretted it."*

Committed individuals are more collaborative. They work together aggressively to further the company's objectives. Their attitude is supportive, not suspicious. You know the suspicious types; individuals so gung-ho for their own interests that they think everyone is out to get them. There are much better environments for building businesses.

- **Be adaptable and communicative**

Adaptable sales people are more likely to be teachable, emotionally secure, and service-orientated. The simple truth is that teamwork and personal rigidity do not mix. As a wine retailer, I remember how hard it was to thrive with inflexible people. Sometimes we would ask an associate to do something just marginally outside his or her job description, and he or she would frown, perhaps expecting a complex renegotiation of our compensation practices (read: a raise!). *No thank you.*

On the other hand, we had associates who *got it.* They understood that great teams require flexibility and adaptability. They would do anything and everything. Since we started this chapter with a basketball theme - do you remember Dennis Rodman? Despite his eccentric personality and multi-colored hair, Rodman understood that his job was to rebound and play defense (and chase Madonna). The Bulls already had enough scorers (Jordan and Pippen). His unselfish play helped the Bulls win three titles.

Another essential attribute of team players is communication. In other areas of this book, I stress the importance of excellent communication with your customers, but it is also vital among teammates. Team players are not isolated from others. They share what they learn with their teammates, readily and enthusiastically, as opposed to the individuals who hide information unless forced to divulge it. Good teammates are candid and handle problems quickly. They *remove the pebble* as quickly as possible.

Perhaps I should explain. Runners often get a pebble stuck in their shoe. Some keep going while others stop and *remove the pebble.* What happens in a long race with a pebble *hanging out* in your shoe? A big, nasty, festering blister! You get the same outcome with your teammates when you do not take the time to air and resolve issues. Address issues with your teammates as soon as possible so those issues do not get past the point of no return.

- **Be dependable and disciplined**

Team players are there for each other.

I recently read an interview about the late Christopher Reeves. As you may remember, Reeves was injured in a horse riding accident and later succumbed to the after effects of his devastating injury. He relied upon a team of caregivers. If his caregiver was mad or unhappy or just felt like doing something else that day, there was absolutely nothing Reeves could do about. He was truly at the mercy of his team, and if a member of that team was having an off day, he was the one who suffered.

Of course, not all teams have such a critical mission, but the truth is that all members of a team are dependent on their teammates. Dependable teammates have a strong sense of responsibility and are known for making a consistent contribution. Their motives are clear because they are worn on their sleeves.

The beverage business is very goal driven. Any sales manager will tell you that the sum of the team's success is dependent on the individual contributions of each sales person. To be a valued teammate, you must work hard to become known as someone who can be counted on.

Also, make sure to be disciplined. Discipline, as defined by noted author John Maxwell is having the ability *to do what you really don't want to do.* Discipline is consistently doing the right thing. Discipline is making all your stops, starting your day early, and finishing late. Discipline is keeping your managers informed and in the loop. Discipline is not getting into silly arguments. Discipline is putting your team's interests before your own, a concept we have talked about elsewhere in this book. Discipline is taming your tongue and stopping yourself from saying words that you know are better left unsaid.

- **Have integrity**

Earlier in this chapter we touched on teammates who may be suspicious of others and how that environment is not conducive to teamwork. Teams succeed by concentrating on the overall goals (in this case taking care of customers), not by looking over their shoulders *at each other.*

What is *your* word worth? Ask somebody on your team. Ask if he or she considers you a person of integrity. Accept (with a smile) the answer if it does not come back like you hoped. Ask for an example in a non-threatening way.

Never put your team at risk with unprofessional or illegal behavior. Unfortunately, every member of the team has the ability to contaminate a winning team. As I write this, the country is in a deepening recession. Just yesterday the jobs report showed more people out of work than in 30 or more years. As a member of a team (and someone with a job), you might be concerned with keeping that job. Always remember that integrity is not an expendable line item on an income statement. Sure, your company may tighten its fiscal belt and jettison certain things, but integrity should never be one of those items. It is a full time job - not a 9 to 5 thing. It is an every day, every act thing.

Ask your sales manager. I believe he or she would rather you not get the business in this economic downturn than have you put the team and company at risk by *buying* the business in some illegal or illicit manner.

## • **Be relatable**

It has been said and written in many places that President Reagan could make you feel like his best friend, even if he had just met you. Americans loved that about the former President. He truly cared about people. How well do you relate to your teammates? How well do you get along with your teammates? Do you care about your teammates?

The more solid the relationship, the most cohesive the team will be, and the goal of selling more cases will be within reach. Another aspect of being relatable is showing respect.

As human relations expert Les Giblin puts it, "*You can't make the other fellow feel important in your presence if you secretly feel that he is a nobody.*" When I read this quote, I was reminded of the interaction between the various members of the sales team, but I know it goes far deeper than that.

Too often, members from within the same company fail to recognize each other's contributions to the overall success of the company. You know - drivers, accounting people, merchandisers, and other individuals from within the company. All functions are important, especially those that support the sales function. Take a moment to get to know other people in your company. Take a moment to appreciate the specific skills and contributions they bring to the table. As George Kienzle and Edward Dare (1950) say in their book, *Climbing the Executive Ladder,* "*Few things will pay you bigger dividends then the time and trouble you take to understand people!*"

In the long run, every position in a company helps the team reach its goals. Focus on others. Ask the *right* questions or, at the very least, just ask *some* questions. Make others feel special. Give a sincere compliment to your teammates once in a while, especially in front of others or a manager. That will pay big dividends.

Remember to bring your enthusiasm to work. Do not be a downer. As Author John Maxwell puts it, *You have the ability to bring people up or let them down – just like an elevator.* In reality, nothing drags a team down faster than one who wants to tell everybody how it *can't be done.* Take responsibility for your own enthusiasm. Spend time with enthusiastic people. Show a sense of urgency. Be willing to go above and beyond for your team and teammates and strive for excellence. Nothing breeds more excellence than a job well done.

### • Commit yourself to long-term achievement

The question that all sales people must ask themselves each day is *"How will I be better tomorrow?"* In other words, if you are a 5 (on a scale from 1 to 10) today, what are you going to do to be more than a 5 tomorrow? Great teams are built upon individuals with the desire to improve, the ability to bounce back, and the ability to maintain a positive outlook in the face of adversity.

I know this for sure - your knowledge and skill base a year from now will be the sum of what you know now, plus what you learn over the next year. That type of growth takes a commitment to long-term achievement.

### • Be a giver, not just a taker

I can sum this one up in a few short sentences. If one person is a giver and the other is a taker, the relationship will not last and there will be no incremental benefit to the team.

You know it and I know it.

So what are some other ways you can be a giver? You can be there for your teammates when they are slumping. Look for underlying issues. Try to determine what is troubling the slumping sales person? Be there when he or she needs you. A good teammate never compares a slumping representative to others on the team but is compassionate and understanding.

Use the proverbial *water cooler* to give your teammate the help he or she may need. Informal exchanges can yield a bunch of information you might not get at a more traditional meeting. The reason is that your teammates may be more *at ease* offering ideas in a casual, one-on-one environment than in a formal, public place.

- **Love your company**

A great teammate decides that he or she is going to make the company great and does not let a teammate badmouth the company.

- **Stop complaining**

Foster a solution-based culture. Change your thought process a bit. Instead of saying *I **have** to see a customer,* say *I get to **see** a customer.*

- **Be generous**

It has been said that the heart of selflessness is generosity. Please do not misunderstand me – I am not suggesting you have bake sales for each other. There are other ways to show generosity than giving of yourself financially. You can give of yourself in so many other ways.

Resist the urge to engage in internal politics. Resist the urge to posture yourself for your own benefit. Resist the urge to take all the credit. Give credit to others. Display loyalty to foster unity – which breeds team success. If you are loyal to your teammates, they will return in kind. That is how relationships work.

In summary, good team players refuse to give up. If your teammate wants to give up, point out the opportunity (which is very relevant in our economically turbulent times). Give all you have for the team. Be tenacious – instead of relying on luck, fate or destiny. Enlarge your heart to accept, love, and admire your teammates. Believe in your teammates before they believe in you. Serve others before they serve you. Ask yourself – what are my teammates good at, and value them for those attributes. Help your teammates go to the next level. They will love you for it.

As it has been said in many places, *you can lose with good team players, but you can't win without them.*
*That's just the way it works!*

# Making Selling a Passion

I am typing this book on my new Mac Book. That's right! I took the plunge and listened to my 13-year old son. For years he has been trying to convince me to *"switch sides"* and give up my PC. He achieved a goal that I know everyone in sales tries to reach each and every day. Instead of selling me on the idea of buying the Mac, he created an environment where *I actually wanted to buy it because I thought it would be a good idea.* The end result was good but it certainly did not start out that way.

Do you enjoy selling? Do you share your passion for your goods or services with your customers, like Josh shared his enthusiasm about his favorite line of computers? Do you always do your research before speaking or meeting with customers? Are you comfortable asking for the sale? The common perception is that great sales people are born and not made. Many people think that sales skills cannot be developed, which is simply not the case! There are many techniques you can use to become better at selling.

Here are some ideas to think about.

- **Determine what the customer wants** – it's not a knowledge contest.

Josh started out telling me every living fact about the Mac Book. I wanted to know three things. Could I transfer my data easily, how much could we get for my current laptop on eBay, and most importantly, would the Apple lock up every 10 minutes like my old computer? As is the case with most pre-teens, Josh was a little hard of hearing. He ignored my impending headache and kept selling. I explained that I was already sold if I was having the conversation with him. He knows my impulsivities! Once he tempered his enthusiasm and gave me the information that I needed to make a comfortable decision, we were on our way. (After I found my car keys!)

In Chapter 10, I suggested that sales professionals *ask first and present second* as a way to present information in a manner that will help their customers feel comfortable. It is essential to determine the customer's needs (and how he or she processes information) before launching into a sales presentation. To be sure, this is simple, but not easy. It is simple to expect to restrain oneself, but not easy to stay silent during a sales call. The most important skills are the most difficult to master!

Years ago, a wine professional asked me to share how I felt she should present a new line of wines to a customer. In this situation, most would show up, open many bottles of wine and start pouring. Alternatively, I recommend leaving the samples in the car at first. Have a conversation to determine which varietals the customer needs (or wants), and then explain (and taste) the virtues (benefits) of each. This approach is much more respectful of the customer's limited time.

- **Know the facts** – before you enter *any* account!

A friend of mine is a wine distributor and he related the following story to me. Seems he had a customer who was not feeling valued. The customer asked for a meeting with the sales manager to *clear the air*, as he had been simmering for several weeks and was ready to explode. Right away the customer was on the offensive. *"Do you know how much business I did with you last month?"* he demanded. The sales manager guessed, and guessed way too little (!), and the customer was deeply hurt.

The customer thought all along that the wine distributor did not value his business, and now, in his mind, he was proven right! The moral: *don't guess.* Know the facts before you enter the account. Had the customer blindsided the sales manager, that would have been one thing, but this situation was different. As I indicated above, the customer's feelings had been simmering for weeks. As the meeting was set up in advance, there was really no excuse for not knowing something as critical as how much business the customer did in December, the busiest month of the year.

Do your homework. Remember how your parents always used to pester you to get your homework done? Perhaps they never mentioned that being prepared is important not just when you are younger, but also for your entire life. As Jeffrey Gitomer (2004) puts it in *The Little Red Book of Selling*, "*Getting ready, preparing, developing questions, creating ideas and every other facet of your sales life presupposes that you have done your homework!*"

- **Love what you sell** – and share that passion with your customers.

If you study sales methods and systems as I do, you come away with many different approaches to the art of selling. One thing is always constant. You have to love the product you are selling. We have all seen people going through the motions. They could be selling life insurance or tires and it would not matter because their passion would be the same – nonexistent.

Brian Tracy puts it very succinctly in many of his teachings. "*If you don't believe or love your product, if you wouldn't use it yourself or sell it to your Mother or Brother, then you should think twice about the career and product you have chosen to sell.*" The point is simple. You must love what you are doing to have the required enthusiasm and confidence. The most effective sales people want the customer to enjoy the benefits of buying their products *more* than they want the personal rewards that they will accrue as a result of selling the products.

- **Ask questions** – that will get your customer thinking.

In my days as a wine retailer, I came face-to-face with many sales people who never took the time to try to intrigue me. Their questions lacked substance. They were developed without any real thought, like some of the ridiculous questioning that takes place every year at the Super Bowl! While listening to the radio one day, I heard a reporter ask the coach of the New England Patriots the following question: *"Do you think the time change (going from the East coast to the West coast) will affect your team this weekend?"* Most people would take their opportunity as a reporter at the Super Bowl to come up with something just a little more thought provoking!

There are several reasons why we ask questions and two that stick out in my mind. First, questions make your prospect feel good. As a rule, people like to talk about their experiences. Asking a retailer or restaurateur how he or she feels about distributor consolidation, or the new wines from South America, will show your customer that you value his or her opinion. Make sure to really listen, however, or those good feelings will evaporate. Insincerity is self-defeating and can be sniffed out a mile away.

Second, the right questions uncover your customer's needs. We are always taught to *know your customers* but what does that really mean? It means ascertaining your customer's problems and bringing solutions that help solve those problems. The great news is that successful questioning will help your sales increase.

For example, if you ask your customers if they feel their Australian red wine selection is up to par, they will probably answer *"yes."* Who would admit otherwise and that type of question does not stimulate any conversation. On the other hand, if you ask *what price range do you feel you could most improve your Australian red wine selection* and you will more likely get information you can use to meet their needs! If the customer indicates he or she is weak in the $35-40 range, then you know where you can provide some value.

The other reason to ask consultative type questions, as we discussed in Chapter 18, is that you will likely not have your customer's attention unless you stimulate their minds a bit.

- **Get face-to-face** – so your prospects can get to know you.

Do whatever you can to get face-to-face. Meeting someone is far more effective than sending an email or making a phone call. Great sales people have a twinkle in their eye and purpose in their step. For example, years ago we had a great wine salesman working in our retail store. This gentleman could sell wine like no other. He had a gleam in his eye and a grin that almost suggested that by showing you a certain bottle, he was sharing a treasured keepsake with you. He really, really loved wine. He loved educating our consumers, but it was a feeling that could not adequately be conveyed over the phone.

Tom Hopkins (2005) in *The Art of Selling* talks about scheduling visits instead of appointments. He points out that people typically associate appointments with trips to the dentist's office, or other similar pleasures. By asking for the time to meet with people and share ideas, you sound more like a person who cares, rather than someone trying to sell something. Try to get in front of the customer as early on in the sales process as possible.

- **Take more chances** – and you will make more sales.

No doubt about it, there is a lot of risk in selling. From time to time, I run into a sales person who dislikes selling or is unwilling to "risk" asking for the sale. Unfortunately, those people should not be in sales until they have some training. Sales managers should help those individuals develop their skills. However, at the same time, they should be candid with their associates if they are incapable of learning how to sell. Sometimes, people just need a push towards something for which they are better suited.

Sales people must possess excellent networking skills. Sales people must be able to make cold calls. They must be willing to ask for the sale, especially when they have exceeded expectations. Remember that *nothing ventured* truly means *nothing gained*, and with that in mind, the time has come to move on to the next chapter. But first, I must repeat myself and leave you with one more thought. You must develop an unshakeable belief in your products or you will not be successful in this business – or any other.

*That's just the way it works!*

# BE A PARTNER, NOT A PRETENDER

Last year was an election year. Millions of Americans headed to the polls and decided on our next President. As you may have heard by now, Barack Obama beat out John McCain to become our nations 44<sup>th</sup> President.

Both candidates had an individual take (or his party's take) on the issues - and one thing is for sure in last year's election or any other election - you may not agree with your candidate on all the issues; however, you must like and trust the candidate for him or her to receive your vote. You must feel comfortable that he or she has your best interests at heart. You must feel that your candidate is sincere, knowledgeable, and committed to receive your vote.

What about your customers? *Are you worthy of their vote?*

A better question is: do your customers cast votes about you in the same fashion? You bet they do! In fact, each time your customer sees you, they cast a pivotal, private vote in their minds about you and your company. They decide, based on many factors, whether you are their trusted partner - or a self-serving pretender. They decide whether or not they want to do business with you.

Are you a partner or pretender?

How would your customer vote?

There are conceivably hundreds of little reasons why a customer would stuff the ballot box in your favor, but in the spirit of simplicity (and the marathon) I have identified 26.2 mistakes that pretenders make and the corresponding way that a partner would handle the same situation.

Think about it this way. Your goal is to be a strategic partner. There is a great deal of difference between *selling* a $15 dollar cabernet and being *asked* for a $15 dollar cabernet. If your customer is lying awake at night, ruminating over a moderately priced cabernet selection, and calls you *first thing* the next morning, you are really close to the finish line. You are a strategic resource, someone whom your customer could not imagine doing business without.

That customer has checked the final box on an imaginary ballot: Motivation.

If your customer is not checking the box on the mental ballot for motivation, then you, your company, and your brands will never reach their true potential. Your customers will not want to do business with you. They will be indifferent – and indifference is the kiss of death for your business. They will never cast their vote for you.

Are you a partner or a pretender? Carefully review the following list and you will learn the answer. Your goal is to have as many of the partner qualities (and as few of the pretender qualities) as possible. If you act like a partner, and more importantly, are considered a partner (by your customers), you will do more business, have a longer career, and be more successful. Say it with me… *That's just the way it works!*

Have a look at the following:

- **Pretenders** enter accounts while talking on their cell phones. Major turnoff for your customers. Always finish your other business before you enter an account. The reason is simple. Your objective is to show that customer that (at least for those precious few moments) he or she is the most important person in the world to you.

  **Partners** leave the cell phone in the car. No, you say, what if a driver has to reach me? Ok, I can see that. My suggestion: put the phone in silent mode and check it periodically and before you check it, let you customer know you may check your cell phone from time to time for emergencies. That is a courteous way to handle the situation. Other than that, give him or her your undivided attention.

- **Pretenders** act like the playground bully. Yelling at people that cannot yell back. Failing to acknowledge the little people. Sadly, bullies exist not only on the playground but also in the halls of corporate America. Do not let this be the case with you. Make time for the little people. Your customers can tell more about you by the way you interact with their clerks than they can by anything you might say to them. Help your customers retain their top people by showing them the proper respect on each visit.

  **Partners** are happy to see people. Does it cost anything to smile or give a kind word?

- **Pretenders** disparage their competition. Some sales people think that bad-mouthing the competition will make their company look better. Not so. Just makes them look worse.

  **Partners** have a professional attitude about other companies in their market. *Oh, the Great Wine Company? They have a nice portfolio. Here is why you should do business with us over them!* With one simple sentence – we acknowledged the other company and immediately started extolling the virtues of our company. When you mention other companies it actually helps because you will look more honest and objective in your customer's eyes.

- **Pretenders** arrive late, disorganized and unprepared. Wasting your customer's time. And your time. Not a good thing! Enough said? Always remember: your customer's time is as valuable as yours. Further, if one cannot arrive on time for a meeting, what makes your customer think the order is going to arrive on time?

  **Partners** have the proper materials before entering an account. Spend time planning your visits. Know what you want to accomplish. Being organized will help you both (your customer and you) achieve your goals. (For more on this topic, see Chapters 5 & 10)

- **Pretenders** fail to control their moods. They take bad moods out on others and have a negative disposition. Think back to a time when you were in less than a positive frame of mind. What did you notice about your performance? Was it good? What about the last time you performed at your absolute best. What was the key difference? The truth is that you were probably in a better mood.

  **Partners** resolve to keep their complaining to a minimum and realize that everyone has his or her own problems, issues and concerns. You are not alone. *I'm not saying that it is easy but it's so vital to your success.* Remember the famous words of former Notre Dame football coach Lou Holtz: *"Never tell your problems to anyone...20% don't care and the other 80% are glad you have them."*

- **Pretenders** lack commitment. Giving up quickly and giving others reasons why it will not work. There are no half-hearted champions. Consider the words of William James, *"most people never run far enough on their first wind to see if they've got a second wind!"*

  **Partners** persist, work hard and ask for the sale and ultimately are rewarded.

- **Pretenders** are slimy, unethical, and immoral and are classified as cheaters and liars. Pretenders let the truth out slowly. Do not let the truth out slowly. Let it out quickly and accurately and remember your reputation follows you wherever you go.

  **Partners** read Chapter 14 of this book!

- **Pretenders** are pessimists and frequently moan and sigh. They have little enthusiasm, low self-belief and low self-esteem. They wear a constant frown instead of a smile. Before you enter an account ask yourself, "Am I a joy to be around?" I guarantee you that your customers are making that judgment about you every time they see you.

  **Partners** smile, are enthusiastic and move with a sense of purpose.

- **Pretenders** blame others when it's actually their fault. Not taking personal responsibility for your life and results – blaming others no matter whose fault it is. Perhaps this is the fault of the car insurance companies that have taught us to never admit blame if we are in an accident!

  **Partners** refuse to play the blame game. Instead of placing blame, take ownership of your life, your feelings and the results you produce. Talk to any successful person and he or she will say that in life there are only results or excuses. Which do you actively seek?

- **Pretenders** are jealous of people who want to move upward and actually do something about it. Having jealousy towards people who identify those they can learn from – those who they can admire – those who set goals and try to achieve them. Some people take chances and inevitably, some may ridicule and explain why the risk takers will not succeed. Not good! As Henry Ford once said, *"You can't build a reputation on what you are going to do."* Some go for it and others react negatively. A real career killer is to be jealous of those who take chances.

  **Partners** are happy for those who are climbing the ladder at their company and want to do the same. Examine the situation and try to determine why it is he or she and not you! Maybe the answer is laying it on the line and being fully committed. You know my most **famous** quote; *"You can't cross the finish line if you don't have enough courage to start the race."* Who am I kidding? *That quote isn't even famous in my own house!*

- **Pretenders** jump to conclusions and rush to judgment. Many relationships have been destroyed because enough time was not taken to observe and gain the facts of a given situation. Knee-jerk reactions are common and understandable; however, they can be devastating. The problem is that these reactions are rooted in emotion, and rarely with a good understanding of the facts.

  **Partners** understand that they rarely have all the information they need at first. Investigate. Never make decisions when you

269

are excessively happy or unhappy with someone. Gather the facts. Calm down before reacting and making any decisions and *especially* before firing off a mean-spirited email.

- **Pretenders** make decisions for the wrong reasons. Managers (and sales people) love to make decisions. It provides validation. It confirms their purpose in an organization, but, unfortunately, many fail to keep the following in mind - that the ability to make decisions is a responsibility, not a right. Decision-making is not for power and authority. Making decisions for the wrong reasons may bring good results in the short term, but will never serve you well in the long term.

  **Partners** ask the following questions. Am I making this decision to save my personal reputation? Bad idea. Am I making this decision to gain prestige? Bad idea. Making a decision solely to become a *bigger* part of the team? Another bad idea! Resist the temptation to make decisions to fit in. Find other ways to contribute. If you have made a mistake, repair your personal reputation another way. Always make decisions for the sake of the team and company, first and foremost.

- **Pretenders** fail to differentiate and fail to add value. Even with all the industry consolidation the last several years, beverage retailers, bar owners and restaurateurs still have many vendors with whom they do business. As you might imagine, business owners are besieged by sales people on a constant basis. Each day these individuals have to make snap decisions about whom to see, whose calls to take, and whose products to carry. Each day these retail owners have to separate the partners from the pretenders, and those sales people who do not differentiate and add value will simply not be able to rise above the clutter.

  **Partners** find ways to stand out. Send a written note once in a while. Help out when your customer's store is busy. Help out when it is not busy. Show up unexpectedly and take initiative. Educate your customer's employees. Bring creative ideas to the table. Build rapport. Take an active interest in all levels of your customer's organization. Be different, be memorable, and be noteworthy in at least one way.

- **Pretenders** are not good listeners. Listening is not hearing. Hearing, according to the dictionary, is the active acquisition and translation of sound waves into meaningful concepts. Listening is different. It is the mental activity of hearing someone with the intent of gaining understanding. It is one of the single most important skills one should posses in their tool kit.

  **Partners practice effective listening**. Yes, actually practice. Concentrate. Do not talk so much. Remove distractions. Make eye contact. Ask relevant questions. Seek to clarify, not judge.

- **Pretenders** fail to "fill their mental tank." You know the expression! *"I've done it this way for 25 years - I know what I'm doing!"* Uh, not necessarily. Longevity does not mean you were doing it right! A major career killer is lack of learning. Maybe we think that our learning is complete when we don the cap and gown, but that is simply not the case.

  **Partners** (and those that are serious about success) make learning a life-long pursuit. Instead of listening to music or talk radio, pop in an audio CD. Listen to others. Listen to their thoughts and opinions. You do not have to agree with every idea, but at least be exposed to different trains of thought. I call it "filling your mental tank." Much like marathon runners eat pasta for energy in the big race, beverage sales people must consistently be filling their brains to not become obsolete.

- **Pretenders** waste time. There is a great line by Harvey Mackay, author of *How to Swim with the Sharks without being Eaten Alive*. *"I've known successful sales people who were alcoholics, gamblers, thieves and liars...but I have never known a successful salesperson who sat on his (rear end) all day."* Beverage sales people that cling to their jobs without exerting themselves will fail, and do so pretty quickly.

  **Partners** make a schedule and stick to it. Make enough sales calls. Provide more than enough information so your customers have confidence in their decisions. Be around to provide service. Be accessible. Be a trusted advisor, an accomplishment

271

only reached after enough face-to-face time with your customers.

- **Pretenders** worry excessively. Are you an excessive worrier? I know many beverage professionals who are, and it is destructive. Excessive worry and the resulting toxic stress lead to decreased productivity, ill health, lack of energy, and damaged relationships. To be sure, there are some situations that warrant an emotional reaction, and bad things really do happen (especially when you least need them to), but much of what we worry about simply never happens. For this point, I am talking about the act of *making a mountain out of a molehill.*

  **Partners** take charge of stress. *Managing Stress* by the *Harvard Business School Press* suggests the following: (1) Stop negative thoughts from flooding your mind, (2) breathe by taking a deep breath and slowly letting the air out, (3) reflect on the situation, and (4) find a solution. In my view, the key is in the initial reaction. Monitoring your thoughts is crucial and if you successfully block negative thoughts, you will be well on the way towards creatively solving your problem.

- **Pretenders** fail to say "thank you." If you have ever read my articles or attended my workshops, then you know what a premium I place on appreciation in the beverage business. I believe that an ounce of appreciation (in some cases) can go so much further than several pounds of anything else. In fact, I am always amazed when a new store opens and the local distributor and supplier fail to send flowers (or a card) or any type of acknowledgement. I mentioned this once and a beverage professional chuckled, *"Yeah, but I sent a ton of vodka!"* Touché! Upon second thought – I am not buying it. Appreciation is a daily activity, and especially important on any day that your customer makes a conscious decision to buy your products.

  **Partners** are appreciative. They send a bouquet of flowers or a note that says, *"Dear Mr. and Mrs. Entrepreneur: I see that you've sunk every last penny into that store (or restaurant or bar) and packed it full of product (much of which is mine) and I appreciate* *that and thank you from the bottom of my heart (or pocketbook).* I'm not talking the whole nursery here - just a $15 floral arrangement. Show your customers you care and they will spend a lot more time *caring* about the sale of your products. Remember: Thank your customers *big and small* for orders *big and small.*

- **Pretenders** are not team players. Who is on your team? Most of the people you interact with on a daily basis are your teammates. For sales people, your teammates include the receptionist in your office, the drivers, merchandisers and accounts receivable personnel. Your team also includes your customers and all the people on their team. The point is the ability to put your team's interests before your interests is a great ingredient of success. Conversely, ego run amok can destroy even the brightest beverage career.

  **Partners** are team players. In your company, create cohesion, not friction. Care about the well-being of the people you meet. Create an inspiring workplace. Strive for a pleasant atmosphere. Most importantly, share credit and shoulder blame. Speak less than you listen. Sometimes, just saying, *"I don't know, what do you think"* can really motivate the person with whom you are talking. Take pride in the success of others and you will truly be a team player.

- **Pretenders** do not know (or care) what is important to their customers. On Fridays all over the country distributors and suppliers try to determine what motivates their customers. In these meetings, a whole host of assumptions are made without asking the critical questions of those that have the answers: the customers. Operating in the dark like that can lead to wasted time and squandered opportunities.

  **Partners** ask questions and accept feedback. Ask what you can do to make your customer more successful. Of course, the first answer will probably be better prices, but probe deeper. *Prices don't put food on the table, but profit does.* Dollars do. There are a great many factors that affect profit and your job is to find them. Find out what truly motivates your customers.

- **Pretenders** are impatient and do not exercise enough patience or give things enough time. Okay, okay I know. I'm impatient. Been so my whole life. If I were a flower, I'd be an *impatient.* I'm *trying* to be more patient. I remember a sales person once told me to make up my g** d**n mind, already. I did after hearing that ludicrous comment, NO THANK YOU! I was not going to be rushed into making the *wrong decision.* As a result of his boneheaded comment, his business suffered but I bet you figured that out.

  **Partners** realize that instant gratification is not always the answer. Try to recognize that people move at their own pace and what may seem like a quick decision to some may take longer for others. Give it some time. Take a deep breath. In the sales environment, keep checking back with customers and prospects. At some point, you will end up in the right place at the right time and your patience will be rewarded.

- **Pretenders** talk too much. I remember this like it happened yesterday. A young salesperson came in to sell me something. He kept talking and talking. I could not get a word in edgewise. What did I want to say? *OK, I'll take it!* But he did not stop. Finally, he talked so long he lost the sale. I know this does not happen every day, but be sure to let your customers talk. Let them hog the conversation. The more they talk the better.

  **Partners** ask questions and then keep their mouths shut. When you do talk, make your points quickly and succinctly. Remember that less is more. Develop a list of questions you feel comfortable asking, ones that are open-ended and then fire away.

So there you have it - a list of behaviors that will help you earn your customer's vote. Why is this important? Well, as a sales person (or sales manager) you have to understand that every time you round the corner or visit your customer's place of business, those customers make a mental determination as to whether or not they enjoy the experience of doing business with you. Whether you are a partner or a pretender.

The great news is that if you do enough of the *partner* actions, you will create customers that are motivated to do business with you, not because they **have to but because they want to!**

*That's just the way it works!*

Would your customers vote for you?

# Improving Cross~Cultural Communication

Many experts say that *understanding* other cultures facilitates effective cross-cultural communication. If you understand even a little about another person's culture, you can communicate more effectively with that person. I think it makes perfect sense! More importantly, in this day and age, it has never been more relevant.

Just one generation ago, most retailers looked pretty similar physically, but now they can look very different. According to the U.S. Census Bureau (2000), there were more than 281 million people in the U.S. population at the turn of the century. Of that number, almost 100 million people were either Latino, African American, Asian or a variety of other races and ethnic groups. That diversity has impacted the beverage business.

These divergent groups represent many cultures, each with a distinctly different communication style. Unfortunately, despite the fact that the U.S. population has become more and more diverse over the years, the reality is that sales people still have a great degree of difficulty communicating with ethnic groups (with different cultures) from the one that prevails in the U.S.

Part of the problem is that English is a second language for many new Americans. To be successful, sales people must be prepared to handle the complexities of interacting with people who speak a different native language, have different customs about buying and selling, are used to different currency, and define some words differently than Americans.

As is my custom, I'd like to share 26.2 ways to *win the customer loyalty marathon* with cross-cultural customers. Will these suggestions guarantee you success in this market? Maybe. But you must be willing to adjust your practices to meet the unique needs of this rapidly growing customer group.

Unfortunately, there is no chart that ***accurately*** summarizes how each group acts or behaves. There are resources that lump people of the same culture or country together that may indicate certain traits, and those can be used as a fundamental guide. Unfortunately, within a given American region, there are so many sub-cultures and other differences that the only way to really understand your new American customers is to take the time to learn the intricacies of their specific culture.

Here are a few things to keep in mind:

- **Be aware of your cultural baggage**

We communicate the way we do because we were raised in a particular culture and learned our own culture's rules and norms. That made sense then, but as the population has diversified, many of us have developed stereotypes or cultural baggage about people that are different from us. Americans, by in large, tend to be ethnocentric. That is, we think *our way is the best way*. Due to our geographic isolation, we tend to be awkward when dealing with other cultures as compared to Europeans, who have many countries touching one or more of their borders. They are accustomed to people who speak a different language and bring with them different cultures.

Often, just because we do something in a specific manner, we are pre-disposed to think that *the other way is wrong* and subsequently develop stereotypes. If you are a sales person and you have difficulty dealing with a diverse customer base, the first step is to identify your own stereotypes so you can do something about it.

- **Don't stereotype**

This is *what* you do about it. Do not assume that things are a certain way because of a pre-conceived notion on your part. That is a stereotype. Stereotypes are assumptions we make about a person's character or attributes based upon a ***general image*** of what a particular group of people are like.

Communication with strangers often relies too heavily on categorization or stereotypes, which are often rooted in ignorance. The decision is yours. Make a conscious effort to correct these inaccuracies to stop stereotyping.

- **Stop asking *why "can't they just act like us?"***

A sales person with a very diverse sales route suggested this to me one day. Maybe *you* silently think that very thought. Maybe you are thinking *why can't they just do it our way? They are living in our country after all!* Thoughts like these are counter productive. The world is changing as diverse cultures intermix as never before because of the Internet and easy transportation. Diversity is here to stay, and those who become more sensitive will cultivate a great opportunity.

- **See diversity as an opportunity**

Yes, diversity is a huge opportunity. According to various population studies, minorities now make up one-third of the population. This represents a huge market opportunity, and if you know how to meet the unique needs of these customers, and are willing to *try*, then you will attract a large share of this emerging market. Avoiding cultural pitfalls can give you a leg up in the marketplace.

- **Don't give up because of myth or hyperbole**

I have spoken to sales people who wrongly believe that people of diversity only want to work with someone of their own culture. That is not the case whatsoever, according to the article *Ten Myths about Multicultural Members* (Michael D. Lee). Mr. Lee suggests "Most of the people that complain about having trouble just need to understand how to meet the unique wants and needs of people from other cultures and to treat them with respect and patience. In fact, many cultural groups prefer to work with a representative outside their group for reasons of privacy."

- **Get information by giving information**

Share information about your personal life and perhaps your customer will open up about his or her personal life. If you would build rapport that way with a member of your own homogenous group, then you should try the same with other groups as well. The weather is always a very safe subject with which to open a conversation that is more personal than just prices and products. You can ask if the American weather is similar to the weather in their home country. It is fairly easy to extend the conversation to children by asking if the other person has children. Most people are quick to talk about their children. It is easy to start a conversation with other people if you ask them about themselves for there is no subject people like to talk about more than themselves!

- **Be patient and forgiving, rather than hostile and aggressive**

Respond slowly when having a conversation. Many people (especially me) talk very rapidly. Remember, English is a second language to diverse customers. It is not their native tongue. Be patient. Talk more slowly. They are not deaf, so do not raise your voice in an effort to make them understand you, which is a common behavior when talking to someone who is speaking with an accent. Throw in a few pauses so your customer can listen at his or her own speed. And don't slur your words one into another. People learn another language one word at a time, and when you slur words it creates new words that bear no resemblance to any word that has been learned one at a time. Do not show your displeasure if your customers cannot ascertain your meaning right away.

- **Check the meaning**

As you converse, stop periodically to make sure your customer is getting your meaning the way you intended. Imagine there are little checkpoints along the course of your conversation. Stop periodically to reassure your customer (and you) that you are still talking about the same thing!

- **Stop and think when things get tense**

When conflict, or the threat of conflict, starts to get out of control, take a step back. Try to get a handle on the situation. Ask: *what could be going on here? Did I misinterpret something? Did they misinterpret me?* It is far better to…

- **…Walk away**

Take a breather. William Ury, noted author on negotiation topics, suggests you *step out on the balcony.* I have mentioned a similar thought in other chapters and I feel especially strong about the concept as it pertains to diverse customers. You never know when the most innocuous comment or an unintended gesture will be misinterpreted by your customer. Take a breather.

- **Watch your non-verbal communication**

Understand that there is a great degree of importance given to non-verbal communication in multi-cultural settings. Facial expressions and gestures are very important. Some cultures place a great value on eye contact. For example, Americans place a premium on eye contact. To not look someone in the eye is a sign of dishonesty. In other cultures, however, looking someone straight in the eye is a sign of disrespect. The best way to learn these courtesies is to observe, do your research, or ask your customer for help to understand this facet of communication.

Do not assume that your way is the right way to communicate.

- **Eliminate ambiguous statements**

It is best to be as clear as possible with diverse customers who often have a different frame of reference. Your customer is likely to see and interpret your comments in a manner consistent with his or her expectations. By the same token, avoid slang and idiom. Expressions like *slam-dunk* and *out of left field* may be hard for your customers to understand. One way to build rapport is to learn some of your customer's native idioms, and then you can share some of yours.

Do make sure that your customers understand slogans and terminology that are prevalent in the beverage business.

## • Watch the tone of your voice

Understand the role of voice level and tonality in conversation. Raised voices are not necessarily a sign that there is conflict. In some cultures, loud conversations are normal, and there is no reason to react with alarm. In other cultures it may be different. Watch your customers to get a sense of their tonality and respond accordingly. Avoid words and phrases that may be considered hurtful. Avoid any hints of a knowing, mocking, or smug tone with your customers.

## • Ask questions

You can learn about different cultures by reading books, doing Internet research, talking to a third party or, most effectively, by asking your customer questions to develop a better understanding of his or her norms and culture. You could ask any of the following questions that are from a list provided by the *National Clearinghouse for Bilingual Education*:

o   In your culture, who is considered to be in the family?
o   In your culture, what are some important stages, periods or transitions in life?
o   In your culture, how do people greet each other?
o   In your culture, what languages are spoken?
o   In your culture, what holidays are observed?
o   In your culture, what holidays are important for children?
o   In your culture, how are history and tradition passed to the young?
o   In your culture, what are the purposes of education?
o   In your culture, what traits and attributes in oneself or others are important?
o   In your culture, what traits and attributes are undesirable?

o   In your culture, what is considered on time?
o   In your culture, what is the importance of punctuality?
o   In your culture, what values are expected to be maintained despite one's degree of formal education?

### •   Take your time with greetings

Do not rush greetings and introductions in an effort to get down to business quickly.  Never assume how your customer wants to be greeted.  Let them determine the most comfortable greeting. If you are not sure, greet the customer verbally and then hesitate for a moment giving your customer the opportunity to offer the kind of greeting that is most comfortable for him or her.

### •   Be supportive

How would you feel if you were doing business in a foreign country?  How would you feel if you had to risk your hard earned money (and maybe your life) to make a living in a distant part of the world? Most diverse customers are trying to learn the language.  Most are trying to fit in. Be supportive and encouraging as they learn our language. As long as you are sincere in your efforts, it will be appreciated.

### •   Study culture continuously

Study the cultures of your diverse customers.  Much of the time we consider differences between our cultures as threatening.  What is logical in one culture may be completely illogical in another. Generally speaking, when we communicate we expect certain responses.  With someone familiar, we are confident in what we may hear.  With diverse customers we are less confident. We can reduce uncertainty (and the underlying tension) by gathering more information about these unfamiliar cultures.

### •   Be careful with humor

Jokes are risky business with diverse customers.  Think about it this way.  Half of our attempts at humor (*3/4's of my attempts*) fall on deaf ears (because we are not comedians) and we speak the language. What if English is not your primary language? Much gets lost in the translation, so humor is probably not a wise choice.

- **Use simple words**

Try to use words with just a few meanings as opposed to words with many meanings. For example, the word *get* has over 20 meanings. It can mean *buy, steal, grab* as well as other meanings. Those to whom English is a second language are likely to know only the first two meanings of an English word.

- **Suspend judgment**

Stop and listen. Do not judge. Perhaps your inability to reach agreement on something is more about a misunderstanding than the fact that you and your customer cannot agree on terms. Control the tendency to think that *different from me is less than me.*

- **Keep your distance**

In some cultures, it is appropriate to stand close to one another, but in other cultures, great separation is required. The best way to recognize this skill is to observe and follow your customer's lead.

- **Understand the need to save face**

Saving face and keeping one's reputation is perhaps one of the most important desires in many cultures. Many cultures frown upon questioning because of the desire to be courteous. One would rather *save face* by pretending he or she understands, even if he or she does not, to seek harmony and confrontation-free relationships.

- **Listen**

Use your best reflective listening skills. Now is a better time than any to say, *"If I hear you correctly, you are saying..."* Repeat back to your customer. Review Chapter 20 for more on listening skills.

- **Acknowledge holidays**

Familiarize yourself with your customer's major holidays and send a card or a small gift. Spend some time learning the customs of gift giving in your customer's culture.

- **Paint a picture**

*A picture is worth a thousand words* could not be truer when working with your diverse customers. Write numbers and other important facts on a piece of paper. Create visual aids. Be creative to get your meaning across and your message will be more effective.

- **Be specific about time**

Time is influenced by culture, so be specific to avoid misunderstandings. In some cultures, the meeting starts at a certain time and in other cultures, the *meeting starts when the meeting starts*. This can be frustrating and it is far better to be *safe than sorry*.

## The Final Straightaway

Pay attention to unique, individual features. Establish personal relationships to break stereotypes down. Learn about your customer. You will likely see that he or she is actually a living, breathing, caring individual, and not a hostile enemy.

Consider the words of multi-cultural expert Professor George Renwick.

> *"You have to first feel genuine respect for others and second, find ways to communicate that respect so that it will be understood."*

Stress similarities not differences. Typically, when people are different, we concentrate on what makes us different instead of seeing what makes us similar. Look for those similarities. Take your customer to lunch. Ask some of the questions I have suggested in this chapter. Ask, listen, and learn.

**There is no magic potion.** As I indicated at the beginning of this chapter, there is no chart that accurately defines how each nationality should behave or wants to be treated. Each customer is different. Take the time to get to know your diverse customers. Show this unique group that you appreciate and value their business. Show that you are trying to adapt and willing to learn their ways and your business with them will increase.

*That's just the way it works!*

# The Final Straightaway

Only 385 yards to go! Thanks for reading my second book, *Winning the Customer Loyalty Marathon!* I hope you will find the preceding 26 chapters useful for improving the relationships you have with your customers. I promised 26.2 ways, and we have to finish the .2! The last yards are the most important. Without those last yards, a runner never has the thrill of hoisting his or her arms in the air and smiling for the finish line photo.

But first - a little review.

We have already discussed how it works in the wine, beer and spirits industry. On and off premise retailers do not have the choices that are evident in most other industries. As I mentioned in the Introduction, I believe some sales people take this for granted. They act like it is a mandate that business has to be done a certain way. They do not try as hard, or provide as much value as they should. They act like they have some pre-ordained right to have the business.

**I want you to pretend you can lose a customer. That he or she can go somewhere else for the same exact product.**

Your number #1 goal should always be to create an environment where your customers do business with you, not because they <u>have</u> to, but because they <u>want</u> to. Make the experience enjoyable and motivating. It is ***then and only then that your products and company will reach their true potential.***

Will it be easy? No, not a chance.

You have to remember that it is simple, but not easy. It's what you do every day, every mile along the way that counts. It's the little things like simple, random acts of kindness. Perseverance is the key! Developing your plan for showing your customers you value them, and then on race day, when they have chosen you, having the dedication, desire, determination and discipline to see it through.

Before you know it, you will have crossed the finish line, in whatever race you're running! You will **win the customer loyalty marathon** and successfully create an environment where your customers do business with you – not because they <u>have</u> to, but because they <u>want</u> to.

And you will be successful. Why? Are you joking?

Because...

*That's just the way it works!*

# 26.2 Ways to Retain and Motivate Terrific People

Recently, my local wine store lost a terrific wine professional. I bought my wine from him and I know he was salt of the earth. He grew up on a farm, if that tells you anything about his work ethic. Whenever I shopped, he was always very busy, but could stop on a dime to help me find a new syrah or zinfandel.

Seeing him leave got me thinking about what it takes to keep talented people at your company. With everything going on in the economy these days, it is simply imperative to keep your best people.

But wait, you say, *they have nowhere to go.*

The day a manager develops that rationale is the day he or she starts losing the cream of the crop.

With that in mind, I offer 26.2 Ways to Retain and Motivate Terrific People. The first point may be the most important.

- **Apologize** – when you make a mistake with someone.

To err is human; to apologize is a sign of respect. Most people will appreciate a sincere apology, but make it specific; otherwise, it will seem empty. Always specify a reason for making the apology. When in doubt: apologize. *It's no big deal. Just say you're sorry.*

- **Say "thank you"** – as often as possible.

One of the greatest things I have learned in business is the power of appreciation. An ounce of appreciation can often weigh so much more than a pound of most anything else. Find creative ways to thank your people. Be specific. Thank you for staying late to help with the important project. Thank you for coming early, etc. Once I sent a thank you note to a manager's wife to thank her for their sacrifice on a busy weekend. Believe me; that was a very well received gesture.

- **Take a time out** – if you are having a sloppy mood.

The book *Love 'Em or Lose 'Em* talks about sloppy moods - moods that are uncontrolled and on any given day will cause whatever you are feeling to come spilling out to slop all over everybody. The result (for the person bearing the brunt of your mood) may be embarrassment, hurt, anger, humiliation and a loss of dignity. Better to take some time to compose yourself, than to risk losing a terrific person on your bad day.

- **Discuss the company's vision** – to energize and inform your troops.

Take some time with your associates to answer the following questions. Where is the company going? What will it look like when we get there? Without answers to these important questions, your sales people and associates will be uncertain as to how to conduct themselves. Motivate everybody by giving them a snapshot of the big picture.

- **Take your associate's temperature** – Do your associates like coming to work?

Convene a focus group or have an informal Internet survey. There are more and more inexpensive and confidential ways to get your associate's opinions - if you want them. And you most certainly do! Create and maintain an environment where your associates *feel* they can speak freely.

Take the top three concerns your associates have about your company and fix them. At the very least, when times are good, show some appreciation to your associates. Let them know and feel that the success that the company is enjoying is due to them. Let them have some credit! Having the right atmosphere in good times will help when things drift the other way in hard economic times – as they have in late 2008 and early 2009.

- **Remove Distractions** – to make your associates feel more important.

We talk about this in reference to our customers but managers, do you give your sales people undivided attention. As I suggest with customers, always let your associates know you are expecting an important call. That way, when it happens, it will be less of an interruption. In the meantime, keep your eyes on your people when they are fortunate to have a few minutes of your time.

- **Set high expectations** – and you will get great things.

Set accessible, but challenging goals for your associates. Great companies set goals their associates can reach, but not too easily. David Packard, one of the founders of Hewlett-Packard once said, "Managers should set some objectives (for employees), provide some incentive, and then let them do their jobs." He set goals for his troops and expected those goals to be reached.

*Conversely, if you expect failure, or accept the status quo, then that's exactly what's headed your way.* In our family's retail wine stores, we always challenged our wine associates to be better. French wine specialists were encouraged to learn about Spanish wines. Spirit specialists were asked to become more familiar with glassware and other accessories. When people were more versatile, the whole team was better. Overall, we were able to serve our customers more efficiently because there were more qualified and knowledgeable people on the floor. It worked out well for both customers and associates.

Look for the best in your sales people. Point out each associate's strengths, not his or her weaknesses. Help them get stronger, but do so with honey, not vinegar.

- **Ask questions constantly (of yourself and others) to make sure you are keeping your eye on what needs to be done to manage a successful team. Here is a list of sample questions:**

  o Does the team need to know more about our company's products and services?

  o Does the team have a high enough level of technical knowledge?

  o Does the team need to know more about the marketplace?

  o Does the team put sales calls above non-sales activities?

  o Am I providing motivation and recognizing success?

  o Am I retaining good people while eliminating bad ones?

  o Do we have effective and accurate measures for monitoring the performance of sales teams?

  o Do I make a public fuss about those that have success, both one–offs and multiple sales?

  o Do I show that I care about our customers? Am I articulating a customer-focused vision?

  o Do I make every customer feel important?

  o Do I sell my people on the quality of our products?

  o Do I participate in sales activities, as I should realize that sales leadership is not a spectator sport?

  o Do I actively manage adversity? Managing adversity is as important as managing goals?

  o Does my sales team know how to overcome obstacles?

  o Do I use some finesse to support my force?

  o Do I compete with my sales stars instead of helping them perform at their best?

  o Do I know what motivates my sales people?

  o Do I know (and appreciate) their challenges?

  o Am I good at organizing the team?

  o Do I give my sales people my undivided attention?

  o Do I share my overall strategy with the team so they know where we are going?

- o Do I motivate with generous praise in public and offer constructive criticism in private?
- o In one-on-one meetings, do I listen more than I speak?
- o Do I do a post-mortem with my team on their sales calls?
- o Do I give complex decisions the time they deserve?
- o Do I resist the urge to do business with liars?
- o Do I build enthusiasm?
- o Am I willing to act boldly when the time is necessary?
- o Do I lead people to improvement?

- **Celebrate achievements** – maintain a light atmosphere.

Honor your associates every chance you can. Birthdays, anniversaries and outside achievements are all great excuses to have some fun. When someone gives notice and moves on to bigger and better things, throw a going-away party. Moving on is an achievement. It means someone is stepping closer to his or her dreams.

Your associates will take note. They will notice that the company is celebrating, even though they now have a position to fill. That is good internal public relations. Of course, celebrate whenever the Cubbies win. *Don't worry about the resulting loss of productivity; the Cubs don't win too often!*

- **Give effective feedback** – that is behavior related, not personal.

When giving feedback that is personal, assume that the recipient will immediately become defensive. Always start with something positive before discussing the problem. Make sure to focus on specific actions or behaviors. Never dwell on the personal attributes of the person causing the problem. The workplace has enough challenges. Do not add petty personal jealousies and animosities to the equation.

- **Find time to listen to everybody** – don't ignore the help.

Let your associates be heard. Solicit their input. I once enjoyed a presentation from the Disney Company. The speaker told an inspiring story about how the housekeeping staff was encouraged to submit ideas to help improve the room cleaning process. The staff developed the idea of putting a basket of linens outside each door before their cleaning rounds began. The results were smaller carts in the hallways and an easier, quicker way for *both* guests and housekeeping personal to get around.

Inspire others. Get people involved in projects *from the start.* Share what you know. Be committed to involving others. Ask people what they would do in a given situation. Support a culture where managers are not expected to have all the answers.

- **Grasp enrichment** – as a way to have your associates enjoy their jobs.

Ask your associates some of the following questions. What do you enjoy the most about your job? How can we make your job more satisfying? How do you like to be rewarded? What part of your job do you consider to be the dullest? What would you like to learn more about?

It is inevitable that talented people might feel trapped over time without choices or the feeling of control over one's professional destiny. To be sure, asking all these questions might lead to answers you would rather not hear; however, the more clued in you are to your associates' aspirations, the better it will ultimately be for your company.

- **Share information** – to make your associates feel more valued.

Has this situation ever occurred in your company? A top person gives notice and you wait a few days to formally tell your troops because you do not want the news to upset everybody. Unfortunately, the whole team knows about it 10 minutes later. The result: the blow is worse because people are frustrated and disappointed that you did not share the information with them sooner.

Share information sooner, rather than later. Share it face-to-face, especially when it is difficult news. Get creative. The more creatively you share news, the more likely the news will be noticed. Of course, there will be times when you simply cannot share the information. When certain things are to be held in confidence, never share no matter how tempting the information might be.

- **Be fair** – talented people will leave a boss that's unfair.

Unfair treatment rises to the level of disrespect in many people's eyes. Be consistent. Be ethical. Remember to always be moving closer to the finish line with your actions. What happens at the finish line? You have competent, happy people who do a good job and want to come to work. Get back to your associates in a timely manner. Be reachable. Do not make people wait for answers that could be easily delivered in a short time.

- **Mentor talented people** – and they will be more likely to stay.

Mentoring is a way not only to transfer important skills and knowledge but also to inspire loyalty in new employees. Encourage your star salespeople and the ones with the most experience to mentor the new ones. Set up a program where, at the very least, they have lunch together once in a while. Management should always be trying to create an environment where the least experienced can learn from the most experienced. That is extremely motivating.

Managers should make it a point to share stories of their mistakes in business. What mistakes did they make before they became managers? What did they learn? Show that managers are human. Let all sales people learn from mistakes so that the same mistakes are not repeated down the line.

- **Cut the underperformers quickly** - and the performers will be more likely to stay.

Long ago I learned that we had to quickly *cut the cord* when someone was not working out, both for the morale of the staff, and in fairness to the underperforming associate. Have you ever worked at a company that retained an associate that was more a liability than an asset? Most people know how uninspiring it is to come to work every day and work alongside someone who is not pulling his or her weight, which is why it is so important to act quickly and decisively. Help your sales people appraise their talents objectively.

- **Ask for opinions** – and keep your people motivated.

You would be very surprised how much your people know. According to Jeffrey Fox, author of many great, common-sense business books, the most powerful words you can say to an associate are, *"I don't know, what do you think?"* Your associates can really help if you let them. Ask questions. Do not disclose your motives. In many cases, people alter their answers to comply with what they think the questioner wants to hear. Say "What would you do in this situation?" rather than "I think we should do xyz; what do you think?" How would you reply if you were asked like that?

- **Know at least one fact** – about each one of your associates.

Always remember that most every individual that punches a clock or toils within your operation has a name, not to mention, dreams, desires and children to put through college, just like you do. Make it your business to know at least one fact about everybody. When I owned my wine stores and one of our associates became a new parent, I may not always have known the baby's name, but I did always acknowledge with a comment as often as possible. The simple act of saying, *"How is the baby?"* could truly brighten somebody's day.

- **Put it in writing** – memorialize the good that your people do.

When people do something wrong, always tell them in private but when they stand out, put it in writing for all to see. The web site of a big wine supplier lists their sales person's achievements. If a sales person places a chardonnay on a restaurant's wine list, they make a big deal about it on the company's intranet site. What a nice touch!

- **Stop gossip** – before it gets out of control.

Do everything you can to slow the spread of gossip from your workplace. To be sure, gossip is almost impossible to eradicate; however, there are a few things you can do. Be open, honest and transparent and you will gain respect from your sales people and associates. If you see problem employees, deal with them swiftly so gossip and negativity have no chance to fester.

Lack of trust leads to low morale, poor service and rampant rumors. At that point, doubt and disappointment are not far behind.

- **See the positive in things** – don't dwell on the negative.

The tendency in life and business is to push positive things to the background and instead to dwell on negative events and occurrences. I remember having a manager who would always complain about orders being filled incorrectly. Of course, I knew that it was important to learn why the problem was occurring; however, I always took time to remind and compliment everybody for all the good things that were happening. I wanted them to remember all the orders that were completed *successfully* and to take pride in the team's accomplishments. Be sure to learn from the negatives, but always take note of the positives.

- **Generate enthusiasm** – have a great sense of expectancy each day.

I started running with my dad when I was twelve. We went to Hermann's World of Sporting Goods to buy the proper clothing and shoes. We bought everything we needed, including shorts that by today's standards were *way too short*, and our first pair of real running shoes. *We didn't need to buy new T-shirts.* We already had drawers that were full of liquor T-shirts with sayings such as "Harvey Wallbanger" (whatever that means). Dad was not dwelling on the fact that Mom was forcing him to quit smoking and get in shape. He wanted me, and more importantly, *him*, to be excited and enthusiastic about our new endeavor. Do the same for your associates. Take the mundane and find creative ways to make the best of every situation.

- **Encourage teamwork** – so your sales people never feel alone.

I recently worked with a beer distributer and a sales person posed a sales scenario and asked for my feedback. As I usually do, before answering I asked the team if the young man had run the scenario by them and was astounded to find out that they never discussed accounts where they were having trouble. Why? Why were they not using their collective brainpower and sales experience to help each other?

Let that be the exception, not the norm, at your company. During every sales meeting, reserve a few minutes for sales people to share their experiences with the group. Encourage an open environment so that sales people can feel comfortable sharing problems they may be having. Brainstorm. Encourage everybody's ideas. The sum of your sales team is far greater than the individual parts so start sharing to solve difficult sales situations.

- **Support balance** - between work and personal life.

Has someone's work habits changed dramatically? This can often mean that there is something going on in his or her personal life. Sure, it is very easy to say that your people should leave their problems at home but that is short sighted. The fact is that personal problems affect performance at work. Take a proactive stance on work/life balance. Many job satisfaction studies show that employees value work/life balance more than compensation/pay. One study even found that Americans would take 15% less pay to have better balance at work.

- **Roam the halls and floors** - of your organization.

Get out there and talk to your associates. Compliment your associates in front of other people. That can be extremely motivating. Help your associates with their tasks when you have time. Make it a priority to find ways to make their lives a little easier. Do not send fancy emails from the corporate office saying you are going to help out at busy times. Just do it! No grandstanding; your efforts will be far more motivating if others notice your actions, rather than just *hearing* about them. No matter how high your position, you simply must get out of the office and coach.

- **Connect with people** – for contagious cooperation.

Theodore Roosevelt once said that the "*most important single ingredient of success is knowing how to get along with people.*" Create a bond with your sales people and associates and they will feel comfortable with you. The goal is for others to easily relate to you. When we feel connected with someone, we feel understood. When we feel understood, a sense of trust ensures. This is the key. Articulating your vision for success will likely fall upon deaf ears if you have not taken the time to sincerely connect with your people.

Also, monitor your language. Use friendly words! I know that may seem a bit goofy but consider the impact of the following: *I'm busy, not today, some other time, ask someone else.* Instead, sprinkle your conversations with the following: *awesome, wonderful, beautiful, appreciate. Not to mention - How can I help? And what can I do?* If you do not believe me, then watch someone's reaction (carefully) when you use unfriendly words.

## The Final Straightaway

**Praise often:** Just like runners need positive reinforcement, especially during the middle miles, your sales people and associates need the same treatment to give great service. The opportunities to *pat* your associates on the back are endless. Managers should always be trying to catch their associates *doing something right.* Upon witnessing positive behaviors - give immediate praise and specific feedback.

*"The sales manager is caught between a boss and an inspirational leader,"* according to Amway founder Rich Devos. He or she has to show what it is possible to do. He or she is really a trainer, manager, counselor and hand holder – all wrapped up into one.

*That's just how it works!*

# ACKNOWLEDGMENTS

There are many people who have helped me bring this book to you and I want to give thanks to a few from the bottom of my heart:

Jill Rosen, my wife. Your support (and editing) is much appreciated, not to mention all the time you've allowed me to *hang out with my laptop*. Thanks for continuing to be my best friend and laughing at my silly jokes.

Josh, Danny and Ben Rosen, my children. I hope you will continue the practice of reading Daddy's books out loud in the car (to your friends) and having a good laugh with me or at me. Who even knows anymore!

I love all you guys.

Thanks to all the beverage company leaders who have allowed me the pleasure of working with their sales teams. And to the thousands of beverage professionals who have seen my workshops and allowed me to enter their lives, if just for a few hours – thank you. As the infamous DJ, Marz, said at my son's Bar Mitzvah, "*I love love doing, what I love do,*" or something like that. (I think I know what that means) and I couldn't have said it any better.

Oh yeah, thanks to my editor and grammarian (Dr. Barbara von Diether), who has always helped me *be me* (but with better grammar). Of course, thanks again to Charlie Bernatowitz, for all your creativity on the cover and all the illustrations. I don't know how you do it, but keep doing it!

# About the Author

Everyone talks customer service, but Darryl Rosen has lived it. He served as President and owner of Sam's Wines & Spirits, a family business started by his grandfather in the 1940's. Under his leadership and unwavering commitment to superior customer service, Sam's grew from a small single operation to a multi-unit retailer with nearly $70 million in sales. Sam's reputation earned Darryl and his team an unrivaled national and international reputation.

Darryl has taken his decades of experience from running a successful business and his interaction with hundreds of hardworking, intelligent beverage professionals and currently delivers presentations and seminars for companies seeking to "win their customer's loyalty" and grow their businesses.

Before joining Sam's, Darryl received a Bachelor's Degree in Accounting from Indiana University and became a certified CPA. He earned his MBA in Marketing and Organizational Behavior from Northwestern University, Kellogg Graduate School of Management in 1997.

He has shared his unique perspective with companies such as Republic National Distributing Company, Jim Beam Brands, Pernod Ricard, Future Brands, Opici Wine Company, Fedway Associates as well as numerous other wine, beer and spirit distributors and suppliers.

Along with his passion for unparalleled sales and service excellence, Darryl spends time with his wife (Jill) and three boys (Josh, Danny and Ben), and is always hoping that this year will be the year for the Cubbies! If you would like more information on Darryl Rosen's speeches, seminars and consulting services, please use the following contact information.

**darryl@darrylrosen.com**

Printed in the United States
137824LV00003B/2/P